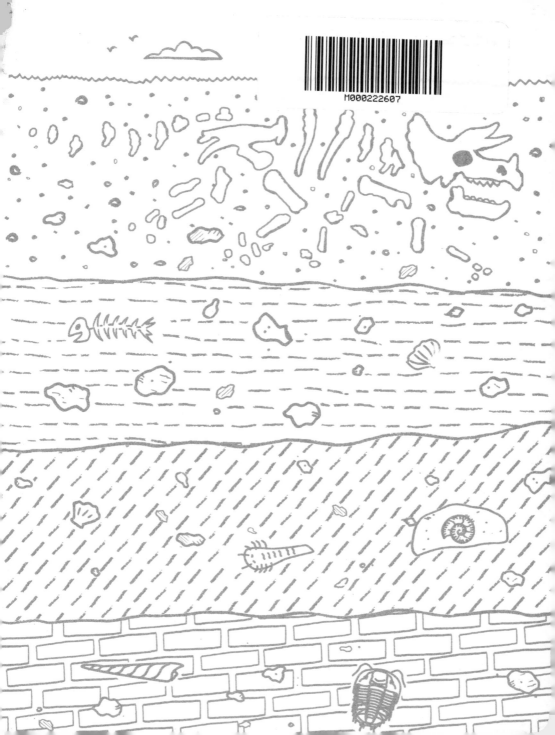

SCIENCE

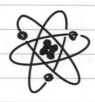

Library of Congress Cataloging-in-Publication Data is available.

ISBN 9780761196877

Illustrator Chris Pearce
Series Designer Tim Hall   Designers Tim Hall, Kay Petronio
Art Director Colleen AF Venable
Editors Nathalie Le Du, Justin Krasner   Production Editor Jessica Rozler
Production Manager Julie Primavera
Concept by Raquel Jaramillo

Workman books are available at special discounts when purchased in bulk for premiums, sales promotions, fundraising, catalogs, subscription boxes, and more. Workman also offers special discounts for schools and educators purchasing books in bulk. For more information, please email specialmarkets@workman.com.

Workman Publishing Co., Inc.
225 Varick Street
New York, NY 10014-4381
workman.com

Printed in Malaysia
First printing June 2020
10 9 8 7 6 5 4 3

THE **COMPLETE** SCHOOL STUDY GUIDE

EVERYTHING YOU NEED TO ACE
SCIENCE
IN ONE BIG FAT NOTEBOOK

Borrowed from the smartest kid in class
Double-checked by Michael Geisen

WORKMAN PUBLISHING
NEW YORK

EVERYTHING YOU NEED TO ACE
SCIENCE

HI!

These are the notes from my science class.
Oh, who am I? Well, some people said I was the
smartest kid in class.

I wrote everything you need to ace **SCIENCE**,
from the EXPERIMENTS to the ECOSYSTEMS,
and only the really important stuff
in between—you know, the
stuff that's usually on the test!

I tried to keep everything organised, so I almost always:

- Highlight vocabulary words in **YELLOW**.
- Colour in definitions in green highlighter.
- Use BLUE PEN for important people, places, dates, and terms.
- Doodle a pretty sweet Charles Darwin and whatnot to visually show the big ideas.

AGREED!

If you're not loving your textbook and you're not so great at taking notes in class, this notebook will help. It hits all the major points. (But if your teacher spends a whole class talking about something that's not covered, go ahead and write that down for yourself.)

zzz...WHAT?

Now that I've aced science, this notebook is **YOURS**. I'm done with it, so this notebook's purpose in life is to help **YOU** learn and remember just what you need to ace **YOUR** science class.

CONTENTS

MY LAWS RULE!

Unit

1

Scientific Investigation

Chapter 1

THINKING LIKE A SCIENTIST

The BRANCHES of SCIENCE and HOW THEY FIT TOGETHER

LIFE SCIENCE, or **BIOLOGY**, is the study of all living things, like plants, animals, and even single-cell organisms.

EARTH SCIENCE deals with Earth and space—things like planets, stars, and rocks. Earth science studies nonliving things and their history.

PHYSICAL SCIENCE is all about matter and energy, the most basic building blocks of the universe. It includes **PHYSICS** (energy interacting with matter) and **CHEMISTRY** (matter and how it transforms).

Science is like thinking about the universe as a Lego world:

1. **PHYSICS** studies a single Lego and all of its properties, like how it moves around and its energy.

2. **CHEMISTRY** studies how Legos fit together to create larger things.

3. **LIFE SCIENCE** studies all of the possible living things made out of Legos.

WOOF!

WHOA.

4. **EARTH SCIENCE** studies all the nonliving things in the Lego world.

SCIENTIFIC INQUIRY

Science is a way to find answers to questions about the world around us. Scientists are very much like detectives, using evidence to solve complex puzzles. Scientists find evidence by conducting experiments and making observations. The process used by scientists to research a question is called **SCIENTIFIC INQUIRY**. Trying to find the answers to a question is also called the SCIENTIFIC METHOD.

A scientific inquiry begins with a question about the world around us and how it works. After a question has been identified, the next step is to collect all of the possible information that relates to that investigation by doing background research, making observations, and conducting experiments.

BACKGROUND RESEARCH looks at the findings of past scientists to predict what will happen in an experiment. This prediction is called a **HYPOTHESIS**. Scientists test their hypotheses by making **OBSERVATIONS** and comparing them to their predictions. Observations require using your senses—the way something looks, smells, feels, or sounds—to describe an event. Some observations are **QUANTITATIVE** and made in the form of **MEASUREMENTS**. Some are **QUALITATIVE** and based on the qualities of something. The findings of the scientific inquiry are referred to as **CONCLUSIONS**.

4

SCIENTIFIC INQUIRY
the strategy used for scientific investigations

HYPOTHESIS
a prediction or proposed explanation that can be tested

OBSERVATION
using all of your senses and scientific instruments to describe a thing or event

CONCLUSION
the findings of your scientific investigation

QUANTITATIVE
information or data based on countable measurements of something

QUALITATIVE
information based on the qualities of something

A **MEASUREMENT** has both a **NUMBER** and a **UNIT**:
3 FEET, 45 MINUTES, 25 DEGREES CELSIUS, 1 LITER, and **115 POUNDS**

5

A **MODEL** is a representation of something that's too small, too big, or too expensive to observe in real life. Since models simplify things to make observing and thinking about them easier, they are very useful tools for scientists. These are a few types of models:

PHYSICAL MODELS, like a globe or a diorama

COMPUTER MODELS, like a simulation of changing weather patterns or 3-D simulations of people or places

MATHEMATICAL MODELS, like the equation of a line or a business using past costs to predict future costs

OOPS! LOOKOUT BELOW!

An experiment isn't a failure if it doesn't work out as predicted. Knowing what is false is an important part of figuring out what is true.

Scientific INQUIRY

① ASK A QUESTION.

② DO BACKGROUND RESEARCH.

③ MAKE A HYPOTHESIS.

④ TEST YOUR HYPOTHESIS WITH EXPERIMENTS AND OBSERVATIONS.

⑤ ANALYZE RESULTS.

⑥ MAKE A CONCLUSION ABOUT YOUR HYPOTHESIS.

IF FALSE: MAKE A NEW HYPOTHESIS AND BEGIN THE PROCESS AGAIN.

⑦ SHARE RESULTS.

7

Scientific Ideas, Theories, and Laws

After making many observations, scientists develop ideas to explain how and why things happen. Scientific ideas start as PREDICTIONS, and evidence may or may not support them.

After a hypothesis has been confirmed through many tests and experiments, scientists can develop a **THEORY**. A theory is a proposed explanation that has been extensively tested and is based on many observations.

A scientific **LAW**, like a theory, is based on many observations. A law is a rule that describes how something in nature behaves, but not necessarily why it behaves that way. For example, SIR ISAAC NEWTON observed that objects naturally fall to the ground. To describe this pattern, he came up with the law of universal gravitation. This law predicts the motion of objects under the force of gravity but doesn't explain why objects move that way.

IT'S TRUE!

LAW	**THEORY**
describes WHAT happens under certain conditions	an explanation of WHY something happens—based on years of testing and observation

CHECK YOUR KNOWLEDGE

1. What are the three main branches of science, and what does each study?

2. What are the basic steps of scientific inquiry?

3. What is a hypothesis?

4. If your observations do not support your hypothesis, what should you do?

5. How is evidence used in scientific investigations?

6. Compare and contrast a theory and a law.

7. What are models, and why are they used in science?

8. Give an example of a physical model, a computer model, and a mathematical model.

ANSWERS 9

CHECK YOUR ANSWERS

1. Life science (or biology) is the study of living things; earth science is the study of the earth and space; and physical science is the study of matter and energy.

2. Ask a question, do background research, make a hypothesis, test your hypothesis, analyze results, draw a conclusion, and share results. Or, if your hypothesis is proven false, make a new hypothesis and start again.

3. It's an educated prediction that can be tested.

4. Make a new hypothesis based on your observations and begin the process over again.

5. Evidence—observations and data—can either support or oppose a hypothesis.

6. A theory explains why something happens. A law identifies what happens in nature but doesn't necessarily explain why it happens.

7. A model is a representation of something. Models are used in science to help us think about things that are difficult to observe in real life.

8. PHYSICAL MODELS: maps, globes, and dioramas
   COMPUTER MODELS: 3-D simulations of people or places and simulations of moving weather fronts
   MATHEMATICAL MODELS: equations, such as the equation of a line, and mathematical simulations, such as business proposals

   #8 has more than one correct answer.

Chapter 2

SCIENTIFIC EXPERIMENTS

Designing a Scientific Experiment

Some good starting points for designing an experiment:

1. **OBSERVE** something you are curious about.

2. **ALTER** a previous experiment to develop your own experimental plans.

3. **REPEAT** past experiments to see if you get the same results.

An experiment requires a detailed list of steps, or a **PROCEDURE**, and a list of materials needed to conduct the experiment. Another scientist should be able to repeat the experiment based on your procedure steps alone, no matter where he or she is. This allows other scientists to evaluate your results.

PROCEDURE
a step-by-step list of how to carry out the experiment

You can have a CONTROLLED EXPERIMENT by running an experiment more than once: first without changing any factors (this experiment is called the **CONTROL**) and then a second time, changing only the factor you want to observe.

CONTROL
a trial where all the variables are held constant. A control is used as the standard of comparison for your experiment.

In a controlled experiment, the factors that are held constant are called **CONSTANTS**, and they don't affect the outcome of the experiment. A VARIABLE is a factor that can alter your experiment's results—a controlled experiment allows you to test the influence of the variable.

CONSTANTS
all the variables in an experiment that remain the same.

In order to test only one factor, all other factors in the experiment are held constant—this ensures that the changes you observe are caused by the one variable you changed.

Different variables play different roles:

An **INDEPENDENT VARIABLE** is the variable that you change in an experiment on purpose.

A **DEPENDENT VARIABLE** is the variable that is influenced by the independent variable, the results of your experiment.

Every couple of weeks, the teacher has to buy a new goldfish after the earlier one has died. The class comes up with a hypothesis that the goldfish is not getting the right amount of food. They devise an experiment to test this factor alone, holding all other variables (type of fish, tank size, water quality, water temperature, food type, and location) as constants.

CONSTANTS
1. Type of fish
2. Tank size
3. Water quality
4. Water temperature
5. Food type
6. Location

In this experiment, the independent variable is how frequently they feed the fish (either once a day or once every other day), and the dependent variable is the health of the fish after two weeks.

FEED DAILY

FEED EVERY OTHER DAY (LIKE USUAL)

FISH FOOD

EXPERIMENTAL   CONTROL

COLLECTING DATA

Good data is specific and detailed. Data with quantitative descriptions, or measurements, is often helpful. Good data is also accurate. Observe and measure things carefully. It is easy to forget things, so in order to ensure accuracy, record data and observations during the experiment instead of after. Without reliable data, conclusions are meaningless!

ANALYZING and PRESENTING DATA

Here are some common ways to organize and display data:

TABLES present data in rows and columns. Because the numbers are side by side, tables can be read quickly and numbers can be easily compared. A table is the best way to record data DURING an experiment.

	week 1	week 2	week 3
PLANT 1	3 cm	5.5 cm	7 cm
PLANT 2	2.5 cm	5 cm	7.5 cm

PLANT GROWTH

Once you've collected data in a table, turn it into a GRAPH to make the information easier to see.

LINE GRAPHS show the relationship between two variables—one plotted on the X-axis (the horizontal line), the other on the y-axis (the vertical line). A SCALE on each axis shows the intervals of measurements. The scale should go up in EVEN INCREMENTS, for example:
2, 4, 6, 8...or 5, 10, 15, 20...—not 2, 5, 7, 15...

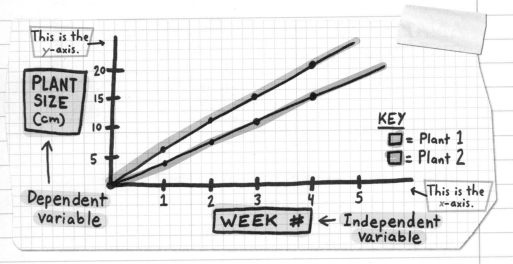

Line graphs help to show how one variable affects another, or in other words, how the dependent variable changes because of the independent variable. The independent variable is on the X-axis, and the dependent variable is on the y-axis. Line graphs work best for experiments that show continuous change over time, such as the growth of a plant or the acceleration of a race car.

A **SCATTER PLOT** is a type of line graph that shows the relationship between two sets of data. Scatter plots graph the data as ORDERED PAIRS (these are simply pairs of numbers—but the order in which they appear together matters).

EXAMPLE: After a math test, Ms. Phinney asked her students how many hours they studied. She recorded their answers, along with their test scores.

NAME	NUMBER OF HOURS STUDIED	TEST SCORE
Tammy	4.5	90
Latril	1	60
Sophia	4	92
Michael	3.5	88
Monica	2	76
Dave	5	100
Eva	3	90
Lance	1.5	72
Becca	3	70
Sarina	4	86

To show Tammy's data, we mark the point whose x-value is 4.5 and whose y-value is 90.

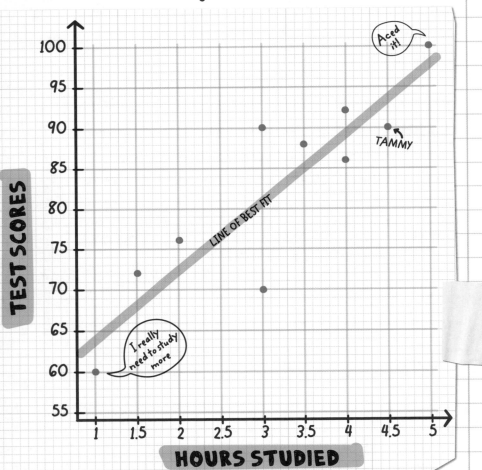

By graphing the data on a scatter plot, Ms. Phinney and her students can see if there is a relationship between the number of hours studied and test scores. The scores generally go up as the hours spent studying go up. This shows that there is a relationship between test scores and studying.

Eva studied 3 hours and got a 90. Becca also studied for 3 hours, but got a 70. A scatter plot shows the overall relationship between the data, while individual ordered pairs (like Eva or Becca) don't show the general trend. Eva and Becca might be considered **OUTLIERS** in this situation because they don't follow the typical pattern.

We can draw a line on the graph that roughly describes the relationship between the number of hours studied and test scores. This line is known as the LINE OF BEST FIT because it is the best description of how the points are related to one another. None of the points lie on the line of best fit, but it's okay! This is because the line of best fit is the line that best describes the relationship of all the points on the graph.

BAR GRAPHS present the data as rectangles of different heights. Each rectangle represents a different part of a category, or variable, such as type of pet or favorite ice cream flavor. The taller the rectangle, the larger the number.

You can think of a **CIRCLE GRAPH** like a pie cut into slices.
(Circle graphs are also sometimes called PIE CHARTS.) ← MMM.

A graph should be titled and labeled with things like
scale and units so readers can interpret the data.

DRAWING CONCLUSIONS

Did your results support your hypothesis? If not, how would
you change your hypothesis to fit your results? Sometimes
conclusions aren't immediately apparent and you will have to
INFER, or use observations and facts, to reach a conclusion
about something you may not have directly witnessed.

For example, if you want to find out what a
Tyrannosaurus rex ate, you might observe the
types of fossilized droppings that could be

found near a *T. rex*'s fossils. If you see crushed bones, you might infer that the *T. rex* ate smaller animals or dinosaurs. When you need to infer, it can help to look at background information and do further research.

Conclusions are also a place to be critical of the experiment and findings: Were there any errors in measurements or otherwise? Was the procedure followed correctly? How precise is your equipment? Even if you carried out the experiment error free, the results aren't always the same. Constants are hard to hold perfectly constant. Unwanted variables may be affecting your results. In order to ensure that findings are accurate, conduct several trials of the experiment.

EXAMPLE: Plant Fertilizer Experiment

Bob wanted to investigate the effects of plant fertilizer. He bought three identical plants and gave plant 1 fertilizer every morning, plant 2 fertilizer once a week, and he kept plant 3 as the control (he didn't give it any fertilizer).

Bob watered each plant once every morning and set all three on the windowsill so they all would have the same amount of sunlight. (The sunlight and water are constants.)

He measured the height of each plant once a week and recorded it in a data table. In order to analyze the data, Bob graphed the results. He plotted height versus time for each plant:

PLANT HEIGHT

PLANT	WEEK 0 (START)	WEEK 1	WEEK 2	WEEK 3
1	6 cm	8 cm	10 cm	12 cm
2	6 cm	7 cm	8 cm	9 cm
3	6 cm	6.5 cm	7 cm	7.5 cm

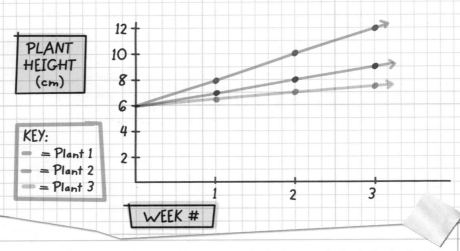

PLANT HEIGHT (cm)

KEY:
● = Plant 1
● = Plant 2
● = Plant 3

WEEK #

With the help of his data and graph, Bob concluded that plants given fertilizer every day grow four times as quickly as plants that are not fertilized. Using the evidence that plant 1 grew more quickly than plant 2, he also concluded that providing fertilizer daily instead of weekly makes the plant grow faster.

22

THE ENGINEERING DESIGN PROCESS

ENGINEERING is a branch of science that studies the design, building, and use of machines and structures in order to invent new products that solve problems. Just as scientists use scientific inquiry

> **ENGINEERING**
> a branch of science that studies the design, building, and use of machines and structures to solve real-world problems

to investigate questions, ENGINEERS use the ENGINEERING DESIGN PROCESS to solve problems through invention, design, and innovation. For example, engineers are currently developing pavement that can collect solar energy and use it to light roadways; this innovation can potentially solve a number of problems—it can help light up roads for safer night-time driving, it uses renewable energy to do it, and it cuts the cost of lighting roadways. To get to a solution like this one, however, engineers usually follow a certain path.

> # The major branches of engineering are:
>
> **MECHANICAL:** deals with mechanical power and designing mechanical systems, machines, and tools; studies forces and motion
>
> **CHEMICAL:** works with raw materials and chemicals; discovers new materials and processes
>
> **CIVIL:** includes designing and constructing buildings, roads, bridges, dams, and more
>
> **ELECTRICAL:** studies electricity and the design of electrical systems such as computer chips
>
> And there are many more types of engineering: computer, aerospace, biomedical, automotive, manufacturing, geological, etc.

Just as scientific inquiry has specific steps to carefully answer a question, the engineering design process has a system to help guide an engineering project. The engineering design process begins with a problem or need that can be solved by design. For example, oceanographers may want to explore and learn about deep seabeds, but divers have a hard time moving in the deep, fast-moving currents. An engineer would do BACKGROUND RESEARCH on the problem, determine all of the **DESIGN SPECS** ← SHORT FOR "DESIGN SPECIFICATIONS" (requirements) needed to start a design, and identify **CONSTRAINTS** (restrictions) that may affect his or her design. For example, an engineer might

DESIGN SPECS
the requirements that an engineer must fulfill in his or her design

research what kind of information
the oceanographers are looking
for in the seabeds. Some design
specs might include how deep divers
must go and how fast the currents

CONSTRAINTS
restrictions or
limitations (can be
physical, social, or
financial)

move. The engineer would also find out about constraints,
like how much money they can spend on the solution and
which materials will work far
underwater.

HEEEELLPPP!

After a problem is identified
and all the necessary information is gathered, the next
step is proposing possible solutions. In scientific inquiry, you
formulate a hypothesis, but in engineering you establish a
DESIGN STATEMENT—this defines what it means to solve
the particular problem. Engineers often brainstorm many
ideas and evaluate each solution in order to choose which
is the best option. For example, the engineer who wants to
solve the problem of exploring deep seabeds may come up
with a motor that a diver can wear or an underwater robot
that pushes against the fast-moving currents and transmits
information. They ask, which approach most likely will work
best? And why?

WRONG WAY!
WRONG WAY!

How do you choose which solution is best? Designers often think about these universal design criteria when deciding which is the best choice:

ROBUSTNESS (strength) • **COST**
AESTHETICS (looks) • **RESOURCES** • **TIME**
SKILL REQUIRED • **SAFETY** • **ELEGANCE**

Then, engineers design and build a **PROTOTYPE** of the solution, which is like the first draft of a paper—it's a rough idea of what the solution might eventually be. Engineers make

> **PROTOTYPE**
> a preliminary model that can be easily adjusted

technical drawings and crunch numbers to construct a simple prototype that can be easily adjusted depending on how it performs. The engineer may decide that an underwater robot that looks and acts like a crab may be the best solution to the divers' problems—it can stabilize itself with its six legs and carry cameras and sonar equipment to send information back to the surface.

ROBO-CRAB

Once the design is complete, engineers construct a simple prototype by using the drawings as a blueprint.

> You can design in many different ways—with drawings, computer models, storyboards, etc. You can also create prototypes with lots of different materials—scrap wood, toy blocks, poster board, or with more advanced materials like metal, plastics, or even by printing out parts with a 3-D printer!

Next, it's time to test how the prototype holds up in the real world!

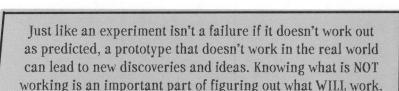

Engineers test the product multiple times to see how it does under different conditions. They collect data on how well the product solves the problem. If it doesn't work well, then they either go back to brainstorming new solutions or redesign the prototype. Often they troubleshoot the ways that the design is not meeting requirements or expectations. As a result of testing the prototype in the real world, they find ways to improve the design, then adjust their prototype or make a new one. After going back through the steps several times and making improvements each time, hopefully, they find a solution that works.

> Just like an experiment isn't a failure if it doesn't work out as predicted, a prototype that doesn't work in the real world can lead to new discoveries and ideas. Knowing what is NOT working is an important part of figuring out what WILL work.

Last, engineers construct a final product. Just like the final draft of a paper, engineers tweak their design until it is perfect. Then, they use final design materials in order to create a final product and present it to the public (and possibly sell their invention!).

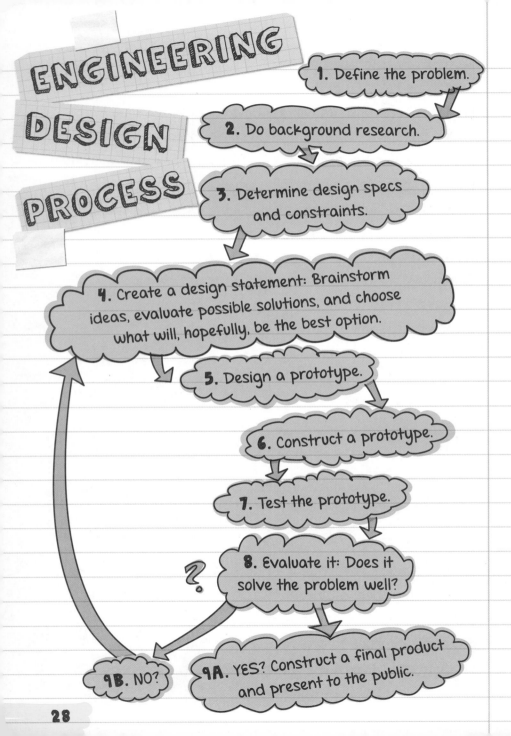

ENGINEERING DESIGN PROCESS

1. Define the problem.

2. Do background research.

3. Determine design specs and constraints.

4. Create a design statement: Brainstorm ideas, evaluate possible solutions, and choose what will, hopefully, be the best option.

5. Design a prototype.

6. Construct a prototype.

7. Test the prototype.

8. Evaluate it: Does it solve the problem well?

?

9B. NO?

9A. YES? Construct a final product and present to the public.

CHECK YOUR KNOWLEDGE

Match the term with its correct definition:

1. Procedure

2. Independent variable

3. Dependent variable

4. Constants

5. Control

6. Infer

A. This factor depends on the independent variable. It is usually the observed outcome (result) of an experiment.

B. A trial where all the variables are held constant

C. The variable that is changed on purpose in an experiment by the scientist

D. Factors in an experiment that remain the same

E. A step-by-step list of how to carry out an experiment

F. Use evidence to draw conclusions about things you may not have directly observed.

In the park, there are 25 pigeons, 15 squirrels, 5 rabbits, and 5 stray cats.

7. Make a table for this data.

8. Draw a bar graph to represent this data.

9. Why can't you draw a line graph using only this information?

CHECK YOUR ANSWERS

1. E

2. C

3. A

4. D

5. B

6. F

7.

ANIMALS IN THE PARK

ANIMAL	NUMBER of ANIMALS
PIGEONS	25
SQUIRRELS	15
RABBITS	5
CATS	5

8.

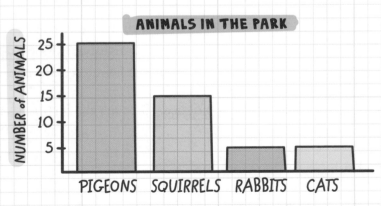

ANIMALS IN THE PARK

9. You can't draw a line graph because there is no data to compare the number of animals to, such as time of day.

Chapter 3

LAB REPORTS
AND
EVALUATING RESULTS

It's important to share your results with other scientists so they can learn from your work, critique it, and build upon it. That's how science knowledge grows. There are many ways to communicate your experiment and findings to others. The most common way is to write a LAB REPORT.

WRITING a LAB REPORT

A lab report usually contains the following:

TITLE: lets the reader know what the investigation was about

PURPOSE: a brief description to answer the question, "What was the purpose of doing this experiment?" or "What is the question I'm trying to answer?"

BACKGROUND INFORMATION: definitions of key words and explanation of key concepts

HYPOTHESIS: the predictions you were testing

MATERIALS AND EQUIPMENT: a list of the materials and equipment necessary to carry out the experiment. You could even add a sketch or description of the setup.

PROCEDURE: a step-by-step description of how to carry out the experiment

Make sure to title charts, graphs, and tables and to label all axes on any graphs.

DATA: all the measurements and observations you made during the experiment. Be sure to present data in an organized way, such as in tables, graphs, or drawings. The best measurements are **ACCURATE** and **PRECISE**.

PRECISION
how consistent and exact your measurements are

ACCURACY
how close to the actual value your measurement is

CONCLUSION: a summary of what you learned from the experiment, whether or not your results supported your hypothesis, any errors, and questions for more experiments

Sometimes exact measurements are not possible or practical—like if you don't have the right tools to measure something or if a decimal continues to infinity. If that is the case, sometimes scientists use **ESTIMATION** or **ROUNDING NUMBERS**.

ESTIMATION
a rough guess of a measurement using reason and observation

ROUNDING NUMBERS
giving a number a nearby value. For example, if you are rounding to the tenth place, and the hundredth digit is five or more, round up. If the hundredth digit is four or less, round down.

EVALUATING SCIENTIFIC RESULTS

When reading another scientist's findings, think critically about the experiment. Ask yourself: Were observations recorded during or after the experiment? Do the conclusions make sense? Does the data conclusively prove the hypothesis, or are there other ways of interpreting the data? Can the results be repeated? Are the sources of information reliable?

You should also ask if the scientist or group conducting the experiment was UNBIASED. Being unbiased means that you have no special interest in the outcome of the experiment. For example, if a drug company pays for an experiment to test how well one of its new products works, there is a special interest involved: The drug company profits if the experiment shows that its product is effective. Therefore, the experimenters aren't objective: They might ensure the conclusion is positive and benefits the drug company. When assessing results, think about any biases that may be present!

CHECK YOUR KNOWLEDGE

1. Describe the difference between precision and accuracy.

2. What does a hypothesis tell you in a lab report?

3. What does a procedure tell you in a lab report?

4. What should you include in a conclusion?

5. Describe some reasons why you might be critical of scientific findings.

6. Describe a situation where you would need to use estimation or round numbers.

7. Define "bias."

ANSWERS

CHECK YOUR ANSWERS

1. Precision is how consistent and exact a measurement is, while accuracy is how close to the actual or true value a measurement is.

2. A hypothesis describes the predictions you were testing.

3. A procedure is a list of the steps necessary to carry out the experiment.

4. A summary of the results, a discussion of whether or not the data supported the hypothesis, errors, and questions for further investigation

5. The person or group conducting the experiment is biased, the data seems unreasonable, and/or the results aren't replicable.

6. Any situation where making an exact measurement isn't possible, or if you are calculating a number with a repeating decimal

7. A bias is having a special interest that prevents you from being objective or conducting a fair test of your hypothesis.

Chapter 4

SI UNITS AND MEASUREMENTS

The **SI SYSTEM** has a base unit, or a standard unit, for every type of measurement.

SI stands for *SYSTÈME INTERNATIONALE*, which is French for "International System." How chic!

SI BASE UNITS:

QUANTITY MEASURED	SI UNIT (symbol)
length (or distance)	meter (m)
mass	gram (g)
weight (or force)	newton (N)
volume (or capacity)	liter (L)
temperature	Kelvin (K)
time	second (s)
electric current	ampere (A)
amount of substrate	mole (mol)
light intensity	candela (cd)

Because we want to use SI units to describe both the distance around someone's bicep and the distance around Earth, we need to be able to change the size of a unit to fit the measurement. Scientists devised a system of prefixes that multiplies the base unit by factors of 10. Just by switching the prefix, an SI unit can be used for measurements big and small:

SI PREFIX (symbol)	MULTIPLIER
giga- (G)	1,000,000,000
mega- (M)	1,000,000
kilo- (k)	1,000
hecto- (h)	100
deca- (da)	10
[base unit]	1
deci- (d)	0.1
centi- (c)	0.01
milli- (m)	0.001
micro- (µ)	0.000001
nano- (n)	0.000000001

Ninety-five percent of the world uses SI units as the everyday system of measurement.

SI UNIT CONVERSIONS

Because the SI prefix system is based on powers of 10, it is really easy to convert between units. If you are converting to a smaller unit of measurement, simply move the decimal point to the right as many places as the difference in place value. If you are converting to a larger unit of measurement, move the decimal point to the left as many places as the difference in place value:

EXAMPLES

0.001 kilometers
=
1 meter
=
100 centimeters

0.0033 kilometers
=
3.3 meters
=
330 centimeters

COMMON SENSE TIP

Remember to use the best-fitting unit. If you measured the volume of the ocean with the same units you use to measure a glass of milk, the numbers would be very difficult to work with. (The volume of the ocean should be measured using much larger units.)

TYPES OF MEASUREMENT

LENGTH: the distance between two points

VOLUME: the amount of space something occupies

MASS: the amount of matter in a liquid, solid, or gas

WEIGHT: the force exerted by a mass

> When you measure someone's weight, you measure the force they exert on the earth.

MASS AND WEIGHT ARE NOT THE SAME!

Mass is the amount of matter in an object, and weight is the force applied by a mass. Weight relies on gravity (a force), but mass doesn't. For example, the moon has less gravity than the earth, so objects weigh less there than on Earth. Mass always remains the same. Weight changes.

DENSITY: the amount of matter in a volume.

TEMPERATURE: how hot or cold something is. While the SI unit for temperature is Kelvin, most scientists use the SI-derived unit, Celsius, to measure temperature.

> Kelvin doesn't use a degree symbol.

SINK OR FLOAT?

Something denser will sink below something that is less dense. When oil is poured into liquid water, it floats on top of the surface because oil is less dense than water. A stone sinks in water, so it is denser than water. Water has a density of approximately 1.0, so oil's density must be less than 1 (or <1) and a rock's density must be greater than 1 (or >1).

This is the formula to convert Celsius and Kelvin:

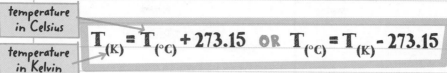

$$T_{(K)} = T_{(°C)} + 273.15 \quad \text{OR} \quad T_{(°C)} = T_{(K)} - 273.15$$

In the U.S., we usually use Fahrenheit to measure temperature. This is the formula to convert Fahrenheit and Celsius:

$$T_{(°F)} = \left(T_{(°C)} \times \frac{9}{5}\right) + 32 \quad \text{OR} \quad T_{(°C)} = (T_{(°F)} - 32) \times \frac{5}{9}$$

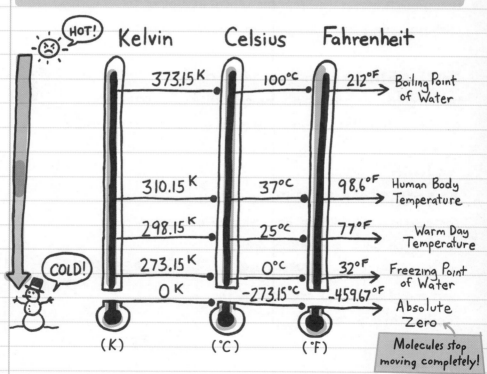

TIME: the period between events, or how long something lasted. The SI unit for time is seconds. Other units for time include hours, days, months, and years.

41

MEASUREMENT TOOLS

Distance

METERSTICK: like a ruler, except it is 1 meter long (100 cm). It is a bit longer than a yardstick.

TRUNDLE WHEEL: To measure long distances, just roll the trundle wheel on the ground, and every time you walk a meter, the trundle wheel makes a clicking sound. Simple—just remember to count the clicks.

TAPE MEASURE: for measuring distances that would be hard to measure using a meterstick or a trundle wheel, such as the distance around a round object

Volume

GRADUATED CYLINDER: a cylinder marked on the outside to indicate how much fluid it contains. Take your volume reading from the bottom of the **MENISCUS** and make sure you are taking the reading at eye level.

VOLUME OF SOLIDS: To figure out the volume of a rectangular solid, simply measure its height, width, and length using any of

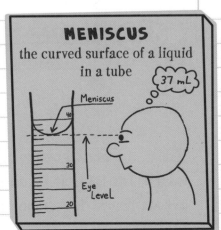

MENISCUS
the curved surface of a liquid in a tube

37 mL

Meniscus

40

30

Eye Level

20

the tools for measuring distance, and then multiply all three:

$$\text{volume} = \text{length} \times \text{width} \times \text{height}$$

For other geometric shapes, look in your math notebook.

VOLUME OF IRREGULAR SOLIDS:

The best way to measure the volume of an irregular solid is to place it in water and find the volume of water it displaces. The difference between the new and old volume measurements is equal to the volume of the object. (Next time you get into a bath, look at the water you displace— that's your volume!)

VOLUME DISPLACED

SOLID

Mass

ELECTRONIC BALANCE: Just put the object on the pan and read the mass.

DOUBLE PAN BALANCE: This compares the weight of objects in pans on each side of a balance. To find mass, place something of known mass in one pan, and in the other pan, place the object of unknown mass. When the pans are level, the masses are equal.

If you are measuring something that needs to be in a container, weigh the empty container on its own first, and then subtract the weight of the container afterward.

TRIPLE BEAM BALANCE: works like a double pan balance, but instead of having a pan on each side of the balance, there is a pan on one side, and three beams, each with sliding weights, called RIDERS, on the other.

Density

Because density is simply the amount of matter in a certain volume, you can calculate density by measuring the volume and mass of an object, and dividing like so:

$$\text{density} = \frac{\text{mass}}{\text{volume}}$$

Time

To measure time, you can use a clock or a stopwatch. If you are using a regular clock, subtract the start time from the end time to figure out how much time has lapsed.

Temperature

THERMOMETER: used to measure temperature. A thermometer can be digital, or it can be a liquid thermometer, which contains a liquid that changes volume with temperature. When taking temperature, make sure the bulb at the end of the thermometer is in the middle of the liquid you are measuring and not touching the sides or bottom of the container.

CHECK YOUR KNOWLEDGE

1. What are the SI units for mass, length, and temperature?

2. What tool would you use to measure the height of your dog?

3. Where do you look to take a volume reading of a liquid in a graduated cylinder?

4. What is the easiest tool used to measure mass?

5. How do you find the volume of a rectangular solid?

6. Describe the difference between mass and weight.

7. Convert 50 centimeters to kilometers.

8. Define "volume" and list some common volumes measured.

9. If the boiling point of water in Celsius is 100°, what is the boiling point in Kelvin?

10. You place a paper clip in a cup of soda and it sinks. Which is denser—the paper clip or the soda? Would the paper clip most likely have a density of 2.8, 1.0, or 0.3 g/mL?

ANSWERS 45

CHECK YOUR ANSWERS

1. Grams, meters, Kelvin

2. A meterstick

3. The bottom of the meniscus

4. An electronic balance

5. You measure the length, width, and height of an object. You then multiply all three numbers to find the volume of the object (volume = length × width × height).

6. Mass is the amount of matter in an object, and weight is the force applied by a mass.

7. 0.0005 kilometers

8. Volume is the amount of space something occupies, such as the volume of liquid in a soft drink, the volume of a serving of cereal, or the volume of a backpack.

9. 373.15° Kelvin

10. The paper clip is denser; 2.8 g/mL.

#8 has more than one correct answer.

Chapter 5

LAB SAFETY
AND
SCIENTIFIC TOOLS

LAB SAFETY

The most important thing is to think before you act. Being thoughtful and cautious while experimenting will help prevent many accidents.

GENERAL LAB SAFETY RULES

Make sure a teacher or another adult is present, and follow directions carefully.

NO SHIRT,
NO SHOES,
NO SCIENCE!

Wear protective clothing—apron and/or lab coat, goggles, and gloves— to protect your eyes, skin, and clothing from burns, chemical spills, splashes, and flying objects. Also, make sure that you aren't wearing loose clothing that could get caught on something or lit on fire.

Wear closed-toe shoes to protect your feet in case something is dropped or spilled.

Tie back long hair—it might get caught in something and yanked, or if you are working with heat, it could even catch on fire.

Wash your hands after handling chemicals and living or once-living things.

Don't eat or drink in the lab—you don't want to mix toxic lab chemicals with things you are consuming.

Keep the lab clean and organized. Put away anything you aren't using, such as backpacks or jackets.

Don't run or throw things—someone could get seriously hurt.

SAFETY EQUIPMENT

Know how to use it and where it is located!

EYEWASH: Use if a chemical spills or splashes into your eye. Rinse your eye immediately for 15 minutes. Sometimes there is a water fountain in the lab just for this.

THERMAL MITTS OR TONGS: Use when handling hot beakers or equipment.

FIRE EXTINGUISHER: Use to put out electrical, chemical, or gas fires.

FIRE BLANKET: Use to smother small fires on people or surfaces. If a person is on fire, wrap them in the blanket and have them roll on the floor.

SHOWER: Use if a chemical is spilled and touches your skin either directly or through clothing. Remove any clothing that is contaminated with chemicals and rinse yourself under water for 15 minutes.

ACCIDENTS HAPPEN

OOOPS! Despite all of the safety precautions we take, things happen. Make sure to tell the teacher or lab supervisor about any accidents.

MINOR BURN: Put under cold running water for at least 5 minutes.

LAB FIRE: Get adult help immediately. A big fire isn't like a birthday candle: Blowing on it will NOT put it out and can make the fire spread. Also, water will not put out an electrical fire.

PERSON ON FIRE: Roll on the ground, preferably in a fire blanket. Again, get an adult to help.

WATER SPILLS: Mop them up so no one slips.

CHEMICAL SPILLS AND BROKEN GLASS: Make sure no one steps in the accident area. Ask an adult for help.

WASTE DISPOSAL

Most labs will have garbage containers labeled with the types of waste you can put inside. Ask the lab supervisor if you're not sure where to dispose of something.

Hazardous Waste

There are six major types of hazardous waste you may encounter in lab, and each type has its own symbol:

 1. BIOLOGICAL WASTE: blood, mold, dead animals, animal waste, or any objects contaminated by these things

 2. TOXIC WASTE: anything poisonous, such as chemicals, solutions, or certain cleaning materials

 3. RADIOACTIVE WASTE: anything contaminated by radiation (the emission of energy through waves or particles), perhaps from lab or X-ray equipment. You probably won't see a lot of this kind of waste in your school lab. *UNLESS YOU'RE ATTEMPTING TO MAKE A NINJA TURTLE BY EXPOSING THE CLASS TURTLE TO RADIATION*

 4. FLAMMABLE WASTE: things that can easily catch on fire such as gasoline, solvents, or alcohol

 5. CORROSIVE CHEMICAL WASTE: highly corrosive (damaging) chemicals such as acids, bases, and old batteries

 6. SHARP OBJECTS AND GLASSWARE: broken glass or sharp objects such as needles or blades

WHEN WORKING WITH...

Heat

Never leave a heat source unattended.

Never heat something in a closed container—it can explode.

Use mitts or tongs to handle hot containers.

Chemicals

Never taste or directly smell chemicals. A safer way to smell a chemical is by wafting it.

Wear gloves and/or an apron/lab coat when handling chemicals, and avoid chemical contact with skin. (It can give you a chemical burn. OUCH!)

Always label containers containing chemicals, and never use chemicals from an unlabeled container.

Biological Materials

Always wear gloves and protective clothing. If you're not careful, **BIOLOGICAL MATERIALS** can transmit **BACTERIA** and disease. YIKES!

Be sure to wash your hands, even after wearing gloves.

BIOLOGICAL MATERIALS
living or once-living materials

Handle living specimens with care, and make sure to provide them with the proper food and habitat. It's important to treat all living specimens ethically.

BACTERIA
single-cell organisms that have cell walls but no organelles or organized nucleus

THAT MUTANT NINJA TURTLE IS PROBABLY A BAD IDEA.

Electricity

Make sure cords are not damaged (damaged cords can cause electrical fires).

Make sure electrical outlets are either grounded (this will usually mean the outlet has a little red button in the middle) or are at least six feet from a water source, such as a sink.

Make sure to keep electrical equipment dry; water on plugs, outlets, or equipment can cause an electrical shock.

Keep cords out of the way so you don't trip on them or snag other equipment on them.

LAB INSTRUMENTS and TOOLS

Hot Plate

A **HOT PLATE** is like a stovetop, and there is a dial to control the heat. Usually, fluid-containing test tubes are heated using a hot-water bath.

SO, ONLY USE WITH ADULT SUPERVISION.

A **BUNSEN BURNER** is also used for heating things. UNLIKE a hot plate, a Bunsen burner is an open flame fed by gas. But LIKE a hot plate, it should be ignited by a teacher or other adult.

Ring stand

Bunsen burner

A **RING STAND** is used to hold up beakers, flasks, and test tubes. It is usually used when heating, mixing, or measuring chemicals.

In a lab, we use many kinds of glassware. Most of the glass is heat resistant and durable, but if it heats or cools too quickly it will crack or shatter.

A **BEAKER** looks kind of like a glass cup with a spout to make pouring fluids easier. Rough measurements can be made using the lines on the beaker's side (these aren't the most accurate).

A **FLASK** is like a beaker, except that its mouth is much narrower, so it can be closed with a stopper. Like a beaker, the measurements on the side only give an estimation.

A **TEST TUBE** is like a long glass tube rounded at the end—sort of like a long, hollow glass finger.

STOPPERS are rubber tops that fit into the neck of test tubes and flasks. Sometimes stoppers have holes in the top for sticking in glass tubing, which can be used to connect the test tube or flask to other things.

A **TEST TUBE BRUSH** helps you clean gunk out of narrow test tubes.

A **STIRRING ROD** is a glass stick used for stirring liquids.

A **FUNNEL** is used to help cleanly pour liquids from one container to another. A funnel is wide at the top and narrow at the bottom, so liquid is caught and pushed out in a concentrated stream.

A **MICROSCOPE** is a tool that allows you to see small things up close. A microscope is essentially a really powerful magnifying glass.

When using a microscope, we usually examine things on a SLIDE, which is either a flat piece of glass or a flat piece of glass with a small depression to hold a specimen.

In lab, we usually use a **COMPOUND MICROSCOPE**, which is a microscope with two lenses for super powerful magnification. You can change the magnification by rotating to a different lens that is closer to the slide. Be careful not to crush the slide when you focus on a high power!

CHECK YOUR KNOWLEDGE

1. What is used to heat things with an open flame?

2. What is a safer way to smell a chemical?

3. What can you use to protect your eyes during labs?

4. Don't ___ or drink in lab!

5. What instrument is like a beaker with a narrower mouth?

6. What is the kind of waste that includes living or once-living things?

7. A _____ stand is used in conjunction with a Bunsen burner.

8. What is used to smother small fires or to wrap a person on fire?

9. Never leave a heat source _____.

10. What holds the specimen when you use a microscope?

ANSWERS

CHECK YOUR ANSWERS

1. A Bunsen burner
2. Wafting it
3. Goggles
4. Eat
5. A flask
6. Biological waste
7. Ring
8. A fire blanket
9. Unattended
10. A slide

Unit 2

Matter, Chemical Reactions, and Solutions

Chapter 6

MATTER, PROPERTIES, AND PHASES

MATTER and ATOMS

MATTER describes everything that we can see, touch, smell, or feel. In other words, matter is anything that has mass and takes up space (including air and almost everything else).

> **MATTER**
> anything that has mass and takes up space
>
> **ATOM**
> the smallest unit of matter

The smallest unit of matter is called an **ATOM**. If you chop a piece of metal into a bajillion pieces, the smallest bit you are left with that still has the properties of the metal is called an atom.

> The word *atom* is derived from a Greek word that means "cannot be divided."

> (And the Greeks didn't even have a particle accelerator!)

ATOMIC MODELS

← Remember that a model is a way to represent something that we can't easily see.

Atoms are made of smaller particles:

PROTONS (positively charged particles)

NEUTRONS (electrically neutral particles, which means they have no charge)

ELECTRONS (negatively charged particles with almost no mass)

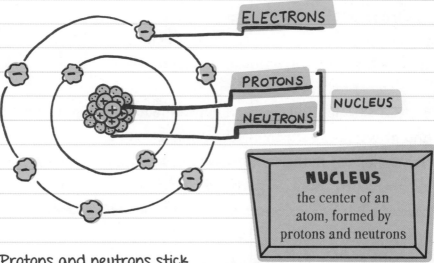

ELECTRONS

PROTONS

NEUTRONS

NUCLEUS

NUCLEUS
the center of an atom, formed by protons and neutrons

Protons and neutrons stick together to form the center of an atom, called the **NUCLEUS**, which has a net positive charge. Electrons orbit, or circle around, the nucleus, but too quickly to pinpoint their exact locations.

The **MODERN ATOMIC MODEL** shows an **ELECTRON CLOUD** rather than individual electrons like the model above. It demonstrates where you're most likely to find an orbiting electron. Denser areas of the cloud mean a higher probability of electrons.

Brief History of the Atomic Models

JOHN DALTON was the first scientist to propose that elements are composed of indestructible atoms. He thought that there were particles so small that we could not see them. He called these particles atoms, and his theory on matter was known as the ATOMIC THEORY OF MATTER.

SIR JOSEPH JOHN (J. J.) THOMSON discovered the presence of negatively charged particles (electrons) in atoms and pictured them embedded with positively charged particles, kind of like raisins in oatmeal-raisin cookies.

YOU'RE SO NEGATIVE ALL THE TIME.

HELLO MY NAME IS ERNEST

HELLO MY NAME IS J.J.

ERNEST RUTHERFORD worked out that each atom had a small and heavy positively charged center, which he called a nucleus. He figured out that electrons were orbiting the nucleus in mostly empty space. He called the positive particles in the nucleus protons. Rutherford's student SIR JAMES CHADWICK proposed the existence of uncharged particles in the nucleus, which he called neutrons.

PHYSICAL and CHEMICAL PROPERTIES and CHANGES

The way something looks, feels, smells, and tastes are all PHYSICAL PROPERTIES. It's easy to classify matter by these characteristics. Some common physical properties used to differentiate matter are:

COLOR   SIZE   DENSITY

MALLEABILITY (how easily something can be flattened, shaped, or pressed)

MAGNETISM (whether or not something is magnetic)

BOILING POINT and **MELTING POINT** (the temperature at which something boils or melts)

SOLUBILITY (how easily something dissolves in another substance)

A **PHYSICAL CHANGE** is any change to the physical properties of matter such as its size, shape, or state (solid, liquid, or gas/vapor). The final product of any physical change is still composed of the same matter. For example, you can revert ice, snow, or vapor back to water by either heating or cooling it. Ice, vapor, and water are all the same matter—just in different states.

CHEMICAL PROPERTIES describe the ability of something to undergo different chemical changes.

Some examples of chemical properties:

FLAMMABILITY (how easily something lights on fire)

REACTIVITY (how reactive something is to oxygen, water, light, etc.)

When any of these chemical properties changes, the matter has gone through a **CHEMICAL CHANGE**. Rust on an iron gate or a log burning and producing ashes are both examples of chemical changes. Some signs of chemical change may include:

> **CHEMICAL CHANGE**
> when matter changes into new substances with new properties

CHANGE IN COLOR—This is like when you leave a sliced apple out and it turns brown.

CHANGE IN ENERGY—The chemicals react, releasing energy in the form of bright lights and heat.

Think of fireworks.

CHANGE IN ODOR

Think of food going rotten.

FORMATION OF A GAS OR SOLID: When you add two substances together, such as vinegar and baking soda, you frequently see bubbles. Bubbles, or gas formation, are a sign that the ingredients have undergone a chemical change.

Chemical changes are often much harder to reverse than physical ones—just imagine trying to turn ashes back into a log of wood.

> **SYNTHETIC MATERIALS** are materials that don't occur in nature, but are instead made from natural resources that undergo a chemical change. For example, polyester is a synthetic fiber made from air, water, coal, and petroleum. Acid and alcohol are used to create a chemical reaction, which results in polyester fibers.

Conservation of Mass

While things may change appearance or composition during physical and chemical changes, one thing remains consistent: the amount of matter present.

This concept is called the **CONSERVATION OF MASS**. So mass doesn't just disappear—it still exists, but it may be in a different form, like in the surrounding gases. The atoms have just rearranged to form different substances.

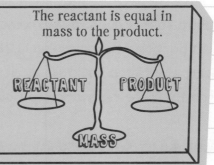

REACTANT
substance that is changed in a physical or chemical reaction

PRODUCT
the resulting substance of a physical or chemical reaction

The reactant is equal in mass to the product.

REACTANT   PRODUCT

MASS

STATES of MATTER

Matter is usually found in three STATES (or PHASES): solid, liquid, and vapor (or gas). The arrangement and behavior of particles is what determines the state of matter. The attraction between particles keeps particles close together, and the energy of their movement allows particles to overcome these attractive forces.

A **SOLID**, like ice, wood, or metal, is matter that has a defined shape and volume. The particles in matter are packed closely together, and they don't move around freely, which is why a solid has a defined shape and volume. Still, particles in a solid vibrate back and forth, but not enough to overcome the attractive force between particles.

LIQUIDS are free-flowing and assume the shape of the container that holds them. Liquids, however, do have a fixed volume. Particles in liquid move around fast enough to overcome attractive forces. While the liquid particles do move freely, they still stick together. The speed at which a liquid flows depends on its **VISCOSITY**. Viscosity is the resistance to flow.

VAPORS (or **GASES**) don't have fixed volume or shape. The shape and volume of a gas depends on its container, and unlike liquids, it will fill any container you place it in. The molecules in gases spread really far apart and move at high speeds. Gas molecules move so quickly that they are able to overcome attractive forces between particles, which allows the molecules to separate on their own. If you spilled the gas from a balloon into the air, it would disperse evenly into the air.

PBBBLT

STATE	FEATURES	MOVEMENT OF PARTICLES
SOLID	Fixed shape and volume	Vibrate, but have fixed positions
LIQUID	Shape can change, volume is fixed. Can flow.	Free-moving— no fixed positions.
GAS	Shape and volume not fixed and depends on container. Can flow.	Particles move quickly and are far apart.

PHASE CHANGES

A state is not permanent. Changes in pressure and temperature alter matter—these are described as PHASE CHANGES.

MELTING is when matter changes from solid to liquid. The melting point is the temperature at which a solid melts. Heat causes solids to melt by increasing the movement of particles. As the particles gain more and more energy from the heat, they move more and more until they are no longer fixed in place.

Above 100°C, water is a vapor.
Between 0°C and 100°C, water is a liquid.
Below 0°C, water is a solid.

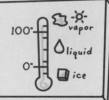

FREEZING is when matter changes from liquid to solid. As liquids cool down, the particles move less and less. At some point, the motion of particles can't overcome the attractive forces between particles, and the liquid turns to solid. The temperature at which a liquid freezes is called the **FREEZING POINT**.

67

VAPORIZATION is when liquid turns to vapor. When sweat disappears and dries up, it has vaporized or evaporated. Evaporation happens slowly and only at the surface (individual molecules get bumped out into the air). When water boils, it has reached the temperature at which water turns from liquid to vapor. Heat causes liquid particles to move around quickly. When the particles are moving around fast enough to overcome all attractive forces between particles, the liquid turns to vapor.

CONDENSATION is when vapor turns to liquid. When you get a really cold drink, the air around the glass condenses and forms little water droplets on the surface of the glass. When water vapor in the air cools down and loses energy, the particles start to slow down. When the particles slow down enough, the attractive forces between particles cause the molecules in the vapor to stick together, forming a liquid.

Sometimes, under extreme conditions, solids can change directly to vapors, which is called **SUBLIMATION**. Dry ice, for example, sublimates when the CO_2 ice turns directly into CO_2 vapor. Vapors sometimes change directly into solids, which is called **DEPOSITION**, like when frost appears on grass overnight.

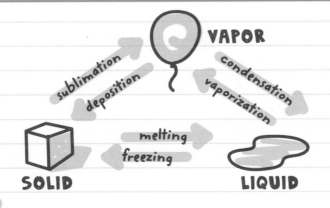

VAPOR

sublimation
deposition

condensation
vaporization

SOLID

melting
freezing

LIQUID

CHECK YOUR KNOWLEDGE

1. What is the positively charged particle in an atom?

2. Describe Thomson's model of an atom.

3. If you turn eggs, flour, and milk into pancakes, what sort of change have the ingredients undergone? If you make a smoothie out of a banana, strawberries, and yogurt, what sort of change have the ingredients undergone?

4. If you burn a piece of paper, is there more or less mass than you started with?

5. Name some things that are not matter.

6. In terms of particles and volume, what is the difference between a liquid and a vapor?

7. What happens at the vaporization point (boiling point) of a substance?

8. Compare the molecular movements in a solid, vapor, and liquid.

9. What is viscosity? Which has a higher viscosity: peanut butter or ketchup?

10. Define vaporization and condensation. Give an example of each.

ANSWERS

CHECK YOUR ANSWERS

1. A proton
2. Thomson thought that electrons and protons were embedded together, sort of like raisins in oatmeal-raisin cookies.
3. The ingredients in pancakes undergo a chemical change—the ingredients have transformed into something else with new chemical properties. For the smoothie, the ingredients have undergone a physical change (the ingredients are the same, they are just cut up into small pieces and blended together).
4. The same. Mass is conserved.
5. Thoughts, light, a vacuum
6. While both can flow freely, the particles in a liquid stick together and don't completely separate. So the volume of a liquid is fixed while the volume of a vapor is not fixed.
7. At the boiling point, a substance changes from a liquid to a gas.
8. Molecules vibrate in a solid, but have fixed positions. Molecules in a liquid flow freely, but they don't completely separate because they don't have enough energy to completely overcome the attractive forces between molecules. Molecules in a gas move freely and so quickly they can overcome all attractive forces between molecules.
9. Viscosity is the resistance to flow. Peanut butter resists flow more.
10. Vaporization is when liquid turns to vapor, like when sweat dries up. Condensation is the opposite—when vapor turns to liquid, like when water droplets form on the surface of a glass holding a cold drink.

#5 has more than one correct answer.

Chapter 7

PERIODIC TABLE, ATOMIC STRUCTURE, AND COMPOUNDS

The PERIODIC TABLE

ELEMENT
one type of atom

Different atoms have different numbers of protons and electrons—accounting for all the differences in the physical properties of matter. Different types

PERIODIC TABLE
a table of all of the elements

of atoms are called **ELEMENTS**, and there are around 118 known elements. Each element is made of unique atoms.

All of these elements are presented in a chart called the **PERIODIC TABLE**, which lists and organizes every element in boxes. Each element is assigned a

CHEMICAL SYMBOL
one or two letters that represent an element

CHEMICAL SYMBOL, which is one or two letters. The first letter is uppercase while the second letter (if there is a second letter) is lowercase. For example, oxygen is represented as O, while zinc is represented as Zn.

THE PERIODIC TABLE

← PERIOD →

1

1
H
Hydrogen
1.0078

Key:
- 3 — Atomic Number
- **Li** — Chemical Symbol
- Lithium — Element Name
- 6.941 — Average Atomic Mass

↑ GROUP ↓

Period 1

1	2	3	4	5	6	7	8	9
1 **H** Hydrogen 1.0078								
3 **Li** Lithium 6.941	4 **Be** Beryllium 9.0122							
11 **Na** Sodium 22.990	12 **Mg** Magnesium 24.305							
19 **K** Potassium 39.098	20 **Ca** Calcium 40.078	21 **Sc** Scandium 44.956	22 **Ti** Titanium 47.867	23 **V** Vanadium 50.942	24 **Cr** Chromium 51.996	25 **Mn** Manganese 54.938	26 **Fe** Iron 55.845	27 **Co** Cobalt 58.933
37 **Rb** Rubidium 85.468	38 **Sr** Strontium 87.62	39 **Y** Yttrium 88.906	40 **Zr** Zirconium 91.224	41 **Nb** Niobium 92.906	42 **Mo** Molybdenum 95.95	43 **Tc** Technetium 98.9062	44 **Ru** Ruthenium 101.07	45 **Rh** Rhodium 102.91
55 **Cs** Caesium 132.91	56 **Ba** Barium 137.33		72 **Hf** Hafnium 178.49	73 **Ta** Tantalum 180.95	74 **W** Tungsten 183.84	75 **Re** Rhenium 186.21	76 **Os** Osmium 190.23	77 **Ir** Iridium 192.22
87 **Fr** Francium (223)	88 **Ra** Radium (226)		104 **Rf** Rutherfordium (267)	105 **Db** Dubnium (268)	106 **Sg** Seaborgium (269)	107 **Bh** Bohrium (264)	108 **Hs** Hassium (269)	109 **Mt** Meitnerium (278)

57 **La** Lanthanum 138.91	58 **Ce** Cerium 140.12	59 **Pr** Praseodymium 140.91	60 **Nd** Neodymium 144.24	61 **Pm** Promethium (145)	62 **Sm** Samarium 150.36
89 **Ac** Actinium (226)	90 **Th** Thorium 232.04	91 **Pa** Protactinium 231.04	92 **U** Uranium 238.03	93 **Np** Neptunium (237)	94 **Pu** Plutonium (244)

18

| 2 | He | Helium | 4.0026 |

| **13** | **14** | **15** | **16** | **17** | |

| 5 B Boron 10.806 | 6 C Carbon 12.009 | 7 N Nitrogen 14.006 | 8 O Oxygen 15.999 | 9 F Fluorine 18.998 | 10 Ne Neon 20.180 |
| 13 Al Aluminum 26.982 | 14 Si Silicon 28.084 | 15 P Phosphorus 30.974 | 16 S Sulfur 32.059 | 17 Cl Chlorine 35.446 | 18 Ar Argon 39.948 |

10	**11**	**12**						
28 Ni Nickel 58.693	29 Cu Copper 63.546	30 Zn Zinc 65.38	31 Ga Gallium 69.723	32 Ge Germanium 72.63	33 As Arsenic 74.922	34 Se Selenium 78.96	35 Br Bromine 79.904	36 Kr Krypton 83.798
46 Pd Palladium 106.42	47 Ag Silver 107.87	48 Cd Cadmium 112.41	49 In Indium 114.82	50 Sn Tin 118.71	51 Sb Antimony 121.76	52 Te Tellurium 127.60	53 I Iodine 126.90	54 Xe Xenon 131.29
78 Pt Platinum 195.08	79 Au Gold 196.97	80 Hg Mercury 200.59	81 Tl Thallium 204.38	82 Pb Lead 207.2	83 Bi Bismuth 208.98	84 Po Polonium (209)	85 At Astatine (210)	86 Rn Radon (222)
110 Ds Darmstadtium (281)	111 Rg Roentgenium (281)	112 Cn Copernicium (285)	113 Nh Nihonium (286)	114 Fl Flerovium (289)	115 Mc Moscovium (289)	116 Lv Livermorium (293)	117 Tn Tennessine (294)	118 Og Oganesson (294)

| 63 Eu Europium 151.96 | 64 Gd Gadolinium 157.25 | 65 Tb Terbium 158.93 | 66 Dy Dysprosium 162.50 | 67 Ho Holmium 164.93 | 68 Er Erbium 167.26 | 69 Tm Thulium 168.93 | 70 Yb Ytterbium 173.04 | 71 Lu Lutetium 174.97 |
| 95 Am Americium (243) | 96 Cm Curium (247) | 97 Bk Berkelium (247) | 98 Cf Californium (251) | 99 Es Einsteinium (252) | 100 Fm Fermium (257) | 101 Md Mendelevium (258) | 102 No Nobelium (259) | 103 Lr Lawrencium (262) |

Each square has information about the element. The top number is its **ATOMIC NUMBER**, and the bottom one is its **ATOMIC MASS**.

3	— Atomic Number
Li	— Chemical Symbol
Lithium	— Element Name
6.941	— Average Atomic Mass

✓ also the number of electrons

ATOMIC NUMBER
the number of protons an atom contains. Elements are differentiated by their atomic numbers because each element has a different number of protons.

The periodic table is organized by row and column. Each horizontal row is called a **PERIOD**, while each vertical column is called a **GROUP** or **FAMILY**. The elements are arranged in order of their atomic numbers—so as you go across, each element has one more electron and has one more proton. Hydrogen has 1, helium has 2, and so on. Elements in the same group (column) share similar chemical and physical properties.

ATOMIC MASS
the average mass of a typical atom of that element

PERIOD
a row of elements across the periodic table

GROUP or **FAMILY**
a column of elements in the periodic table. Groups of elements have similar physical and chemical properties.

To remember that a period is across while a group is down, think: A period comes at the end of a sentence, and a sentence goes ACROSS a page.

Atomic Structure and Energy Levels

The nucleus of the atom contains the positively charged protons, neutral neutrons, and a negatively charged electron cloud, which contains electrons and surrounds the nucleus. Electrons orbit the nucleus at really high speeds. Because electrons are constantly moving, it's hard to say exactly where an electron is at any moment in time, but scientists can predict the probability of finding an electron in certain zones. Most of these zones are shaped like rings around the nucleus, because electrons orbit the nucleus.

Each of these rings is called an ENERGY LEVEL. The lowest energy levels are the rings closest to the nucleus, and the higher energy levels are farther from the nucleus. Since electrons are attracted to the nucleus (remember that + and − forces attract), the electrons closest to the nucleus are hardest to remove. The energy level closest to the nucleus can hold up to 2 electrons. Every energy level beyond that can hold up to 8 electrons. For example, the first level of an oxygen atom has 2 electrons, and the second has 6 electrons.

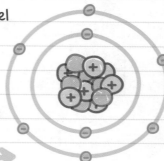

oxygen = 8 electrons

Isotopes

While atoms of the same element have the same number of protons, the number of neutrons can vary. More neutrons mean the atom is heavier! Atoms of the same element that have a different number of

> **ISOTOPES**
> atoms of the same element that have a different number of neutrons

neutrons are called **ISOTOPES**. The atomic mass is actually the average weight of the isotopes of a single element.

Neutral Elements and Ions

The number of protons in a NEUTRAL ELEMENT is equal to the number of electrons—the positives balance out the negatives to make the element neutral.

All atoms at first have a neutral charge. Therefore, if you know the atomic number of an element, you know the element's number of protons as well as the electrons. You can also figure out how many neutrons are in the atom by subtracting the atomic number from the atomic mass:

3
Li
Lithium
6.941

— Atomic number: number of protons.
Also, number of electrons.

— Average Atomic Mass

$6.941 \cong 7$ (Round atomic mass to nearest whole #.)

$7 - 3 = 4$ (Subtract atomic number from atomic mass.)

Lithium has 4 neutrons.

atomic mass − atomic number = number of neutrons

If we round the average mass to 7, we know there must be a total of 7 neutrons and protons combined. Because we know from reading the atomic number that there are 3 protons, we know there must be 4 neutrons.

From all this information, we can draw a model of the atom:

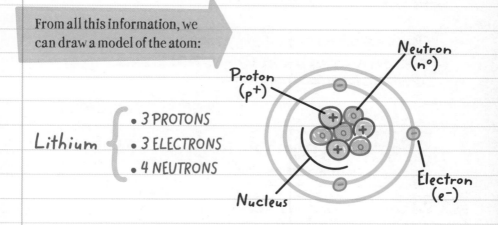

Lithium
- 3 PROTONS
- 3 ELECTRONS
- 4 NEUTRONS

If an atom has a charge, it's called an ION, and it has either more or fewer electrons than protons. If an atom is negatively charged, it has more electrons (fewer protons). If it is positively charged, it has more protons (fewer electrons).

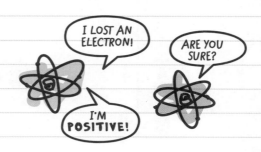

MOLECULES and COMPOUNDS

When two or more atoms combine, they form **MOLECULES**.

Molecules frequently combine with other molecules to form **MOLECULAR COMPOUNDS**.

The simplest molecular compound has two atoms and is called a **DIATOMIC MOLECULE**.

The prefix *DI* means "two."

Nitrogen and oxygen are frequently found as diatomic molecules—N_2 and O_2.

We can use simple models like these to represent the atomic composition of different molecules, or we can get fancy with computer-generated 3-D models.

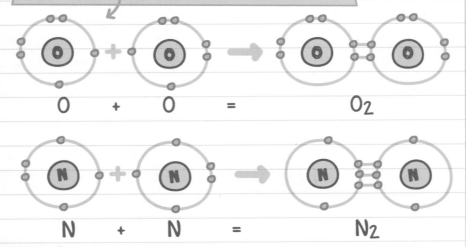

O + O = O_2

N + N = N_2

Compounds have different properties from those the individual elements have on their own—water wouldn't seem anything like water if it were a bunch of separate hydrogen and oxygen atoms.

WHY ATOMS FORM COMPOUNDS

Atoms always want to be in a stable state. Many atoms find stability by combining with other atoms. That means giving away, taking, or even sharing electrons with other atoms.

Electrons move in all directions, but they are limited to different ELECTRON SHELLS around the nucleus. When electrons from different atoms pair up, they form a CHEMICAL BOND. This chemical bond is the force that holds atoms together. Only electrons in the outer rings—VALENCE SHELLS—form bonds.

The VALENCE ELECTRONS are the first to interact and decide how an atom will react in a chemical reaction.

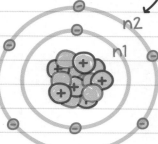

Each shell (n) is numbered.

n2

n1

Oxygen = 8 electrons

6 valence electrons

How to Write a Chemical Formula

Every compound contains a specific ratio of elements. A CHEMICAL FORMULA is sort of like the compound's recipe—it describes the ingredients and their quantities. In a chemical formula, each element is written using its chemical symbol, which is a one- or two-letter symbol, with a subscript beneath the symbol defining the number of atoms.

EXAMPLE: Sugar contains 12 carbon, 22 hydrogen, and 11 oxygen atoms. So the chemical formula is $C_{12}H_{22}O_{11}$.

CHECK YOUR KNOWLEDGE

1. How many known elements are there?

2. Elements are differentiated by their _ _ _ _ _ _ _   _ _ _ _ _ _ _ _ because each element has a different number of protons.

3. What is the name of a column of elements in the periodic table? What do these elements have in common?

4. What do two or more atoms combine to form?

5. What is the atomic mass of an atom?

6. If the atomic number of an element is 6 and the atomic mass is 15, how many neutrons are present?

7. What is an isotope?

8. What is a chemical bond?

9. Why do atoms bond?

ANSWERS

CHECK YOUR ANSWERS

1. 118

2. Atomic numbers

3. A group is a column of elements in the periodic table. Groups of elements have similar physical and chemical properties.

4. A molecular compound

5. The atomic mass is the average mass of a typical atom of that element. It's also the combined number of protons and neutrons.

6. Nine neutrons are present ($15 - 6 = 9$).

7. Atoms of the same element that have a different number of neutrons are isotopes.

8. A chemical bond is when atoms share electrons.

9. Atoms make chemical bonds so that their electrons can pair up and become more stable.

Chapter 8

SOLUTIONS AND FLUIDS

SUBSTANCES, MIXTURES, and SOLUTIONS

A SUBSTANCE is something that can't be broken down into simpler parts and physical changes won't alter its composition. A substance is made of a single compound. For example, water (H_2O) is a substance. No matter what physical processes you put water through (like freezing or boiling), water will remain H_2O.

A MIXTURE, on the other hand, is made of different substances mixed together that aren't chemically bonded. Salad dressing is a mixture of different things, like oil, herbs, and lemon juice.

A SALAD IS ALSO AN EXAMPLE OF A MIXTURE.

There are two kinds of mixtures:

1. HETEROGENEOUS MIXTURE: a mixture where the substances aren't evenly mixed. A salad is an example of a heterogeneous mixture; every bite of a salad is different no matter how many times you mix the salad.

HETERO is Greek for "different," so the mixture has different parts; it's not all the same.

2. HOMOGENOUS MIXTURE: a mixture where the molecules of each substance are equally mixed, and you can't see the different parts of the mixture. Sugar that is dissolved in water creates a homogenous mixture—you can't see the sugar and the water, just a liquid that contains molecules of both.

HOMO is Greek for "same," so the mixture is the same throughout.

Sometimes homogenous mixtures are called **SOLUTIONS**. A solution is made of a **SOLUTE** and a **SOLVENT**. A solute is the substance that gets dissolved, and the solvent is the substance that dissolves the solute. For example, some sports drinks are a solution that is made of water (the solvent) and powdered sports drink mix (the solute).

SOLUTION
a homogenous mixture

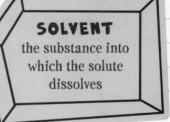

SOLUTE
the substance that is dissolved into the other substance

SOLVENT
the substance into which the solute dissolves

SOLUTE

SOLVENT

SOLUBILITY

SOLUBILITY is the ability of a substance to dissolve in another substance. Lots of things affect solubility:

Temperature is one factor: Usually solid solutes are more soluble in water at higher temperatures, which is why it is easier to dissolve sugar in hot water.

GASES CAN BE DISSOLVED IN LIQUID, TOO!

Gas solutes, like carbonation, are the opposite of solid solutes. Gases are more soluble in liquids at colder temperatures. Carbonated beverages remain fizzy longer when they are cold because gas is more soluble in cold liquids.

PRESSURE and the **CONCENTRATION** of other solvents in a solution also affect solubility.

CONCENTRATION

The CONCENTRATION of a solution is the amount of solute contained in a solution. A CONCENTRATED SOLUTION has a lot of solute, while a DILUTED SOLUTION has very little solute. For a lemon sports drink solution, a concentrated solution would be really sour and sweet, and a diluted solution would taste watery.

The side of a juice box will usually tell you the concentration of fruit juice. If the concentration of fruit in a fruit punch is 7 percent, that means 7 percent of the drink is made of juice, and the rest is stuff like water and sugar.

PRESSURE

A FLUID is anything that can flow, like liquids and vapors. A fluid, like all other forms of matter, exerts PRESSURE, or pushes, on its surroundings. For example, air that fills a balloon exerts pressure on the sides of the balloon to keep it inflated. Meanwhile, pressure from the atmosphere pushes on the outside of the balloon. As long as the pressure from the inside is greater, the balloon stays inflated. Pressure is proportional to both the force of the push and the area on which it pushes. More force means more pressure, and more area means less pressure:

$$\text{pressure} = \frac{\text{force}}{\text{area}}$$

The units most commonly used for pressure are a PASCAL (Pa), or an ATMOSPHERE (atm). One atmosphere is the pressure the atmosphere exerts on Earth at sea level. As you go higher up, there are fewer air molecules above you—so there's less pressure. The change in pressure between low and high altitudes is what causes your ears to pop when you go over a high mountain pass

LITTLE WEIGHT ABOVE YOU

LOTS OF WEIGHT ABOVE YOU

in a car. It's also why water boils at a lower temperature in the mountains: There's less pressure holding the molecules, so they can escape more easily.

The amount of pressure exerted on an object depends on the amount of water or air molecules above it. Think of a huge pile of books. The books deeper in the pile have more books on top of them, so they feel more pressure. If you go deep underwater, you feel much more pressure than you do at the surface of the water for the same reason.

CHECK YOUR KNOWLEDGE

1. Define "substance."

2. A bowl of beef-barley soup is a _ _ _ _ _ _ _ _ _ _ _ _ _ _ mixture.

3. If the force exerted remains the same, pressure increases as area _ _ _ _ _ _ _ _ _.

4. The deeper you go in the ocean, the _ _ _ _ _ _ the pressure gets.

5. What is the concentration of a solution?

6. What word describes anything that can flow, including water, air, and oil?

ANSWERS

CHECK YOUR ANSWERS

1. A substance is something that can't be broken down into simpler parts, and physical changes won't alter its composition.

2. Heterogeneous

3. Decreases

4. Higher

5. Concentration is the amount of solute contained in a solution.

6. Fluid

Unit 3

Motion, Forces, and Work

WHEW

Chapter 9

MOTION

MOTION

MOTION is the change of position. Motion is everywhere you look. Turning the page of this notebook is motion and the earth revolving around the sun is also motion. Any time your position changes, YOU are in motion.

RELATIVE MOTION

If you're standing by a road and a truck drives by at 30 miles per hour, to you, the truck appears to be moving 30 miles per hour down the road. However, if you were in a car also driving 30 miles per hour next to the truck, the same truck wouldn't seem to move. MOTION IS RELATIVE: It is always described in relation to a REFERENCE POINT.

For example, Earth rotates more than 1,000 miles per hour at the equator, but we can't see or feel it spinning. Why? Because everything we see around us is rotating along with Earth. So from our reference point, nothing is moving.

SPEED and VELOCITY

SPEED is the distance something travels in a certain amount of time:

$$\left\{ \text{speed} = \frac{\text{change in distance}}{\text{change in time}} \right\}$$

In SI units, distance is measured in METERS (m), time is measured in SECONDS (s), and speed is therefore measured in METERS PER SECOND (m/s).

When something is in motion, it doesn't necessarily stay at the same speed the entire time—it can change speeds and move faster or slower between its stopping and starting points. If that is the case, we use AVERAGE SPEED, or the total distance something has traveled divided by the total time it has traveled. INSTANTANEOUS SPEED is the speed at a certain given moment. For instance, an Olympic sprinter who runs the 100-meter dash in 10 seconds might seem like she would be going 10 m/s, but that's just her AVERAGE speed. Near the finish line she's probably going much faster.

VELOCITY

VELOCITY is just like speed except that it includes direction. If you were jogging at 2 meters per second and all of a sudden you turned and jogged 2 meters per second in the opposite direction, your speed before and after would remain the same, but your velocity would be different. You would be jogging 2 meters per second first, and negative 2 meters per second after turning around. The velocity would be equal in magnitude but opposite in direction.

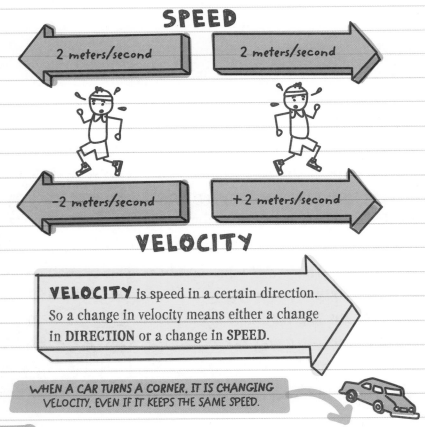

SPEED

2 meters/second   2 meters/second

−2 meters/second   +2 meters/second

VELOCITY

VELOCITY is speed in a certain direction. So a change in velocity means either a change in **DIRECTION** or a change in **SPEED**.

WHEN A CAR TURNS A CORNER, IT IS CHANGING VELOCITY, EVEN IF IT KEEPS THE SAME SPEED.

94

ACCELERATION

The rate at which velocity changes with time is called **ACCELERATION**. Whenever an object changes velocity, it is accelerating. Something can accelerate by:

SPEEDING UP,　　　　　　**SLOWING DOWN,** or

CHANGING DIRECTION.

The formula for acceleration is:

$$\text{acceleration} = \frac{\text{final velocity} - \text{initial velocity}}{\text{time}}$$

Final and initial (starting) velocities are usually measured in METERS PER SECOND (m/s), and time is measured in SECONDS (s). Acceleration is therefore measured in units of METERS PER SECOND SQUARED (m/s²).

Because velocity takes direction into account, so does acceleration. Therefore, when your car goes around a corner (even if it keeps the same speed), you feel the acceleration as a force that seems to push you toward the outside of the corner.

UGH!

Acceleration is positive when it is in the same direction as the object's motion, and positive acceleration means the object is speeding up. Acceleration is negative when it is in the opposite direction of the object's motion, and it means the object is slowing down. Negative acceleration can also be called DECELERATION.

BRAKE
("decelerator")

GAS PEDAL
("accelerator")

CHECK YOUR KNOWLEDGE

1. What is the formula for speed?

2. A dolphin swims 56 meters in 8 seconds and a walrus swims 30 meters in 6 seconds. Which is faster, the dolphin or the walrus?

3. Explain why motion is relative. Give an example.

4. What is required to know the velocity of an object?

5. If you walk around a square block going at the same pace, how many times does your velocity change, and how many times does your speed change?

6. If a truck driver is driving at 30 kilometers per hour and she makes a U-turn, then starts driving at 30 kilometers per hour in the opposite direction, did the driver's speed or velocity change after changing direction? Why?

7. If a bee is flying in a circle at a constant speed, is the bee accelerating?

8. What are the three ways something can accelerate?

ANSWERS

CHECK YOUR ANSWERS

1. speed = $\dfrac{\text{change in distance}}{\text{change in time}}$

2. dolphin speed = $\dfrac{56 \text{ m}}{8 \text{ s}}$ = 7 m/s

   walrus speed = $\dfrac{30 \text{ m}}{6 \text{ s}}$ = 5 m/s

   The dolphin is faster.

3. Motion is relative because it is always described in relation to a reference point. For example, we don't see the earth rotating because everything around us is moving with it (including us).

4. The speed and the direction of motion

5. Your velocity changes four times (because you are walking in a different direction on each side of the block). You are going at the same pace the entire time, so your speed doesn't change.

6. The driver's velocity changed because the driver changed directions. The driver's speed did not change.

7. Yes, the bee is accelerating. Because acceleration is the change in velocity per unit of time, and the bee is constantly changing direction, the bee is also constantly changing velocity and is therefore accelerating.

8. When something speeds up, slows down, or changes direction

#3 has more than one correct answer.

Chapter 10

FORCE AND NEWTON'S LAWS OF MOTION

FORCE

What makes something move? What makes a car speed up?
What makes the wheels on a bike turn? The answer is FORCE.
A force is a push or pull, and force is required to change the
motion of an object. The force you exert on the pedals of a
bike makes the wheels turn. In a car, the force behind motion
is an engine.

Force always has MAGNITUDE (size) and direction. Forces can
set an object in motion or change the speed and direction
of motion. Movement doesn't have to be moving from one
location to another; it can also be changing the shape of
something. Think about squeezing an empty soda can until it
crumples—you haven't thrown the can in the recycling bin,
but you have caused motion by changing its shape.

Net Force

Sometimes there is more than one force working on an object.
For example, when you pull a magnet off the fridge, there are
two forces at work: the magnetic force holding the magnet
to the fridge and the force you exert
on the magnet. The combination of all
of the forces acting on an object is
called the NET FORCE. The net force
on an object can be calculated by
adding all of the forces on an object
together.

FORCE + FORCE = NET FORCE

Force, like velocity and acceleration, has direction. So, to
calculate net force, you need to take direction into account.
If the forces are in the same direction, you add them; if the
forces are in opposite directions, you subtract them.

ISAAC NEWTON

ISAAC NEWTON figured out force, so the
unit that measures it is named after him. The SI
unit for force is a **newton (N)**. One newton is the
force needed to accelerate an object with a mass
of 1 kilogram at 1 meter per second squared:

$$1N = 1kg \times 1\frac{m}{s^2}$$

In fact, to hold up an apple against the
force of gravity requires about 1N of force!

FORCE and MOTION

Isaac Newton figured out all of this force and motion stuff, and he came up with the LAWS OF MOTION to describe the motion of all objects in the universe.

> ## NEWTON'S FIRST LAW OF MOTION is:
> "An object in motion will remain in motion and an object at rest will remain at rest unless there is net force acting on the object."

For example, a soccer ball is lying in an open field. It will remain sitting there unless an outside force acts on the object, like someone kicking the ball. Once the ball is in motion, it will remain in motion unless an outside force acts on it, like friction between the ball and the grass, air resistance, gravity, or another soccer player stopping the ball with his foot. On the other hand, if you kick a ball in deep space, it would keep going (until gravity from a star or planet bent its path).

HONEY, TIME TO GET UP!

BUT...INERTIA...

Inertia and Momentum

Matter doesn't like to change what it's doing. If it is in motion, it likes to stay in motion, and if it is at rest, it likes to remain at rest. INERTIA is matter's resistance to change in motion. Matter will remain at rest or in constant motion unless acted on by an outside force. That's why Newton's first law is sometimes referred to as the LAW OF INERTIA.

Objects with more mass have more inertia. Think about catching a tennis ball as compared to catching a basketball:

If they have the same velocity, it is easier to stop the motion of a tennis ball because the tennis ball has less mass than the basketball.

MOMENTUM is a measure of how difficult it is to change the inertia of an object. You can calculate it with this formula:

$$\{\ \textbf{momentum = mass × velocity}\ \}$$

Conservation of Momentum

If energy isn't lost during a collision (maybe through friction or heat), the amount of momentum in a group of objects before and after a collision is the same. For example, when you play pool, the momentum of the cue ball is transferred to the ball it hits, and the amount of momentum in the system remains constant (except for the little bit of energy transferred to heat when they collide). The LAW OF CONSERVATION OF MOMENTUM can be used to predict the velocity of objects of any mass and velocity before and after they collide.

NEWTON'S SECOND LAW of MOTION

> **NEWTON'S SECOND LAW OF MOTION** is:
> "The acceleration of an object is equal to the net force
> on an object divided by the mass of the object."

Newton's second law basically says that the more force
applied to an object, the faster it will accelerate. It also
says that the more mass an object has, the more force
you'll need to accelerate it. The relationship between force
and acceleration is often expressed
like this:

Net force is sometimes
abbreviated as F_{net}.

$$\{ \quad acceleration = \frac{net\ force}{mass} \quad \}$$

We can also use our algebra skills to rearrange this formula
to find net force:

$$\{ \quad net\ force = mass \times acceleration \quad \}$$

Think about pushing a shopping cart and pushing a car. If
you apply the same amount of force to both, the shopping
cart will zoom off, but the car won't move. So a larger mass
will accelerate less if the same amount of force is applied.

A force can cause something to either speed up or slow down. This is how you can tell which will happen:

When the net force (and therefore acceleration) is in the SAME DIRECTION as the velocity, the object will **SPEED UP**.

When the net force is in the OPPOSITE DIRECTION to the velocity, the object will **SLOW DOWN**.

When you are coasting on a bike with the wind at your back, the net force is in the same direction, so you accelerate forward.

Don't forget that:
$$acceleration = \frac{final\ velocity - initial\ velocity}{time}$$
Acceleration is related to force because velocity is motion, and force causes motion.

UNBALANCED FORCE

When you are coasting on a bike against the wind, the net force is pushing in the opposite direction, so you slow down.

BALANCED FORCE

An **UNBALANCED FORCE** has a net force in one direction.	**BALANCED FORCES** cancel each other out so there is no acting force.
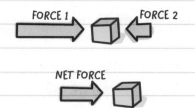	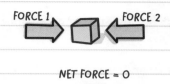

NEWTON'S THIRD LAW of MOTION

NEWTON'S THIRD LAW OF MOTION is:
"Forces act in pairs: For every action, there is an equal but opposite reaction."

Imagine holding a bowling ball near your chest and throwing it forward. You can probably shove it a few feet, but it also shoves you backward. Newton's third law refers to equal size of force and opposite direction of force.

Meaning: The size of the force on the bowling ball equals the size of the force on your body; the direction of the force on the bowling ball (forward) is opposite of the direction of the force on your body (backward).

COUPLED FORCES are called ACTION-REACTION PAIRS, and they have equal but opposite forces. You exert a force when you land on a trampoline, and the trampoline exerts an equal but opposite force on you, sending you up into the air.

Newton's third law also applies to running. When you strike the ground with your foot, you exert force on Earth, and Earth exerts equal but opposite force on you, propelling you forward. So if you exert a force on Earth, how come Earth doesn't also move? Remember Newton's second law:

"The acceleration of an object is equal to the net force on an object divided by the mass of the object."

Because Earth is so much more massive than we are, the same force that causes us to accelerate doesn't really affect Earth much (but it's there).

CHECK YOUR KNOWLEDGE

1. Describe the difference between a balanced and an unbalanced force.

2. You and your brother are playing tug-of-war. You pull with a force of 15 N, and your brother pulls with a force of 10 N. What is the net force?

3. What is Newton's first law of motion?

4. If a 2,000-kilogram car accelerates at a rate of 3 meters per second squared, what is the force the engine applied to the car?

5. What is Newton's second law of motion?

6. What is the unit of a force, and what is 1 unit equivalent to?

7. What is Newton's third law of motion?

8. Explain why when you jump up in the air, you move but the ground doesn't move much?

CHECK YOUR ANSWERS

1. An unbalanced force has a net force in one direction. Balanced forces cancel each other out so there is no acting net force.

2. 15 N – 10 N = 5 N

3. Objects in motion will remain in motion unless acted on by a net force, and objects at rest will remain at rest unless acted on by a net force.

4. $F = m \times a = (2{,}000 \text{ kg}) \times (3 \frac{m}{s^2}) = 6{,}000 \text{ N}$

5. The acceleration of an object is equal to the net force on an object divided by the mass of the object.
$$a = \frac{F_{NET}}{m}$$

6. A newton. $1 \text{ N} = 1 \text{ kg} \times \frac{m}{s^2}$

7. Forces act in pairs: For every action, there is an equal but opposite reaction.

8. While the force you apply on Earth is equal to the force Earth applies on you, you have different accelerations because your masses are so different. The force Earth exerts on you is large enough to send you into the air, but the force you exert on Earth is not significant enough to send Earth moving noticeably away from you.

Chapter **11**

GRAVITY, FRICTION, AND MORE FORCES IN EVERYDAY LIFE

Everywhere we look in our day-to-day lives, we see forces in action.

> **GRAVITY**
> the attractive force between objects with mass

GRAVITY

GRAVITY is not just the force we see when objects fall to the ground—gravity

> GRAVITY IS ALWAYS A PULL— NEVER A PUSH.

affects all masses. Gravity is the force of attraction between all things that have mass. The strength of gravity depends on both the mass and the distance between masses. Larger masses have more gravity. Also, objects that are closer will always pull on you with more gravity. If gravity affects all objects, why aren't we pulled to a building when we walk past it? The force of gravity between objects on Earth is so tiny that we don't even feel it—especially when compared to the force of gravity from Earth itself.

Gravity is also what keeps the earth in orbit around the sun. The sun has so much mass that it exerts a gravitational

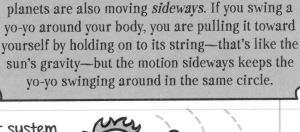

Why aren't planets in orbit around the sun pulled toward it? Because, despite the sun's gravity, the planets are also moving *sideways*. If you swing a yo-yo around your body, you are pulling it toward yourself by holding on to its string—that's like the sun's gravity—but the motion sideways keeps the yo-yo swinging around in the same circle.

force on our entire solar system, keeping all of the planets, including Earth, in orbit.

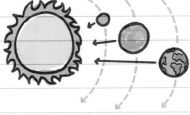

WEIGHT

WEIGHT is actually a measure of gravitational force. Weight depends on both the force of gravity and the mass of the object. If you weigh two objects on a scale, the object with more mass will weigh more.

Mass doesn't depend on location, but weight does because gravitational force can change depending on your location. For example, the force of gravity is less on the moon than it is on Earth. (The force of gravity depends on mass, and because the moon has less mass than the earth, it has a smaller gravitational force.) Therefore, the same object will weigh less on the moon than it will on Earth (about one-sixth as much).

Because gravity pulls you down toward the earth, there is a constant acceleration toward the ground. The force of gravity on Earth is approximately $9.8 \frac{m}{s^2}$. So, when you throw something up into the air, it gets slower until it stops in midair, and then comes back down toward the earth, accelerating down until it crashes into the ground.

This is **NEGATIVE ACCELERATION**.

FRICTION

Newton's first law states that an object in motion will remain in motion unless acted on by a net force. Try sliding this notebook across the table. It slows down and eventually stops. So what is the net force that is affecting the book? FRICTION! It's the force that opposes movement between touching surfaces and always acts against the direction of motion. When you ride a skateboard, the wheels slow down due to friction with the sidewalk and with the bearings in the wheels.

In general, rougher surfaces have more friction. Sandpaper is harder to slide than normal paper because it has a rougher surface and therefore more friction. On the other hand, you can minimize the force of friction by greasing surfaces. Even our bodies have ways to reduce friction: We have fluid in our knees to reduce joint friction.

There is also friction with air and water. The more technical term for friction with the air is **AIR RESISTANCE**. When you drop a feather, it floats from side to side because air resistance opposes the downward movement. Because friction is the force that opposes movement between surfaces in contact, objects with more surface area will have more air resistance.

SOME OTHER TYPES OF FRICTION ARE:

STATIC FRICTION: the force of friction between surfaces not in motion. Static friction is the result of molecules on one surface adhering to the other surface.

NO MOTION   FORCE→   ←STATIC FRICTION

SLIDING FRICTION: also known as KINETIC FRICTION, the force of friction that affects surfaces in motion. When you are pushing a box, the force of friction that resists the motion is sliding friction. Because the surfaces aren't always bonded like they are in static friction, sliding friction is less powerful than static friction.

UMPH!

SLIDING MOTION   FORCE →   ← SLIDING FRICTION

ROLLING FRICTION: the friction between surfaces, when an object, such as a wheel or a ball, rolls freely over a surface. The friction between the wheels of a skateboard and the sidewalk is rolling friction. Rolling friction is weaker than sliding friction, which is why it is much easier to move something on wheels!

ROLLING MOTION   ← FORCE   ROLLING FRICTION →

TERMINAL VELOCITY

When an object is falling to the ground, there are two forces acting on it: the force of gravity and the air resistance that is opposing its motion. When the air resistance equals the force of gravity on the object, there is no net force on the object; the forces are balanced. Without a net force, the object stops accelerating and it continues falling at a constant speed. TERMINAL VELOCITY is the speed at which the force of gravity equals air resistance. This speed depends on many factors, including the object's surface area, mass, how the object is oriented, and even the thickness of the air!

MAGNETIC and ELECTRIC FORCES

When you play with magnets, you can feel either an attractive or a repelling force. A MAGNET is a material that is attracted to iron, steel, or other magnets. Magnets have a positive and negative end. ← Sometimes referred to as a north (N) and a south (S) end

OPPOSITE CHARGES ATTRACT and LIKE CHARGES REPEL. So, when you place a positive with a negative end, the MAGNETIC FORCES pull together. If you try to touch a negative end with another negative end, or a

ATTRACT

REPEL

positive with a positive, you will feel a repulsive force (they push each other away).

ELECTRIC FORCES are like magnetic forces in that they are caused by positive and negative

charges in the matter. While magnetic forces are created by unmoving charges, electric forces are created by moving charges. The strength of both electric and magnetic forces is related to the amount of charge and the distance between charges. Electric and magnetic forces increase when the charge is stronger and when the charges are closer together.

ELECTROMAGNETISM is the interaction of electric forces and MAGNETIC FIELDS—any electric charge in motion has a magnetic region around it. A wire that carries an electric current is surrounded by a magnetic field. You can make an ELECTROMAGNET by wrapping a current-carrying wire around an iron core. Just like other magnets—one end is a north pole, and the other is a south pole.

The north and south ends of the bar are determined by the direction of the flow of electricity. If you reverse the flow, the charges reverse!

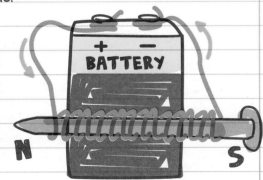

CENTRIPETAL FORCE

Because velocity includes both speed and direction, an object in circular motion is constantly changing its velocity, and therefore accelerating. Because an object in circular motion is accelerating, there must be an outside force acting on it (according to Newton's second law, force equals mass multiplied by acceleration). The force affecting an object in circular motion is called a **CENTRIPETAL FORCE**.

A centripetal force always points toward the center of the circular path of motion.

CENTRIPETAL FORCE
the force that causes an object to follow a curved or circular path and is directed inward toward the center of rotation

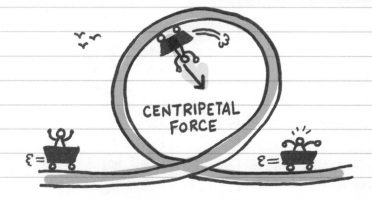

CENTRIPETAL FORCE

A centripetal force can be any number of things. The moon moves in a circular orbit around the earth and is affected by the centripetal force of gravity. If you swing a yo-yo around in a circle, tension from the string is the centripetal force that keeps the yo-yo in circular motion.

BUOYANCY and DENSITY

The force that keeps a rubber ducky floating is
called the BUOYANT FORCE. The buoyant force
is an upward force exerted by a fluid onto
an object that is immersed in the fluid.

YAY, BUOYANCY!

The buoyant force depends on the density
of the fluid and the amount of fluid that the object displaces.
The denser the fluid and the less fluid displaced, the
stronger the buoyant force. The buoyant force is actually
equal to the weight of the fluid that has been displaced,
which is a principle called ARCHIMEDES' PRINCIPLE.

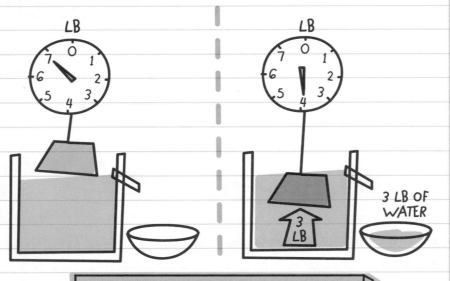

3 LB OF
WATER

DON'T FORGET: An object placed in fluid will
FLOAT if it is less dense than the fluid, and it
will SINK if it is denser than the fluid.

CHECK YOUR KNOWLEDGE

1. What is the force that attracts masses together?

2. Why does a bowling ball have more gravity than a soccer ball?

3. When you push a shopping cart, the friction that is opposing the motion is called _ _ _ _ _ _ _ friction.

4. What is centripetal force?

5. Centripetal force always points toward the _ _ _ _ _ _ of the circular path of motion.

6. Why does a feather drift back and forth as it falls?

7. The force of gravity decreases as the _ _ _ _ _ _ _ _ between masses increases.

8. In magnetic and electric forces, likes _ _ _ _ _ and opposites attract.

9. When the force of air resistance equals the force of gravity, a falling object reaches _ _ _ _ _ _ _ _ velocity.

10. What is the name of the upward force exerted on a boat in the water?

11. What is the buoyant force of a dog that displaces 10 pounds of water?

ANSWERS

CHECK YOUR ANSWERS

1. Gravity

2. As mass increases, so does the force of gravity.

3. Rolling

4. Centripetal force is the force that causes objects to have circular motion.

5. Center

6. Because of air resistance

7. Distance

8. Repel

9. Terminal

10. Buoyancy

11. 10 pounds

Chapter 12

WORK AND MACHINES

The scientific definition of **WORK** is different from how we use the word every day; in science, work is when an applied force makes an object move in the same direction as the applied force. So towing a car is work because the applied force and resulting motion are both in the same direction. Lifting a book off of the ground is also work: You apply a force upward and the book moves upward. The amount of work depends on both the amount of force applied and the distance across which the force is applied:

$$\text{work} = \text{force} \times \text{distance}$$

Work is measured in joules (J), force is measured in newtons (N), and distance is measured in meters (m).

119

To calculate work, we can only input force that is in the same direction of motion, meaning, if you are holding a basket of laundry, you won't be doing work as you walk down a hall, but as soon as you walk up the stairs you are doing work. Why? The force applied to the laundry basket to overcome gravity and pick it up

WORK

applying a force over a distance. The force must be in the same direction as movement.

WORK = FORCE × DISTANCE

$$J = N \times M$$

NO WORK

WORK

is vertical; when you walk down the hall, the motion of the basket is horizontal (not vertical), so you cannot include the horizontal distance in your calculation of work. When you walk up the stairs, the force is vertical (because you have to overcome gravity) and the motion is also vertical, so you are doing "work"!

Sometimes the force is only partially in the direction of motion. For example, if you can't fully carry the

trash, you lift up a little as you drag the bag (to overcome sliding friction), so you apply force in two directions: vertical and horizontal. However, because the bag is only moving across the floor, only the amount of force that is applied in the horizontal direction is considered "work."

POWER

POWER is the rate at which work is done—in other words, how quickly or slowly work is done. More powerful machines perform work faster.

$$\text{power} = \frac{\text{work}}{\text{time}}$$

Power is measured in watts (W), and time is measured in seconds (s).

SIMPLE MACHINES

To make work easier, humans invented MACHINES. When you think of a machine, you might think of a tractor or car, but a machine can be super simple. A machine is anything that makes work easier—even a RAMP is a machine. A simple machine doesn't reduce the total amount of work that is accomplished, but it decreases the amount of force required to do the same amount of work by increasing the distance.

A **SIMPLE MACHINE** is a machine that does work with a single motion, as opposed to a **COMPOUND MACHINE**, which combines a number of simple machines to produce a more complicated machine, like a can opener.

Inclined Plane

An INCLINED PLANE or ramp is an example of a simple machine. It reduces the amount of effort required by increasing the work's distance. Think about pushing a really heavy box into the back of a truck. With a ramp, you can roll the box up the ramp, which requires much less force than lifting the box into the truck. The box ends up at the same height, so the same amount of work is accomplished. However, because you pushed the box across a greater distance, less effort was required at any given time. The longer the inclined plane, the less force required to raise the object the same distance.

WHEW

EGYPTIANS BUILT THEIR PYRAMIDS USING REALLY LONG RAMPS.

Wedge

A WEDGE is a movable inclined plane, and it reduces the amount of work required to split or lift objects.

←WEDGE

Some examples of wedges are knives, axes, doorstops, and plows. To reduce the amount of effort required to cut firewood, people use wedge-shaped axes to split wood. It has to travel farther, but an axe requires less force than simply pulling a log in half with your bare hands.

Screw

A SCREW is a wedge (an inclined plane) wrapped around a shaft or post. As you turn the screw, the wedge pushes the object up the shaft (or the screw into the object). The amount of force required to secure a screw into the wall is less than it would be to hammer a nail of the same size. That's because the spiral of the screw has to go a much farther distance because it is turned so many times.

SCREW

Lever

A LEVER reduces the amount of effort required to lift something. A lever is like a seesaw: a rigid bar or plank with a pivot point, called a FULCRUM. When you apply a force, called effort, to one side of the fulcrum, the load on the other side also moves. Think about sitting on a seesaw with a friend— when you push down on the seat, your friend goes up into the air. Even if your friend is twice your mass, you can lift him by having him sit closer to the fulcrum. You push over more distance, so you need less force.

Levers are classified according to where the fulcrum and load are placed and where you apply the force, or effort:

FIRST CLASS: The fulcrum is somewhere in the middle, and the load and effort are on each side of the fulcrum (like a seesaw).

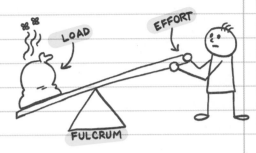

SECOND CLASS: The fulcrum is to one side, the load is in the middle, and the effort is on the other side (like a wheelbarrow).

THIRD CLASS: The fulcrum is to one side, the effort is in the middle, and the load is on the other side (like your arm when you lift a weight).

Wheel and Axle

A WHEEL and AXLE make it easier to
turn something by attaching a larger

wheel to an axle, or rod, which is essentially a smaller wheel.
There are two ways wheels and axles are used:

THEY INCREASE THE OUTPUT FORCE:

Turning a larger wheel requires less force than turning a
smaller wheel (the larger wheel is moved a farther distance,
so it requires less force for the same
amount of work). Think about twisting open
a faucet: It is much easier to turn a faucet
handle a few inches than it would be to
turn the pencil-thin neck. The axle exerts
the output force.

THEY DECREASE THE DISTANCE REQUIRED
TO MOVE THE WHEEL:

Turning the smaller wheel requires more force than turning
the larger wheel, but the smaller wheel must be turned a
much smaller distance to accomplish the same work output.
This mechanism is used on a bike: You apply the force over a
shorter distance with the pedal, and
the back wheel exerts less force
over a longer distance. The wheel
exerts the output force.

Pulleys

A PULLEY is a wheel with a rope wrapped around it. The rope fits into a groove on the wheel, and it is used to either magnify the force you apply to the rope (if you arrange a system of two or more pulleys) or change the direction of the force so it is easier to pull.

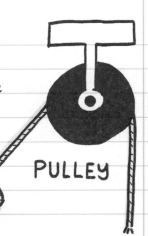

PULLEY

WORK as
ENERGY and EFFICIENCY

The energy of an object increases as you do work on the object. For example, when you push an object, it begins to move, and that motion is a form of energy. Work is equivalent to energy, so all of the work done on an object is conserved in the form of energy.

Energy comes in many forms, such as heat and motion. If you are doing work on an object and some of the energy you expend is lost in the form of heat (such as the heat that friction produces), you have lost some of your work. How much work, or energy, you lose to heat determines EFFICIENCY. A machine that doesn't lose much energy to heat produces more work and is therefore more efficient.

CHECK YOUR KNOWLEDGE

1. When is a person doing work? List some work you do on a daily basis.

2. When you drop a book, the earth exerts an upward force of 10 newtons on the book. If the book drops 0.5 meters, how much work did the earth do?

3. What is the difference between a simple machine and a compound machine?

4. Name an activity that uses a lever.

5. A pivot point on a lever is called a _ _ _ _ _ _ _.

6. How does an inclined plane make work easier? Are you still doing the same amount of work?

7. What are the two ways a wheel and axle can make work easier?

8. A pulley is a _ _ _ _ _ with a _ _ _ _ wrapped around it.

ANSWERS 127

CHECK YOUR ANSWERS

1. Any time a person applies a force in the direction of motion, he or she is doing work. Jumping up in the air, lifting a backpack, and throwing a ball are all examples of work.

2. work = force × distance
   10 newtons × 0.5 meters = 5 joules of work

3. A simple machine does work with one motion, and a compound machine combines different machines to produce work.

4. Transporting dirt by using a wheelbarrow is an example of an activity that uses a second-degree lever.

5. Fulcrum

6. An inclined plane reduces the amount of force necessary to lift an object a certain height by increasing the distance the object has to travel. An inclined plane increases the distance over which the force is applied, but you're still doing the same amount of work.

7. They increase the output force, or they decrease the distance required to move the wheel.

8. Wheel, rope

> #1 and #4 have more than one correct answer.

Unit 4

Energy

Chapter 13

FORMS OF ENERGY

CONSERVATION of ENERGY

ENERGY is a property of matter, and it comes in many forms, such as heat, sound, light, and motion. Energy, like matter, is always conserved. The amount of energy in a system remains the same, although it may change forms and be transferred between objects. For example, when a golfer strikes a golf ball, the energy from his or her swing is transferred to the ball (which, hopefully, lands in the hole).

The LAW OF CONSERVATION OF ENERGY states that energy can neither be created nor destroyed—it simply changes form. An example of energy transformation is light energy from the sun being absorbed by plant leaves to grow and thrive. The energy produced in the plant leaves is transferred to energy in our bodies when we eat our veggies. When we run or move, we release the stored chemical energy into mechanical energy.   ← SO, TECHNICALLY, WE'RE SOLAR-POWERED!

POTENTIAL and KINETIC ENERGY

When you drop a pen, **POTENTIAL ENERGY** is converted to **KINETIC ENERGY**.

Both are forms of MECHANICAL ENERGY, which is the energy of an object based on its motion or position. For example, when you kick a ball up a hill, it has kinetic energy because it is moving. As it slows and stops, the energy of motion is transferred to the potential energy in the ball's position. The potential energy of the ball can quickly be converted back to kinetic energy when the ball rolls back down the hill. The energy of the ball gets transferred between potential and kinetic forms, so energy is conserved.

We call this **GRAVITATIONAL POTENTIAL ENERGY** because it has the POTENTIAL to release its stored energy due to gravity.

KINETIC ENERGY the energy of motion

POTENTIAL ENERGY stored energy

Kinetic energy can be transferred to other objects through collisions. Think of bumper cars—when one car bumps into another, it transfers its energy, causing the other car to move.

The amount of kinetic energy an object has depends on both its mass and its velocity. More mass and/or more velocity means more energy. The amount of potential energy depends on both the mass and the height of the object. More mass and/or more height means more energy.

More mass and/or more velocity means more energy. In plain English, this means you'd rather have a tennis ball dropped on your head than a bowling ball, because the tennis ball has less mass. You'd also rather have that tennis ball drop from two feet above your head rather than from the top of a skyscraper, because the ball would develop less velocity.

The amount of potential energy of an object can change based on the way it is arranged. For instance, a book on the top shelf of a bookcase will have more potential energy than a book on the bottom shelf, since the higher book has more potential distance to fall.

Some scientists say there are only two types of energy (kinetic and potential energy), some say seven, others say nine! The important thing is to understand that energy comes in many forms (both moving and stored) and that energy is constantly changing from one form to another.

KINETIC ENERGIES

MECHANICAL KINETIC ENERGY
moving objects

THERMAL ENERGY
vibrating molecules that affect temperature

ELECTROMAGNETIC ENERGY
light waves (both visible and invisible)

SOUND ENERGY
molecules bumping into each other to transmit sound

ELECTRIC ENERGY
the flow of electrons

POTENTIAL ENERGIES

GRAVITATIONAL POTENTIAL ENERGY
(or MECHANICAL POTENTIAL ENERGY)
stored in the height of an object

ELASTIC ENERGY
stored in the compression or stretching of elastic materials

133

NUCLEAR ENERGY

is stored in the nucleus of radioactive atoms. In a process called **NUCLEAR FISSION**, atoms are split and that energy is released.

WE PRODUCE ELECTRICITY FROM NUCLEAR ENERGY THIS WAY.

CHEMICAL ENERGY

is the energy stored in chemical bonds. Before a bond is broken, the chemical energy stored in the bond is a form of POTENTIAL ENERGY. Once the bond is broken, the chemical energy can be released. Food, oil, gas, firewood, and coal are all sources of chemical energy. Anything that is considered fuel (for living and nonliving things) has chemical energy stored in its bonds.

CHECK YOUR KNOWLEDGE

Match the term with the correct definition:

1. Conservation of energy

2. Potential energy

3. Kinetic energy

A. Stored energy

B. Energy can never be created or destroyed. The amount of energy in a system remains constant.

C. The energy of an object based on its motion

4. When a cow eats grass, it digests and breaks chemical bonds in the grass to release thermal and kinetic _ _ _ _ _ _.

5. What is chemical energy?

6. What two factors influence the amount of potential energy of an object?

7. Energy is constantly _ _ _ _ _ _ _ _ from one form to another.

8. Your bumper car hits your friend's bumper car, causing her to move forward. What kind of energy was experienced?

ANSWERS

CHECK YOUR ANSWERS

1. B
2. A
3. C
4. Energy
5. Chemical energy is the energy stored in chemical bonds.
6. Mass and height
7. Changing
8. Kinetic energy

Chapter 14

THERMAL ENERGY

TEMPERATURE

Our everyday definition of **TEMPERATURE** is how hot or cold something is, but the actual definition of "temperature" is the average kinetic energy of molecules in a substance. The molecules in a liquid, solid, or vapor are always in motion. These molecules move around and bump into each other. Because the molecules are moving, they have kinetic energy, and the faster the molecules move, the more kinetic energy they have. If you compare the molecules in a cup of hot cocoa to the molecules in a glass of cold chocolate milk, the hot cocoa molecules would be zipping around much faster than the cold chocolate milk molecules.

> **TEMPERATURE**
> the average kinetic energy of the molecules in a substance

Measuring Temperature

Usually, when things heat up, they expand, and when they cool down, they contract. Thermometers are based on the expansion or contraction of material according to temperature. When something is at a higher temperature, the liquid contained in the thermometer expands and indicates a higher temperature.

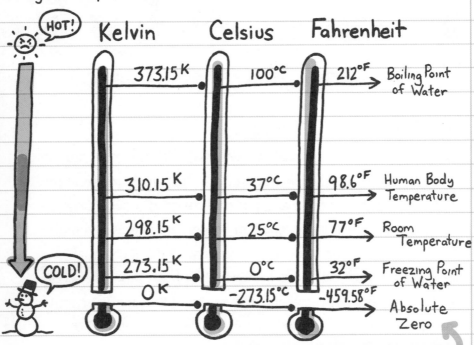

Molecules stop moving, so the temperature can't get colder—molecules can't get slower than stopped.

Converting Temperatures

We usually measure temperature either in Celsius (C), which is the metric scale, or Fahrenheit (F). You can convert between Celsius and Fahrenheit with these formulas:

$$T_{(°F)} = \left(T_{(°C)} \times \frac{9}{5}\right) + 32 \qquad T_{(°C)} = \left(T_{(°F)} - 32\right) \times \frac{5}{9}$$

Scientists frequently use the Kelvin (K) scale, which is the SI unit for temperature. To convert between Celsius and Kelvin, use the following:

$$T_{(K)} = T_{(°C)} + 273.15 \qquad T_{(°C)} = T_{(K)} - 273.5$$

THERMAL ENERGY

The total amount of kinetic and potential energies in the molecules of a substance is its **THERMAL ENERGY**. The difference between temperature and thermal energy is that temperature is the

> **THERMAL ENERGY**
> the sum of the kinetic and potential energies of all molecules in a substance

AVERAGE KINETIC energy of molecules in the substance, and thermal energy is the SUM of the kinetic and potential energy of all of the molecules in a substance. For example, a single brick has less thermal energy than a stack of bricks because it has less potential energy, but the single brick and stack of bricks may have the same temperature.

Heat

When we feel that something is hot, it's because the object is warmer than our hand.

> **HEAT**
> the transfer of thermal energy from warmer to cooler objects

HEAT is technically the transfer of thermal energy from a warmer substance to a cooler one. Thermal energy always moves from high to low energy, or, in other words, from warmer to cooler objects. Thermal energy continues to transfer between substances until both are at the same temperature.

Thermal transfer can occur through:

CONDUCTION: the transfer of heat from
a warmer object to a cooler object
through direct contact. The molecules
in the warmer object collide with the
slower-moving molecules in the colder
object, transferring energy. For example,
touching a hot stove with your hand. OUCH!

RADIATION: the transfer of heat
through electromagnetic rays. For
example, the sun heating the earth
or the warmth you feel when you sit
next to a fire.

CONVECTION: the transfer of heat through the movement
of a fluid (such as air or water). Air in your home moves in
CONVECTION CURRENTS—the warm air from a heater
rises, cools down, then sinks back down to the floor. You can
enhance the flow of air (convection) with a ceiling fan.

| **CONVECTION CURRENT** a current in a fluid that moves heat around | COOL AIR | WARM AIR | COOL AIR |

CHECK YOUR KNOWLEDGE

1. What's the difference between temperature and thermal energy?

2. If you have a large and a small glass of juice, both at room temperature, which one has more thermal energy?

3. _ _ _ _ _ _ _ _ _ _ is the transfer of heat through the movement of a fluid such as water or air.

4. What kind of heat transfer happens in a microwave?

5. When you lick a Popsicle, how does the thermal energy travel between the Popsicle and your tongue? What kind of heat transfer is that?

6. What is the formula to convert Celsius to Kelvin?

7. Thermal energy always moves from _ _ _ _ to _ _ _ energy.

8. When an object heats up, it _ _ _ _ _ _ _ .
When an object cools down, it _ _ _ _ _ _ _ _ .

ANSWERS 141

CHECK YOUR ANSWERS

1. Temperature is the average kinetic energy of molecules in a substance, and thermal energy is the sum of kinetic and potential energies of all the molecules in a substance.

2. The larger glass of juice because it has more molecules. More molecules means more thermal energy—it has more kinetic and potential energy.

3. Convection

4. Radiation

5. Heat travels from warmer to cooler objects, so thermal energy is transferred from your tongue to the Popsicle, melting the Popsicle. This kind of heat transfer is conduction.

6. $T_{(°C)} = T_{(K)} - 273.5$

7. High, low

8. Expands, contracts

Chapter 15

LIGHT AND SOUND WAVES

WAVES

WAVES are **OSCILLATIONS** that carry energy. Waves can move through matter or **VACUUMS**. Waves that move through matter are called MECHANICAL WAVES, and waves that move through vacuums are called ELECTROMAGNETIC WAVES.

> **OSCILLATION**
> an up-and-down or back-and-forth motion

> **VACUUM**
> space that has no matter in it.
> (Think of a vacuum cleaner sucking every bit of matter out of a space.)

Two examples of mechanical waves:

1. Waves in water created from the back of a speedboat. The energy travels from water molecule to water molecule, making ripples.

In outer space, you wouldn't hear any sounds because there isn't air for the waves to travel through!

2. Talking creates sound waves, which travel by transferring vibrations from molecule to molecule and move the sound from mouth to ear.

Unlike mechanical waves, electromagnetic waves don't need to travel in matter—they can travel in a vacuum, such as outer space. Some examples of electromagnetic waves include:

LIGHT WAVES   **X-RAYS**   **RADIO WAVES**

Wave Properties

The four main characteristics of a wave are:

1. AMPLITUDE is one-half the distance between a wave's high point, or **CREST**, and low point, or **TROUGH**. Amplitude measures how much a wave is displaced from its resting point. More energetic waves have larger amplitudes. Think of waves in an ocean: Waves that carry more energy are taller and are farther displaced from the regular waterline, so they have larger amplitudes.

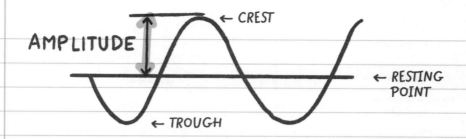

AMPLITUDE

← CREST

← RESTING POINT

← TROUGH

2. **WAVELENGTH** is measured from a point on one wave to the same point on the next wave—like crest-to-crest or trough-to-trough—and is written as λ (the Greek letter lambda). The difference between colors is caused by different wavelengths of light. Red has a longer wavelength than blue.

WAVELENGTH

You can measure wavelength any of these three ways. →

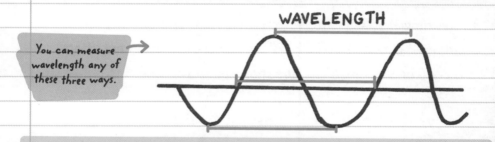

3. The number of waves that pass a fixed point in a given unit of time is called **FREQUENCY**, written as f. The unit for frequency is a hertz (Hz), which is the number of waves per second. Frequency and wavelength are inversely proportional if the waves are traveling the same speed, meaning: When frequency is higher, wavelength must be smaller (and vice versa).

Ten waves pass a dock in 10 seconds (higher frequency waves).

10 SEC

Two waves pass a dock in 10 seconds (lower frequency waves).

In the first situation, ten waves have to pass in the same amount of time it takes two waves to pass! Because the waves are traveling at the same speed, the ten waves must be closer together (they have a shorter wavelength).

(Higher frequency = smaller wavelength)

4. The time it takes a wave to move from one point to another is called **WAVE SPEED**, represented in equations as V (for velocity). The equation for wave speed is:

wave speed = frequency × wavelength
(abbreviated as $v = f \times \lambda$)

Wave speed is measured in METERS PER SECOND (m/s), frequency is measured in HERTZ (Hz), and wavelength is measured in METERS (m).

Waves travel at different speeds in different mediums. For example, mechanical waves, such as sound waves, travel faster in water than they do in air. Electromagnetic waves, such as

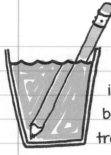

light, are the opposite: They travel faster in air than they do in water. When you stick a pencil into a glass of water, the pencil looks distorted because the light waves reflecting off the pencil are traveling faster in air than they are underwater.

Wave Behavior

REFLECTION is when a wave bounces off a surface. When you look into a mirror, you see yourself because the light waves have reflected off of the mirror. An ECHO *is also a reflection of a sound wave.*

The LAW OF REFLECTION explains that waves get reflected in a particular way—a wave reflects at the same angle as the angle that it moved toward the barrier. So, if a wave moves toward a wall at 90 degrees, it will also bounce off at 90 degrees.

Called the incident ray

Called the reflected ray

BARRIER

REFLECTED RAY

INCIDENT RAY

The bending of waves as they travel through different mediums (like the distorted light waves of a pencil in a cup of water) is called REFRACTION and is caused by waves traveling at different speeds in different mediums (or substances).

This is also why your legs sometimes look really short when you're standing in the pool!

DIFFRACTION is the bending of waves around a barrier or the spreading of waves past small openings. You can see diffraction when ocean waves come through a jetty or pier.

The result of waves colliding with each other is called INTERFERENCE. When waves collide, they either combine to form a larger wave, a process called CONSTRUCTIVE INTERFERENCE, or they interfere with each other and cancel each other out, a process called DESTRUCTIVE INTERFERENCE. When you jump on a trampoline with friends, you experience constructive and destructive interference. When you jump at just the right time, you get launched into the air! Other times, you hardly move. And sometimes the interference is somewhere in between constructive and destructive.

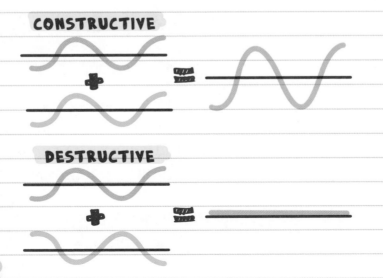

CONSTRUCTIVE

DESTRUCTIVE

ABSORPTION

If a wave passes through a substance, ABSORPTION may happen. Absorption is the transfer of energy from a wave to matter as the wave passes through it. For example, waves of light from the sun enter the ocean and are absorbed as they travel down, which is why the deeper you swim, the darker the water becomes.

The way a wave is absorbed depends on the nature of the substance it goes through and the substance's thickness. For example, recording studios often use sound insulation to absorb sound waves. When sound waves hit the insulation, most waves are absorbed, some are reflected, and very few pass through. Some substances absorb only specific wavelengths, which is how we see color. When we see a red apple, it's because every other color EXCEPT red is being absorbed and red is being reflected.

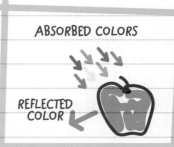

ABSORBED COLORS

REFLECTED COLOR

Furthermore, when a wave is being absorbed, the energy can be transformed. When light rays are absorbed, they are transformed into a different form of energy, such as heat. This is why colors that absorb more light rays (dark colors) heat up when in the light.

LIKE PAVEMENT ON A HOT SUMMER DAY

ELECTROMAGNETIC SPECTRUM

Electromagnetic waves are TRANSVERSE WAVES, which means they oscillate perpendicular to the direction of motion. Electromagnetic waves are made of electric and magnetic fields oscillating at 90-degree angles to each other, thus the name "electromagnetic" waves. Electromagnetic waves are basically "light waves," although not all of them are visible.

TRANSVERSE WAVE IN A ROPE

Up-and-down motion perpendicular to the direction of the wave

Direction of wave

The ELECTROMAGNETIC SPECTRUM ranges in wavelengths from thousands of meters to a trillionth of a meter long. The only kind of electromagnetic wave we can see with our bare eyes is visible light, which is only a tiny fraction of all electromagnetic waves—the visible **SPECTRUM** only ranges from 700 to 400 nanometers (billionths of a meter).

> **SPECTRUM**
> the wavelengths and frequency range of electromagnetic waves

Waves

Waves along the entire electromagnetic spectrum vary in energy, wavelength, and frequency. At the low-energy end of the spectrum, waves have longer wavelengths and lower frequencies. At the high-energy end of the spectrum, the waves have shorter wavelengths and higher frequencies.

THE ELECTROMAGNETIC SPECTRUM

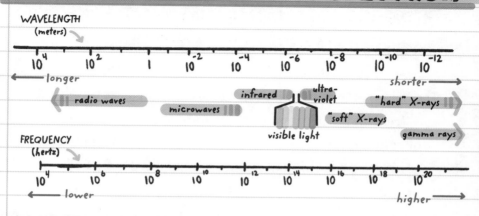

WAVELENGTH (meters)

longer ← | → shorter

radio waves

microwaves

infrared

visible light

ultra-violet

"soft" X-rays

"hard" X-rays

gamma rays

FREQUENCY (hertz)

lower ← | → higher

The spectrum of electromagnetic waves from low to high energy are:

RADIO WAVES
→ Lowest-energy electromagnetic waves
→ Longer than 0.3 meters
→ Transmit the music you hear on the radio

MICROWAVES
→ Between 0.3 meters and 0.003 meters
→ The waves that cook your food in a microwave

The frequency of the invisible waves in your microwave oven is just right for vibrating water molecules, which heats up the wet parts of your food.

INFRARED WAVES
→ Just longer than red light in the visible spectrum (which is why its called infrared)
→ Warm objects emit infrared waves, so night-vision goggles are sensitized to infrared waves to help see warm-blooded animals and people at night.

VISIBLE LIGHT

→ Light that humans can see is in this spectrum—between 700 nanometers and 400 nanometers

The colors of a rainbow are in the order of longest wavelength (red) to the shortest (violet). To remember the order of colors in the visible spectrum from longest to shortest wavelength, think of a person named **ROY G. BIV** (or **R**ed, **O**range, **Y**ellow, **G**reen, **B**lue, **I**ndigo, **V**iolet).

ULTRAVIOLET WAVES (UV RAYS)

→ Smaller frequency and higher energy than visible light— between 400 nanometers and 10 nanometers
→ The sun emits UV rays—they cause the sunburn you get at the beach.

X-RAYS

→ Higher energy and higher frequency than UV rays
→ X-rays can pass through skin and flesh, but not through bone, so they are used to examine bones.

GAMMA RAYS

→ Highest-energy, highest-frequency waves
→ These radioactive rays are harmful to humans and other living things.

Remember the visible light spectrum, from low to high energy with this mnemonic:

Roger Makes Instruments:
Violins, Ukuleles, Xylophones, and Guitars

(or **Radio, Microwaves, Infrared, Visible, Ultraviolet, X**-rays, **Gamma** rays).

The Perception of Light and Color

Electromagnetic waves travel incredibly fast—nearly 300,000 kilometers per second. It takes about 8.5 minutes for light to travel about 150 million kilometers from the sun to Earth. Light waves reflect off objects and enter our eyes. Usually, we think of light as white, but actually white light is every color combined. When light is refracted, the colors in white light separate out into each distinct wavelength of light.

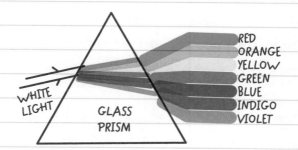

A RAINBOW IS THE RESULT OF LIGHT BEING REFRACTED THROUGH SMALL RAINDROPS IN THE AIR.

Sound

Noise is caused by sound waves, which are simply molecules vibrating. A sound wave is a LONGITUDINAL WAVE, which means that it oscillates in the same direction as it moves. A sound wave can travel in matter only because it needs to transfer its energy from molecule to molecule. So, if you sent your alarm clock to outer space, which is a vacuum, it wouldn't make a sound! No need for a snooze button!

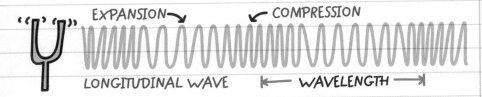

EXPANSION → ← COMPRESSION

LONGITUDINAL WAVE |← — WAVELENGTH —→|

Speed of Sound

Sound waves travel more slowly than light waves—light waves travel in air at about 300,000,000 meters per second and sound waves travel in air at about 340 meters per second. That's why you see distant lightning before you hear its thunder.

Although light waves travel slowest in solids, sound waves travel fastest in solids. Molecules are closer together in solids, so the molecules can bump into each other faster and transfer sound waves more quickly.

Intensity of Sound

The INTENSITY of a sound wave is how much energy the sound wave carries past a certain area. The amplitude of the sound wave causes the intensity—the larger the amplitude, the higher the intensity and the louder the sound. The intensity of a sound wave decreases as you get farther away from the sound's source, which is why things sound quieter at a distance. As the waves travel, they are absorbed by the air and other objects.

The loudness, or intensity, of sound is measured on the decibel scale (dB). For every increase in intensity of 10 dB, the sound wave carries 100 times more energy. People generally speak at 50 dB. The sound of a plane taking off is 150 dB, which is why airport employees sometimes wear ear protection.

Pitch

When you listen to a song, you hear many different tones. The different tones we hear are related to the sound's frequency, or the number of vibrations per second. Higher sounds have higher frequencies (short wavelengths), and lower sounds have lower frequencies (long wavelengths). Our perception of sound wave frequency is called PITCH.

BASS SOPRANO

The difference between a low-pitched bass and high-pitched soprano is the sound's frequency or wavelength. Higher-pitched sounds have higher frequencies (and thus smaller wavelengths).

A sound wave is an example of an **ANALOG** signal. Analog signals carry information but vary continuously in both amplitude and frequency. Alternatively, **DIGITAL** signals send information as wave pulses, and communicate only through 1s and 0s, so the form that the information takes is much simpler. When you speak into a cell phone, the analog sound waves of your voice are converted into a digital signal by your phone. The digital signal of your voice is then sent through a cell tower, bounced off a satellite, sent through another cell tower, and then finally to your friend's phone. When the sound comes out of your friend's phone, the waves become an analog signal again. Because a digital signal is simply sent through 1s and 0s, your friend will hear your voice perfectly, because any interference will not translate into the simple digital signal. (Since analog waves can hold so many different values, they are much more susceptible to interference, and therefore are more unreliable for sending information.)

CHECK YOUR KNOWLEDGE

1. What is the mnemonic for the order of colors in the visible spectrum? What is the order of the colors?

2. A high-intensity sound wave has a large _ _ _ _ _ _ _ _ _.

3. Between vapor, liquids, and solids, sound waves travel fastest in _ _ _ _ _ _.

4. What are the kind of waves you use to warm up food?

5. Which high-energy electromagnetic wave is harmful?

6. What kind of wave causes sunburn?

7. What are the electromagnetic waves that we can see?

8. What kind of waves do warm bodies emit?

9. Why would a cell phone not make a sound in space?

10. Why do higher-pitched sounds have higher frequencies?

ANSWERS

CHECK YOUR ANSWERS

1. ROY G. BIV: red, orange, yellow, green, blue, indigo, violet

2. Amplitude

3. Solids

4. Microwaves

5. Gamma

6. Ultraviolet

7. Visible

8. Infrared

9. Sound waves need matter so they can travel from molecule to molecule. There is no matter in space.

10. Higher-pitched sounds have shorter wavelengths, which means they have more vibrations per second.

Chapter 16

ELECTRICITY AND MAGNETISM

Electricity and magnetism are intertwined because they are both caused by the interaction of positive and negative charges in matter. When charges in matter interact, they can produce both electric and magnetic forces.

ELECTRICITY

Electric Charge and Force

All atoms have electrons, which are negatively charged particles, and protons, which are positively charged particles. When the number of protons and electrons in an atom are the same, the positive and negative charges cancel each other out and the atom is neutral.

However, atoms lose and gain electrons pretty easily. When an atom gains electrons, it has more negative than positive charges, so it carries a NEGATIVE CHARGE. When an atom loses electrons, it becomes POSITIVELY CHARGED. Positively or negatively charged atoms are called IONS.

Because like charges repel and unlike charges attract, ions create attractive and repulsive forces, called ELECTRIC FORCES. The negative electrons want to move to where it's more positive. And that's what electricity is all about: the flow of electrons!

The size of the electric force depends on how charged the atoms are and how far apart they are. Electric force increases with increasing charges and decreasing distance between charges.

Static Electricity

Electrons move relatively easily from one atom to another. When an electric charge builds up on an object and transfers from  one body to another it is called a STATIC CHARGE or STATIC ELECTRICITY. Things rubbing together, like rubbing a balloon on your hair, can create static charges because you're literally rubbing the electrons off your hair and onto the balloon!

When you feel an electric shock, you're experiencing the opposite—the quick discharge of electrons, called an ELECTRIC DISCHARGE or STATIC DISCHARGE. Lightning is actually an enormous electric discharge.

Electric Fields

The area around an electric charge that experiences the force exerted by that charge is called an **ELECTRIC FIELD**. The farther you are from the charge, the weaker the field is; an electric field gets stronger as you get closer to the charge.

Also, the larger the charge is, the larger the field is. ELECTRIC FIELD LINES show the direction of the electric force, and the field lines point toward a negative charge and away from a positive charge.

ELECTRIC FIELD
the area around an electric charge that experiences the force exerted by the electric charge

Induction

When you place a charged object near another object, it can cause the nearby objects to become charged as well. For example, if you put a balloon that is negatively charged close to a wall, the balloon will repel other electrons in that part of the wall, pushing them

161

away from the surface, and creating a localized temporary positive charge. Sometimes you can get a balloon to stick to a wall or window because of this temporary charge. The separation of charges caused by an electric field is called **INDUCTION**.

INDUCTION
the separation of charges caused by an electric field

Insulators and Conductors

An INSULATOR is a material that doesn't allow electrons to move easily, so charges don't flow. A CONDUCTOR, on the other hand, is a material that is good at transmitting energy because it

EXAMPLES INCLUDE GLASS, PLASTIC, RUBBER, PORCELAIN, AND STYROFOAM.

is made of a material through which electrons move easily. Gold, copper, and most other metals are good conductors. Usually, electrical wires are made of a conductor wrapped in an insulator, like plastic, to prevent the electricity from flowing into other conductors, such as your body. OUCH!

A RESISTOR is something that resists the flow of electrons but still lets them through. They usually either heat up, light up, or both when electrons flow through them. Examples include the thin wire (filament) in a regular lightbulb, the heating coils in your toaster, and even the human body.

ELECTRIC CURRENT

When electric charges move, they create an
ELECTRIC CURRENT. Electric current
is measured by the amount of charge
that flows by a certain point every
second, and the SI unit for electric
current is an ampere (A), or amp.

> ### ELECTRIC CURRENT
> the number of electrons that pass a given
> point in a certain amount of time

There are two types of current:

DIRECT CURRENT(DC): the electric charges in the
current move in one direction the entire time, like the
electrical current created by a battery.

ALTERNATING CURRENT(AC): a flow of electrical
charges that alternate direction periodically. The
electricity from an outlet provides AC current.

Electrical Circuit

An electric current will continuously flow if the charges can travel in a closed conducting loop, called a CIRCUIT. The electric field keeps the charge moving.

The components of a circuit are:

ELECTRICAL CONDUCTOR, such as a **WIRE**, which connects to the power source to form a **CLOSED LOOP** (a connection with no openings or breaks)

LOAD (not necessary, but usually there), a device that the circuit is powering, like a lightbulb, fan, or speaker

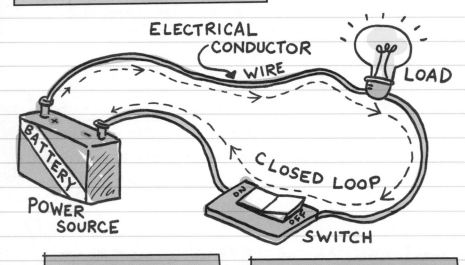

ELECTRICAL CONDUCTOR
WIRE
LOAD
BATTERY
CLOSED LOOP
POWER SOURCE
SWITCH

POWER SOURCE of electrical energy, such as a **BATTERY**

SWITCH (not necessary, but frequently there), a device to open and close a circuit

IT'S LIKE A DRAWBRIDGE ON A ROAD.

Series and Parallel Circuits

If an electron is like a car, a circuit is like the road: The circuit provides an electron with all the paths it can take. When there is only one way an electron can travel through a circuit, the circuit is called a SERIES CIRCUIT. In a series circuit, all of the current flows in one direction through every element in the circuit, and if the circuit is opened at any point, the electrical flow in the entire circuit will stop. So if a lightbulb in a circuit burns out, causing a break in the circuit, electricity will stop flowing.

SERIES CIRCUIT

A PARALLEL CIRCUIT is like traveling on a road with a fork in it—a car can take either a right or a left. In a parallel circuit, the electrons can take more than one path. When one path is broken, the current can continue to flow because the electrons still have an alternate path to follow.

PARALLEL CIRCUIT

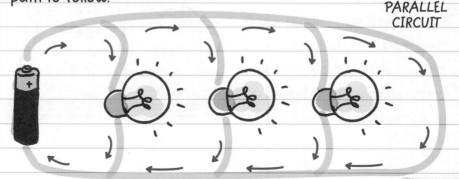

165

Batteries

Batteries provide the energy source that pushes the electric charges around a circuit. When connected to a circuit, a battery creates an electric field with a positive and negative terminal at each end of the battery (which is the + or − sign you see on different sides of the battery). The electrons, which are the moving charges in a current, are attracted to the positive terminal and repelled by the negative terminal. They travel like traffic on a road (as long as the circuit is a closed loop).

Voltage

The energy of flowing electrons in a circuit is called **VOLTAGE**. Voltage, measured in volts (V), is the electric potential difference between two points in a circuit, such as the positive and negative terminals of a battery. Voltage provides potential energy to an electron, just like gravity provides potential energy to a ball held above the ground. The higher the voltage, the greater the potential difference, and the more energy the current can supply. So a 9-volt battery will make a small lightbulb glow much brighter than a AA battery would (which is 1.5 volts).

VOLTAGE
the amount of potential energy an electron in a circuit can gain

Resistance

As electrons move in a current, they can bump into things, which makes it harder to travel. RESISTANCE, measured in ohms (abbreviated as R and symbolized as Ω), measures how difficult it is for electrons to travel through something—in other words, the resistance to flow.

Wires with less resistance can hold more efficient circuits— energy in high-resistance wires can be lost in the form of thermal energy from collisions. Resistance in a wire increases as the wire gets thinner and/or longer.

Think of a wire like a water hose: As the hose gets longer and/or narrower, the water has a harder time making it through the hose. Longer and/or narrower hoses have more resistance to flow. The same rules apply for a wire.

A lightbulb provides resistance in a circuit: The filament of a lightbulb is really thin, and as electrons flow through the filament, they collide and heat up the filament, releasing energy in the form of heat and light.

Ohm's Law

Ohm's Law shows the relationship between the voltage, current, and resistance in a circuit:

$$\text{voltage} = \text{current} \times \text{resistance}$$

Current is sometimes abbreviated as I.

Voltage is measured in volts (V), current in amperes (A), and resistance in ohms (Ω). Ohm's Law shows that if voltage increases, current, resistance, or both will increase as well. It also shows that if voltage stays the same:

{ When resistance decreases, current increases. }

{ When resistance increases, current decreases. }

Electric Power

Power is the rate at which electrical energy is transformed into other forms of energy; for example, the power of a toaster is the rate at which the toaster converts electricity into heat. The equation for power is:

$$\text{power} = \text{current} \times \text{voltage}$$

Remember, power is measured in watts, current in amperes, and voltage in volts.

APPLIANCE	WATTS PER HOUR
TOASTER	1,000 W
CLOTHES WASHER	500 W
CLOTHES DRYER	5,000 W
COMPUTER	200 W

Conservation of Energy in Circuits

Electrical energy also follows the law of the conservation of energy. So where does the energy from a battery go? As the current travels through a circuit, electrical energy is converted to thermal energy, light, or kinetic energy, such as the movement of a battery-powered toy.

MAGNETIC FORCE

Remember that a magnet has a positive and a negative end, or pole (a POLE is a strongly charged region of a magnet). Magnetic force is the attractive and repulsive force between poles. Opposite charged poles attract and like charged poles repel (just like electric charges).

SOMETIMES REFERRED TO AS NORTH AND SOUTH POLE

Magnetic Fields

The area around a magnet that exhibits magnetic force is called a MAGNETIC FIELD. MAGNETIC FIELD LINES show the direction and strength of the magnetic field. Magnetic field lines go from the north to the south pole, and the closer the field lines are, the stronger the force.

Electromagnetism

Electric charges in motion create magnetic fields. Because a current is a moving charge, any wire that has an electrical current flowing through it is also surrounded by a magnetic field. When a current-carrying wire is wrapped in a coil, the magnetic field lines around each piece of wire create a stronger magnetic field. The more times the wire is wrapped around the coil, the stronger the magnetic field.

The earth is like a giant magnet and has a magnetic field, too. A compass needle is actually a small magnet, which has a north pole and a south pole. When a compass is pointing north, the north pole of the compass's magnet is being attracted to the south pole of the earth's magnetic field—which is actually the geographical North Pole.

Motors

Because a current-carrying wire has a magnetic field, the wire can either be attracted to or repelled by other magnets. Some **MOTORS** use the attractive and repulsive forces between current-carrying wire and magnets to create movement in the wire. When the current-carrying wire is made into a loop and placed in a magnetic field, it continually spins, which creates kinetic energy that can be transformed into electric energy.

> **MOTOR**
> a device that converts electric energy into kinetic energy

Generators

Using the same concept (but reversed), we can transform mechanical kinetic energy into electric energy by moving a wire through a magnetic field (or moving a magnet through a coil of wire). By doing so, we cause electrons to move, creating current.

A **GENERATOR** turns the kinetic energy of a wire in a magnetic field into electricity. In a generator, a power source spins a loop of wire through a magnetic field, producing a current in the loop, a process

GENERATOR

called ELECTROMAGNETIC INDUCTION. Power plants use generators to create electricity, and a variety of sources provide the kinetic energy used to rotate the coils of wire through a magnetic field.

GENERATOR
a device that converts kinetic energy into electric energy

1. Which pole of a compass needle points north?

2. Two wires each have a current running through them and are placed next to each other. Will one wire be affected by a force from the other, and if so, why?

3. How does an electric field change with distance and increasing charge?

4. You have to change the lightbulb in a flashlight, and the new lightbulb has a larger resistance. If the voltage of the battery doesn't change, what happens to the current going through the flashlight?

5. When does an atom have a negative charge?

6. If you place a negatively charged hairbrush close to your hair, what kind of charge will your hair have?

7. What happens to the resistance of a wire as it gets wider?

8. What happens to the resistance of a wire as it gets longer?

9. If Christmas tree lights are wired in a series, and one burns out, do all of the other lights go out as well?

10. If Christmas tree lights are wired in parallel, and one burns out, do all of the other lights go out as well?

ANSWERS ▸ 173

CHECK YOUR ANSWERS

1. The south pole of the needle (opposite poles attract)

2. Yes, it will be affected by a force from the other wire because both wires have a current running through them and therefore both have magnetic fields.

3. Electric fields get weaker with increasing distance from the charge, and the larger the charge, the stronger the field.

4. V = IR, so if resistance increases and voltage stays the same, there is less current.

5. An atom is negatively charged when it has more electrons than protons.

6. The negative charge on the hairbrush will induce a positive charge on your hair. As a result, your hair will be attracted to the brush (and repelled by other strands of hair).

7. As a wire gets wider, it has less resistance.

8. As a wire gets longer, it has more resistance.

9. If the lights are in series and one burns out, all of the others go out as well because the circuit is broken—it is no longer a closed loop.

10. If the lights are wired in parallel, the electricity can still flow in a closed loop through the other lights, so the lights continue to work.

Chapter 17

ELECTRICAL ENERGY SOURCES

Where does all the electrical energy that we use day-to-day come from?

GENERATING ELECTRICAL POWER: TURBINES

A power source turns a TURBINE, which is a propeller-like piece that turns a metal shaft in an electric generator.

For example, a hydropowered plant uses falling water to turn the turbine. The spinning turbine converts kinetic energy into electricity (and some heat due to friction).

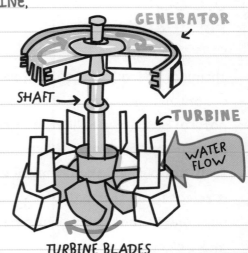

GENERATOR

SHAFT →

←TURBINE

WATER FLOW

TURBINE BLADES

175

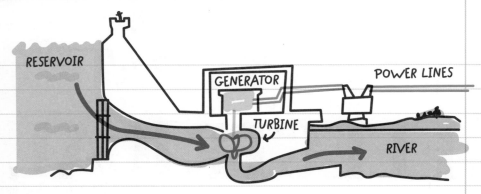

Using the concept of conservation of energy, we transform different forms of energy into electricity. Some of the most common energy sources are:

- **NUCLEAR ENERGY**
- **FOSSIL ENERGY**, such as oil, coal, and natural gas
- **RENEWABLE ENERGY**, such as hydropower and solar, geothermal, tidal, and wind energy

NONRENEWABLE RESOURCES
Fossil Fuels

FOSSIL FUELS use the stored chemical energy of ancient fossilized organisms that turn into oil, coal, and natural gas after millions of years of heat and pressure. When fossil fuels are burned, the chemical energy is released as thermal energy, which boils water that spins a turbine to make electrical energy.

Fossil fuels are considered NONRENEWABLE RESOURCES, which means that sooner or later, fossil fuels will run out.

← WE'RE USING THEM MUCH FASTER THAN THEY CAN BE REPLENISHED.

Burning fossil fuels also creates a lot of pollution, which is bad for the environment. The CO_2 that is released while burning fossil fuels contributes to **GLOBAL WARMING**.

GLOBAL WARMING
an increase in the overall temperature of the earth's atmosphere partially due to manmade causes

Nuclear Power

NUCLEAR POWER uses the energy contained in the nuclei of enriched uranium. When a nucleus breaks apart, it releases an enormous amount of energy that can be used

NUCLEAR

STEAM

to heat water, creating steam to spin an electrical generator. Although nuclear energy produces very little air pollution, it does produce nuclear waste, which is very toxic.

Earth's mineral, energy, and groundwater resources are unevenly distributed around the planet because of ongoing processes such as weathering, erosion, and removal by humans. For example, as glaciers move, they carry minerals away from some areas and deposit them in others. Humans also change the land—sometimes in irrevocable ways. When we build a city or even just a new building, we cut off access to the resources in that area or destroy them. All of this leads to the uneven distribution of resources, and many of these resources are not renewable or replaceable during our lifetimes.

RENEWABLE RESOURCES

A RENEWABLE RESOURCE is a resource that can be replenished. Hydropower, solar power, geothermal, tidal, biomass, and wind power are all examples of renewable resources.

Hydroelectricity

HYDROELECTRICITY collects water's gravitational potential energy to create electricity. Running water from a river is piled up high

HYDROELECTRIC

behind a dam, then let out (thanks to gravity) in a controlled stream, and the kinetic energy from the flowing water turns a turbine, which generates electrical energy.

Solar Power

SOLAR POWER captures the energy from the sun's radiation. There are two types of solar energy collectors:

SOLAR

- **THERMAL COLLECTORS** absorb the sun's radiant energy to heat up water. The hot water can then be used to heat a home or to produce steam to power a steam turbine, which generates electricity.

- **PHOTOVOLTAIC COLLECTORS** directly transform radiant energy from the sun into electrical energy.

Only about 0.1 percent of our energy comes from solar energy because it is expensive to capture. But maybe in the future!

Geothermal Power

The center of the earth is incredibly hot—so hot that it melts rocks. In places, this molten rock, called MAGMA, is close to the earth's surface, and it can heat water to form steam. Wells are drilled to reach these underground sources of steam and hot water. The steam is then used to generate electricity. Once the steam cools off in a cooling tower, it condenses and becomes water again. The cool water is injected back into the ground so the process can begin again.

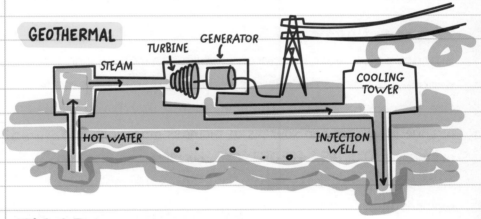

GEOTHERMAL

TURBINE   GENERATOR

STEAM

COOLING TOWER

HOT WATER

INJECTION WELL

Tidal Power

TIDAL POWER captures the energy of the ocean's tides. Oceans are in constant flux—they shift between low tide and high tide around twice a day. In places where the differences between the high and low tides are really large, underwater turbines capture the endless energy of water flowing in and out.

TIDAL

Wind Power

WIND POWER can also be captured to produce electricity.

The kinetic energy of wind is used
to turn wind turbines, which
generates electricity. Wind
energy is a leading source of
renewable energy, despite the
fact that turbines must be located in
windy spots in order to be efficient.

WIND

Biomass Power

Biomass power uses the stored chemical energy of living
things—you've created biomass power if you've ever made a
fire for cooking or staying warm. Plants, wood, and waste
are the most common sources of biomass materials, and
are called BIOMASS FEEDSTOCKS. Burning, dehydrating,
or stabilizing a biomass feedstock creates thermal energy,
which is then converted
into electricity. One of the
most common ways to create
biomass energy is to burn scraps from paper or lumber mills,
or even municipal solid waste. GROSS, BUT GREEN! Although
biomass feedstocks are renewable, they do produce air
pollution.

> If the biomass feedstock is not replanted,
> biomass power is nonrenewable.

CHECK YOUR KNOWLEDGE

1. Name some renewable and nonrenewable power sources.

2. Name some problems with using fossil fuels as our main energy source.

3. What is a problem with using nuclear power?

4. What is a turbine?

5. Which electrical energy sources use turbines to produce energy?

6. What are the two types of solar energy collectors, and how are they different?

7. Where does the energy in nuclear power come from?

8. How does hydroelectricity produce energy?

9. Geothermal energy requires what to heat water and produce steam?

10. What is biomass power? Give a few examples of biomass feedstocks.

CHECK YOUR ANSWERS

1. Renewable: hydropower, solar, geothermal, wind, biomass, and tidal energy. Nonrenewable: fossil fuels and nuclear.

2. When we use all of the fossil fuels in the earth, we'll have none left for millions of years. Burning fossil fuels also releases a lot of air pollution into the environment. The CO_2 released contributes to global warming.

3. Nuclear energy creates really toxic waste, and disposing of and storing this waste is problematic.

4. A propeller-like piece that turns a metal shaft in an electric generator

5. All electrical energy sources use them!

6. Thermal collectors and photovoltaic collectors: Thermal collectors absorb the sun's radiant energy to heat up water, which then creates electrical energy. Photovoltaic collectors directly transform the sun's energy into electrical energy.

7. Nuclear power uses the energy contained in the nuclei of enriched uranium.

8. Water from a river is piled up high behind a dam and let out (with the help of gravity) in a controlled stream. The kinetic energy from the flowing water turns the turbine and generates electricity.

9. Magma, or molten rock produced by the earth's core

10. Biomass power uses the stored chemical energy of living things. Some examples of biomass feedstocks are plants, wood, and waste.

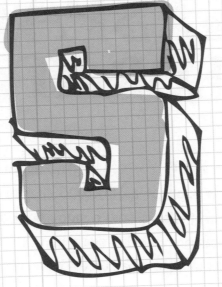

Unit 5

Outer Space: The Universe and the Solar System

Chapter 18

THE SOLAR SYSTEM AND SPACE EXPLORATION

Our solar system is **ENORMOUS**! The distance from the earth to the sun is about 150,000,000 kilometers (about 93,000,000 miles), and that is only a small part of the solar system. Our solar system includes everything affected by the sun's gravity. It includes the sun and everything orbiting around it—eight planets and numerous other objects, such as moons, asteroids, and comets.

THERE COULD BE A NINTH PLANET! SCIENTISTS RECENTLY FOUND EVIDENCE OF THE GRAVITATIONAL PULL OF A LARGE OBJECT BEYOND NEPTUNE, BUT NO ONE HAS SEEN IT . . . YET!

 The average distance from Earth to sun (150,000,000 kilometers) is a number that is pretty hard to work with. So scientists decided to call it one **ASTRONOMICAL UNIT (AU)**.

Our Solar System* *TRUE TO SCALE

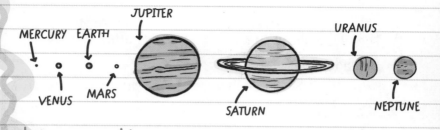

INNER PLANETS   OUTER PLANETS

> When looking at models, look closely at the measurements to understand how changes in **SCALE** affect the model. A scale model stays "true to scale," which means it will physically represent a system while keeping the relationship between the objects in proportion.

INNER PLANETS

SCALE MODEL
a representation of an object that is larger or smaller than the actual size of the object

The four planets closest to the sun are called the INNER PLANETS. All of the inner planets are TERRESTRIAL PLANETS, which means "earthlike." The terrestrial planets are made of rocks and have iron cores, just like Earth. Many of the inner planets have craters, or holes on their surfaces, caused by rocks smashing into them. These are the inner planets (listed in order from closest to the sun to farthest from the sun) and their characteristics:

MERCURY

- Has extreme temperatures (-180°C to 430°C) because it has no atmosphere
- Looks like Earth's moon—has many cliffs and craters
- Has no moons

VENUS

- Close in size and mass to Earth
- Has a dense atmosphere of mostly carbon dioxide that collects heat—remains around 464°C

EARTH

- Only planet known to support life—helped by its unique properties, such as liquid water, atmosphere, and an ozone layer
- Has one large moon

MARS

- Looks red because it contains iron oxide (rust)
- Has ice caps and rift valleys and the largest volcano in the solar system, Olympus Mons
- Has a thin atmosphere that is mostly carbon dioxide
- Has huge dust storms and seasons
- Has two small moons, Phobos and Deimos

OUTER PLANETS

The OUTER PLANETS of the solar system are the planets that are farthest from the sun. The outer planets are all called gas giants, because although they have rocky or metallic cores, they are mostly made of gassy sludge. Gas giants don't have defined outlines and are much larger than the terrestrial or inner planets.

JUPITER

- Largest planet in solar system
- Made mostly of hydrogen, helium, ammonia, methane, and water vapor
- Has at least 66 moons, including the largest moon in our solar system ← CALLED GANYMEDE
- Has white, red, and brown stripes, which are gas storms. The Great Red Spot (which is a giant red spot on the planet) is a huge storm.

SATURN

- Second-largest planet, with the lowest density
- Mostly hydrogen and helium
- Has a complex system of rings, which are made of ice, rock particles, and dust
- Has at least 60 moons (one of the moons has active volcanoes)

URANUS

- Bluish-green in color, caused by methane in its atmosphere
- Atmosphere is hydrogen, helium, and methane
- Has at least 27 moons
- Probably mostly ice and rock
- Uranus looks like it's flipped on its side—its **AXIS** of rotation is parallel to its orbit (unlike the other planets).

AXIS
an imaginary line about which a body rotates

NEPTUNE

- Farthest planet from the sun
- Also bluish-green in color
- Atmosphere can change rapidly (gets lots of storm spots)
- Has at least 13 moons and several rings

Here's a mnemonic to keep those eight planets in order:

My Very Energetic Malamute Just Swam Until Nighttime

(**M**ercury, **V**enus, **E**arth, **M**ars, **J**upiter, **S**aturn, **U**ranus, **N**eptune).

DWARF PLANETS

Dwarf planets are smaller than the inner and outer planets, but they still orbit the sun like other planets. Also, they are unlike planets because their gravity isn't strong enough to pull in and clear their orbital "neighborhood" of other major debris. The largest dwarf planets are CERES, PLUTO, and ERIS, but there are likely to be hundreds of dwarf planets discovered as scientists continue to explore the outer reaches of the solar system.

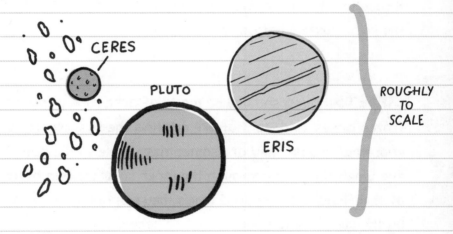

CERES

PLUTO

ERIS

ROUGHLY TO SCALE

Pluto was once considered the ninth planet, but after scientists discovered Eris in 2005, they redefined the term "planet," and Pluto was renamed a dwarf planet. Pluto is actually so cold that it is made of rock and gases frozen into ice. Ceres is located within the asteroid belt that is between Mars and Jupiter.

OTHER OBJECTS in the SOLAR SYSTEM

Besides planets and moons, there are other objects in our solar system:

ASTEROIDS: huge chunks of irregularly shaped rocks, mostly located in an area called the **ASTEROID BELT** between Mars and Jupiter, or scattered throughout the solar system. They're the largest objects in the solar system besides planets and moons.

COMETS: "dirty snowballs" made of dust, rock particles, frozen gases, and ice that are orbiting the sun, usually with enormous orbits. They are sometimes visible to the naked eye when they pass through the inner solar system because of their long tails—caused when they're partly vaporized by the sun. (The tail doesn't follow behind the comet; it always points away from the sun.)

The **OORT CLOUD** is a cloud of billions of comets beyond Pluto, named after astronomer **JAN OORT**, who first proposed the model.

METEOROIDS, METEORS, METEORITES:

METEOROIDS are small pieces of rock and dust (such as disintegrated comets). Meteoroids become **METEORS** when they enter the earth's atmosphere and burn from all of the atmospheric friction into a bright streak. A meteor that makes it to Earth without burning up in the atmosphere is called a **METEORITE**.

> The average meteor you see at night is only about the size of a grain of sand!

HOPE THAT'S NOT A METEORITE...

A "SHOOTING STAR" IS ACTUALLY A METEOR.

SHOOTING STAR?

METEOR.

METEOROID
a piece of space dust or rock

METEOR
a meteoroid burning as it enters the earth's atmosphere

METEORITE
when a meteor strikes Earth

ONLY A SMALL PERCENTAGE OF ALL METEORS

SPACE EXPLORATION and STUDY

Telescopes

Stars and other objects in space emit electromagnetic radiation, such as radio waves and visible light. On Earth, we study this radiation with telescopes to help us understand space.

OBSERVATORIES are buildings that house telescopes. Other telescopes are on satellites orbiting the earth (to reduce distortion caused by the atmosphere).

OPTICAL TELESCOPES collect light from space and magnify images of objects.

RADIO TELESCOPES collect radio waves instead of light waves. Unlike light rays, radio waves reach the earth's surface twenty-four hours a day regardless of weather conditions. Some radio telescopes are composed of many large dishes spread over a large geographic area.

OTHER TELESCOPES can collect different wavelengths of light (such as X-rays, gamma rays, etc.) to tell us more about our solar system and universe.

Space Exploration

ROCKETS are powerful engines that are used to send objects such as satellites and space probes into space.

MOONS CAN BE SATELLITES TOO!

A **SATELLITE** is anything that revolves around a planet or other object. Artificial satellites collect data such as weather patterns and pictures and relay the information back to Earth.

SPACE PROBES are crafts that travel through space collecting and transmitting data back to Earth using radio waves. Much of what we know about the planets and objects in our solar system comes from data collected by space probes.

A reusable **SPACE SHUTTLE** can transport satellites and astronauts to space, sort of like an airplane to space.

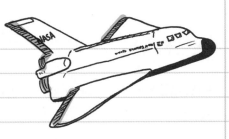

A **SPACE STATION** is like a combination lab and apartment in space for astronauts.

HOME SWEET HOME.

Measuring Distance in Space

Because objects in space are so far apart, we have to use huge units for measuring distance. Scientists use LIGHT-YEARS to measure distances in space. One light-year is the distance light travels in one year, which is about 9.5 trillion kilometers. The star closest to Earth is about 4.3 light-years away.

LOTS OF ROCKS HERE ON MARS...YEP.

CHECK YOUR KNOWLEDGE

1. List the planets in order from closest to farthest from the sun.

2. The asteroid belt is between ____ and _____.

3. The "dirty snowballs" of space are _____.

4. Why are the outer planets called gas giants?

5. The terrestrial planets are the _____ planets.

6. Explain the difference between a meteoroid, a meteor, and a meteorite.

7. The Great Red Spot is a _____ on the planet of _____.

8. Explain what a dwarf planet is.

9. The planet of _____ has a complex system of rings.

10. Earth is the only planet known to support ____.

11. Long distances in space are measured in _____-_____.

ANSWERS

CHECK YOUR ANSWERS

1. Mercury, Venus, Earth, Mars, Jupiter, Saturn, Uranus, Neptune

2. Mars, Jupiter

3. Comets

4. Because they are mostly made of gassy sludge with rocky or metallic cores.

5. Inner

6. A meteoroid is simply a piece of space dust or rock in space. A meteor is a meteoroid that enters the earth's atmosphere and burns up. A meteorite is a meteor that hits Earth.

7. Storm, Jupiter

8. Dwarf planets are smaller than the inner and outer planets, but they still orbit the sun like other planets. They can't sweep up their orbital neighborhood with their gravity.

9. Saturn

10. Life

11. Light-years

Chapter 19

THE SUN-EARTH-MOON SYSTEM

We observe the sun, the earth, and the moon in action daily. Ocean tides, sunsets, the length of days, seasons, and the moon rising are all caused by interactions among the sun, the earth, and the moon.

The EARTH
Earth's Characteristics

Earth is shaped like a slightly squashed SPHERE, sort of like a rubber gym ball squeezed a bit between your hands. As a result, Earth is longer around the equator than it is around the poles (but not enough to notice just by looking at it). It's stretched slightly because of its rotation, much like a flying, spinning ball of dough stretches out to form a pizza crust.

The earth's movements and iron core give it a magnetic field. A compass is simply a magnet that points toward the earth's magnetic north, which is actually not under the geographic North Pole! Magnetic north changes a bit every year as the earth's magnetic field wanders around.

Earth's Motion

ROTATION: Earth spins around an imaginary vertical line that runs from the North Pole to the South Pole, ← JUST LIKE A GLOBE a motion called ROTATION. The earth completes one rotation, or one complete turn, about every twenty-four hours. This rotation makes the sun appear to move across the sky.

REVOLUTION: As Earth rotates, it also revolves around the sun, which means it moves in a circle around the sun. Earth makes one REVOLUTION, or one full circle around the sun, every 365.25 days. Our calendar year is based on the earth's revolution (1 year has 365 days). The path Earth takes around the sun is called an ORBIT. The earth's orbit

WE ADD AN EXTRA DAY EVERY FOUR YEARS (OUR LEAP YEAR) TO MAKE UP FOR THE EXTRA 6 HOURS AND 9 MINUTES.

is actually shaped like an ELLIPSE, which is an elongated circle, like an oval. This means that Earth is not the same distance from the sun year-round.

THE EARTH'S TILT: Earth is also at a tilt. The earth's axis is tilted 23.44 degrees from the line perpendicular to its orbit (meaning at a 90-degree angle to its revolution around the sun). Because of the earth's tilt, light strikes the surface of Earth at different angles at different stages of its orbit.

SEASONS: The earth's orbit, combined with its tilt, creates seasons. When the northern hemisphere is tilted toward the sun, the sun's rays hit it at a higher angle and for longer periods of time, which means it gets more energy from the sun. The increase in solar energy and the longer periods of sun exposure create summer for the northern hemisphere. During summer, temperatures get warmer because the days get longer and the sunlight is more intense at that angle.

When the northern hemisphere is tilted away from the sun, the sun's rays strike it at a lower angle and for fewer hours of the day. The result is winter: cooler temperatures because of the shorter days and less intense sunlight.

The northern and southern hemispheres are always in opposite seasons. When the northern hemisphere is tilted toward the sun, the southern hemisphere is tilted away from the sun, and vice versa. When it is winter in the U.S., it is summer in Australia. The tilt doesn't wobble back and forth to create the seasons—the seasons happen because the earth revolves to the other side of the sun.

SOLSTICES: The days that Earth is most tilted toward the sun are called SOLSTICES. On solstices, the sun reaches its greatest distance north or south of the equator, so the sun is at its highest or lowest in the sky at noon. The solstices are around June 21 and December 21, and they mark the longest and the shortest days of the year. The sun is highest in the sky on the summer solstice, and the sun is lowest in the sky on the winter solstice. The longest day of the year is on the summer solstice, and the longest night of the year is on the winter solstice.

EQUINOXES: Earth is not tilted toward or away from the sun on EQUINOXES, so the length of the day is the same all over the world. On equinox days, the sun is directly above the equator, causing day and night to each be twelve hours everywhere on Earth. The equinox happens in the spring and fall around March 20 and September 22.

The spring equinox is called the **VERNAL EQUINOX**, and it marks the beginning of spring.

The fall equinox is called the **AUTUMNAL EQUINOX**, and it marks the beginning of fall.

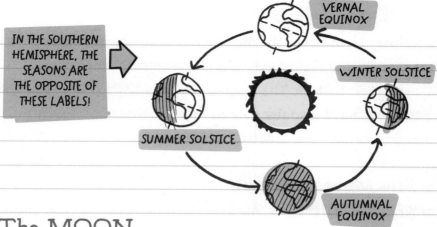

IN THE SOUTHERN HEMISPHERE, THE SEASONS ARE THE OPPOSITE OF THESE LABELS!

VERNAL EQUINOX

WINTER SOLSTICE

SUMMER SOLSTICE

AUTUMNAL EQUINOX

The MOON

A MOON is an object that revolves around a planet. A moon is a natural satellite, which is any object that orbits a planet. Our moon was most likely formed early in Earth's history when our young planet collided with debris about the size of Mars. Gravity pulled the debris into a large ball that became our moon.

The Moon's Surface and Composition

When you look at the moon on a really clear night, you can see different types of surfaces. The moon has mountains, craters, and smooth, dark regions composed of hardened lava from

volcanic eruptions. The mountainous regions of the moon are called LUNAR HIGHLANDS, and the smooth, dark regions are called MARIA. The moon even has MOONQUAKES! Space missions have also discovered that the moon's poles may contain areas of WATER ICE.

NOT QUITE ICE OR WATER— LUNAR SORBET! MMM. ↰

The Moon's Motion

REVOLUTION AND ROTATION: The moon is in constant motion and completes a revolution around Earth every 27.3 days. As the moon orbits Earth, it also rotates around its axis once every 27.3 days (sort of like how Earth rotates around its axis and revolves around the sun at the same time). Because the moon rotates and revolves at the same speed, we see the same face of the moon all the time.

YOU COMPLETED YOUR ROTATION THIS MONTH, BRO?

YUP! 27.3 DAYS. BRO!

When you ride a Gravitron at a carnival, you are constantly spinning, but always facing toward the center of the circle. This is exactly what the moon does—it spins, but it always shows the same face to Earth.

HOW DID THE MOON GET ON THIS RIDE??

GRAVITRON

MOON PHASES: The moon glows at night because it reflects sunlight. The sun always lights half of the moon, but because the

positions of the earth and moon change, we see a different part of the lighted side of the moon every night. The changes in appearance of the moon are called MOON PHASES, and they depend on the relative positions of Earth, the moon, and the sun. When the moon is getting larger in appearance each night, it is WAXING (which means "growing"); when the moon is getting smaller, it is WANING (which means "shrinking").

The moon goes through eight phases:

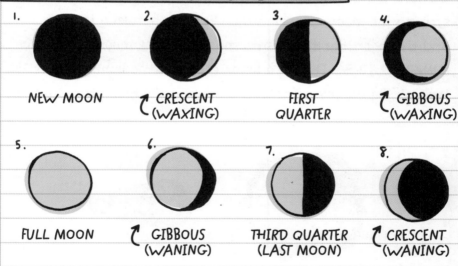

1. NEW MOON
2. CRESCENT (WAXING)
3. FIRST QUARTER
4. GIBBOUS (WAXING)
5. FULL MOON
6. GIBBOUS (WANING)
7. THIRD QUARTER (LAST MOON)
8. CRESCENT (WANING)

The moon is waxing from the new moon until the full moon and is waning from the full moon until the new moon. A LUNAR CYCLE, which is 29.5 days, is how long it takes the moon to complete all eight phases.

We call it one month!

SOLAR ECLIPSE: A SOLAR ECLIPSE happens when the moon is between Earth and the sun. In this position, the moon can block the light from the sun, casting a shadow on Earth. During a solar eclipse, Earth can be either completely in shadow or only partially in shadow.

LUNAR ECLIPSE: Earth can obstruct the sun's light from striking the moon, as well. When Earth is between the sun and the moon, Earth casts its shadow on the moon, causing a LUNAR ECLIPSE. During a lunar eclipse, some light refracts through the earth's atmosphere, causing the moon to glow red.

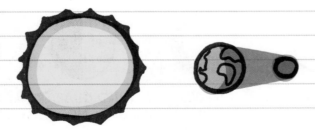

Eclipses are somewhat rare events because the sun, the moon, and Earth all need to be perfectly aligned, which doesn't happen very frequently.

Tides

THE MOON'S EFFECT: While the earth's gravity pulls on the moon, keeping it in orbit, the moon's gravity also pulls on Earth, causing tides. TIDES are the regular rise and fall of ocean water levels. The part of Earth that is either close to the moon or directly opposite the part facing the moon experiences high tide—the water is being pulled toward the moon. The high-tide point moves across Earth as our planet rotates under these "tidal bulges." Therefore, most places experience two high tides and two low tides per day. Because it takes twenty-four hours for our planet to rotate, the time between high tide and the next low tide is usually about six hours.

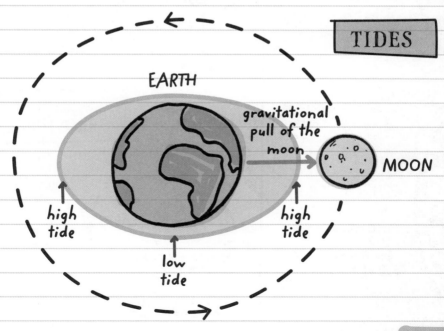

TIDES

EARTH

gravitational
pull of the
moon

MOON

high
tide

high
tide

low
tide

THE SUN'S EFFECT: When Earth, the sun, and the moon are all lined up, the gravity of the moon and the sun add up, resulting in higher high tides and lower low tides, called SPRING TIDES. When the sun and the moon are at a 90-degree angle to each other relative to Earth, the gravitational forces are not aligned, so they don't add up. As a result, the tides, called NEAP TIDES, are less pronounced.

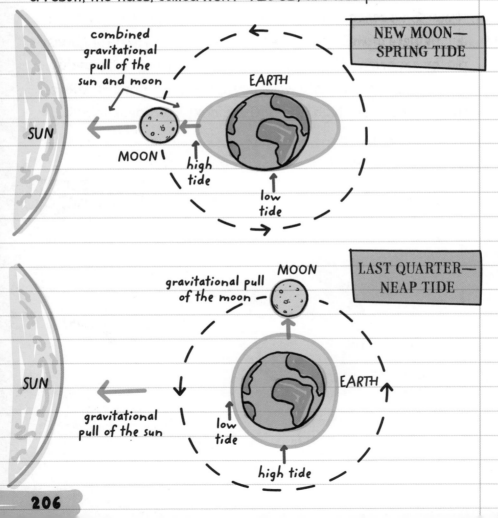

SUN

combined gravitational pull of the sun and moon

EARTH

MOON

high tide

low tide

NEW MOON—SPRING TIDE

MOON

gravitational pull of the moon

LAST QUARTER—NEAP TIDE

SUN

gravitational pull of the sun

low tide

EARTH

high tide

CHECK YOUR KNOWLEDGE

1. What is the imaginary line that runs between the earth's poles and around which Earth rotates?

2. Describe the motion Earth completes every year.

3. When is it summer for the northern hemisphere, and why?

4. How do you think our seasons would be affected if Earth were at more of a tilt? Why?

5. Explain the difference between solstice and equinox.

6. Why do we always see the same side of the moon?

7. Explain what happens in a solar eclipse and what happens during a lunar eclipse.

8. How does the moon's gravity affect water on Earth?

ANSWERS

CHECK YOUR ANSWERS

1. Its axis

2. Earth completes one revolution around the sun every 365.25 days.

3. When the northern hemisphere is tilted toward the sun, sunlight strikes it at a higher angle and for longer periods of time, resulting in longer, warmer days.

4. The seasons would be much more extreme. The sunlight in summer would be at an even more direct angle, and days would be even longer. The opposite would be true of winter.

5. A solstice is when Earth is most tilted toward the sun, marking the longest and shortest days of the year. Equinoxes happen on days that Earth isn't tilted toward the sun, so the length of a day is equal everywhere in the world: twelve hours of light, twelve hours of dark.

6. We see the same side of the moon because it rotates and revolves around Earth at the same speed.

7. In a solar eclipse, the moon blocks the sun's light from Earth because it aligns perfectly between the sun and Earth. In a lunar eclipse, Earth aligns perfectly with the sun and the moon, blocking the sun's light and casting a shadow on the moon.

8. The moon's gravity pulls on Earth, causing tides (the rise and fall of ocean water levels).

Chapter 20

STARS AND GALAXIES

STARS

A STAR is an object in space that emits energy in the form of light and heat. Stars are made of gas and dust that are attracted to each other by the force of gravity. As the dust and gas get closer together, temperatures in the core of the star become so hot that the nuclei of the atoms begin to fuse together! Two hydrogen atoms combine to form a helium atom. This reaction is called a NUCLEAR FUSION reaction, and it emits tremendous amounts of energy, which is transmitted through space in various wavelengths of light (electromagnetic energy).

Life of Stars

This is the life of a typical star from start to finish:

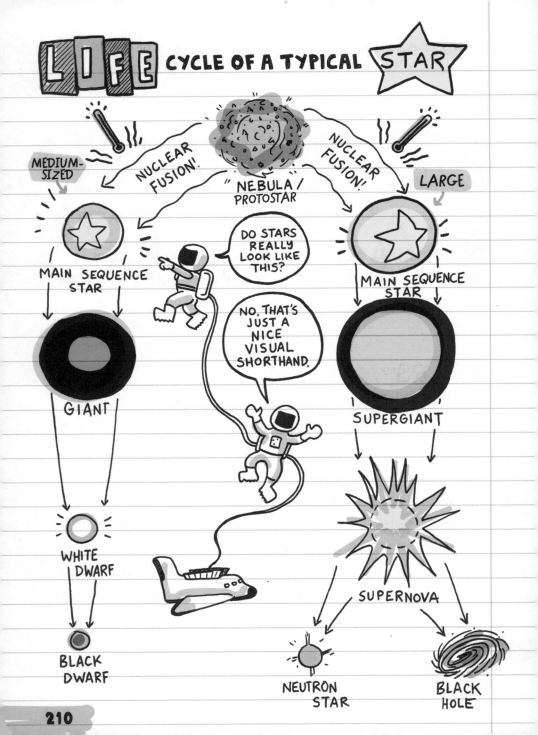

NEBULA: a large cloud of gas and dust. Over time, gravity draws the nebula together. A condensing nebula is known as a **PROTOSTAR**.

NUCLEAR FUSION: As the nebula contracts, the temperature increases until it gets to be so hot (more than 10 million Kelvins!) that nuclear fusion of hydrogen to helium begins. The nuclear fusion releases energy in the form of light and heat, forming a star.

MAIN SEQUENCE STAR: The fusion of the star creates outward pressure that balances the force of gravity. The star continues to fuel its fusion with the hydrogen at its core. Large stars may last only a few million years because they burn through their fuel so fast. A medium-sized star (like our sun) might last around 10 billion years (we're halfway there!) and small stars can last trillions of years.

GIANTS: As a medium-sized star converts all of its hydrogen to helium, it loses its source of energy and begins to cool. The cooling reduces the outward pressure, and the core contracts. The contracting core causes high temperatures, and the outer layers of the star expand and cool and get ejected into space. A star in this phase of the life cycle is called a **GIANT**. Large stars form **SUPERGIANTS**, while regular stars form giants. When the core of the giant becomes incredibly hot from all of the compression, it begins fusion again.

Next, a giant can become either a white dwarf or a supergiant can explode in a supernova.

WHITE DWARFS: After a giant uses all of its helium, it forms a dense, hot core called a white dwarf. When a white dwarf cools and stops emitting light, it becomes a **BLACK DWARF**.

SUPERNOVA: A supergiant, which is formed by a really large star, compresses very quickly. As it comes together, its core temperatures get REALLY hot. Fusion of larger elements begins in the core, until it forms heavier and heavier elements, like iron. Iron can't release energy through fusion, so iron causes the core to collapse violently, sending waves through the outer layers of the star and causing an explosion of bright light called a supernova. After the supernova collapses on itself, it contracts to a super dense ball called a **NEUTRON STAR** because only neutrons can exist in its core. Smaller supernovas form neutron stars because neutrons can resist the force of gravity pulling the supernova together. In larger supernovas, the force of gravity is so powerful that nothing can stop it from collapsing. The force of gravity sucks everything nearby in so strongly that not even light can escape, forming a **BLACK HOLE**.

Dust and gas ejected from a star over the course of its lifetime can form new nebulas, starting the process all over again! In fact, many of the elements that we find on Earth (from hydrogen to carbon to oxygen to iron) were fused together in ancient stars.   WE'RE LITERALLY MADE OF STARDUST!

> The larger the star, the quicker its evolution. Usually, smaller stars, such as white dwarfs, can live the longest, because they don't burn fuel as rapidly.

Starlight

When you look in the sky, stars all seem to be the same color. But actually, stars give off different colored light. Different stars give off different amounts of energy, which affects the color of light. That's all down to the type of star they are—or the stage in the timeline of a star's life.

For most stars, known as main sequence stars, as the temperature of a star increases, it gives off brighter, bluer light. When a star has lower temperatures, it gives off dimmer red light. White dwarfs and giants are exceptions because their temperatures don't correspond to their brightness: White dwarfs are tiny stars that are hot but not bright, and giants and supergiants are enormous stars that are really bright, but not as hot as other stars.

Different elements in a star's atmosphere release different SPECTRA. Spectra are a combination of light wavelengths, and each element releases a unique combination. Astronomers can determine the composition of stars by looking at the different wavelengths of light emitted by a star.

Constellations

When you stare up at a clear night sky, you can see all sorts of stars. The shapes and pictures people see in the starry night sky are called CONSTELLATIONS. The Big Dipper (part of a larger constellation called Ursa Major,

or the "great bear") is perhaps
the most recognizable
constellation in the
northern sky.

Constellations are like maps projected onto the night sky.
Long ago, travelers used the stars to help them navigate.
POLARIS, also known as the North Star, is located directly
above the North Pole. In the northern hemisphere, the
constellations appear to slowly rotate around Polaris.
Different constellations come into view at different times
of the night and at different parts of the year.

The SUN

The sun is a star just like every other star in the night
sky. Astronomers describe the sun as a medium-sized main
sequence yellow dwarf star at the center of our solar
system. The sun is somewhat unique in our galaxy because
it is far away from other stars. Many other stars are in
clusters or in orbit with each other. In fact, more than half
of the stars you see at night might actually be two "binary"
stars revolving around each other, but they're close enough
together that they look like a single star.

THE SUN'S LAYERS

CORE: Like any other star, the sun produces light and heat through the fusion of hydrogen, forming helium at its core.

RADIATIVE ZONE: The energy from fusion travels from the core to the radiative zone.

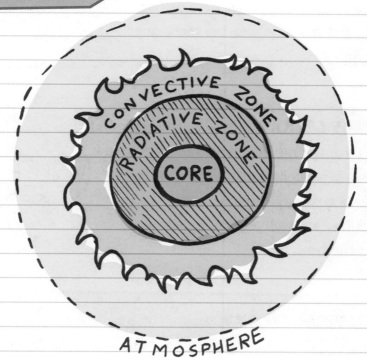

CONVECTIVE ZONE: The energy from the radiative zone travels to the convective zone, where gases circulate and swirl the energy around in convection currents.

ATMOSPHERE: The sun's atmosphere extends several million miles outward from the sun.

GALAXIES and the UNIVERSE

GALAXIES are huge groupings of stars, gas, and dust. The sun is in the MILKY WAY galaxy. The Milky Way galaxy measures about 100,000 light-years across. That milky bright streak across the middle of the night sky is made up of about several billion stars in our galaxy. Our galaxy is a spiral galaxy, but there are other types:

The Milky Way is only one galaxy among a few hundred million galaxies in our universe (each with hundreds of billions of stars!).

SPIRAL GALAXY: galaxies that have spiral arms that emerge from the center. Our solar system is located on one of the arms of the Milky Way galaxy. Our galaxy has a huge black hole at its center that billions of stars revolve around.

ELLIPTICAL GALAXY: shaped like a huge egg

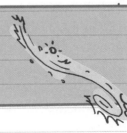

IRREGULAR GALAXY: There are many other shapes of galaxies that aren't spiral or elliptical. They all fit into this category.

CHECK YOUR KNOWLEDGE

1. A large main sequence star will expand outward to become a _ _ _ _ _ _ _ _ _ _.

2. What causes a supergiant to become a supernova?

3. Different stars give off different amounts of energy, which affects the _ _ _ _ _ of emitted light.

4. Stars at higher temperatures usually emit _ _ _ _ _-colored light.

5. Why is the sun in our galaxy unique compared to other stars?

6. Scientists can figure out the composition of stars by analyzing their _ _ _ _ _ _ _ _.

7. When a white dwarf cools and stops emitting light, it becomes a _ _ _ _ _ _ _ _ _ _.

8. An _ _ _ _ _ _ _ _ _ _ _ _ _ _ _ _ _ _ is shaped like a huge egg.

ANSWERS

CHECK YOUR ANSWERS

1. Supergiant

2. As a supergiant compresses, its core temperatures become very hot. Fusion causes larger elements in its core to form heavier and heavier elements, like iron. Because iron can't release energy, the core violently collapses, sending waves through the outer layers of the star and creating an explosion of bright light called a supernova.

3. Color

4. Blue

5. Our sun is unique because it is far away from other stars, which are usually clustered together or in orbit around each other.

6. Spectra

7. Black dwarf

8. Elliptical galaxy

Chapter 21

THE ORIGIN OF THE UNIVERSE
AND OUR SOLAR SYSTEM

The ORIGIN of the UNIVERSE

There have been many ideas throughout the centuries about the origin of the universe, but few have had much evidence to support them. Here are three theories that were supported at various times in the past century:

CONSTANT STATE THEORY: The universe has always existed in a steady state; as it expands, new matter is created, keeping the density of the universe consistent. Observations and a pile of evidence collected since the 1960s have pretty much ruled out this possibility.

OSCILLATING MODEL THEORY: The universe is in a cycle of expanding and contracting, sort of like blowing up a balloon, letting it deflate, and blowing it up again. However, we don't have evidence that indicates that the universe will contract.

219

BIG BANG THEORY: Our universe began around 14 billion years ago from a single point smaller than an atom. It was extremely hot and dense and started expanding outward (the "bang"). The new matter cooled to form different objects, like planets, moons, and stars. And it's still expanding.

The most accepted and supported theory is currently the big bang theory. It is constantly being refined as new evidence is discovered.

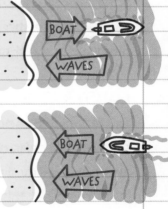

EVIDENCE that the UNIVERSE IS EXPANDING

We perceive waves at different frequencies depending on our movements. The change in perceived frequency of a wave is called the DOPPLER SHIFT. Think about a speedboat heading out to sea—it will slam through the oncoming waves rapidly. But when it comes back to shore, traveling in the same direction as the waves, it feels like you go over the top of the same waves much less frequently.

In a similar way, when an ambulance is driving toward you, the siren sounds higher pitched. When it is driving away from you, the siren sounds lower pitched. The change in sound is caused by a change in the frequency of the sound waves hitting your ears: As the siren is moving toward you, you perceive the sound waves to be closer together, producing a higher-pitched sound. When the siren is moving away, you perceive the sound waves at a lower frequency, producing a lower-pitched sound.

Scientists use the Doppler shift of light waves to determine whether stars and galaxies are moving toward or away from us. Instead

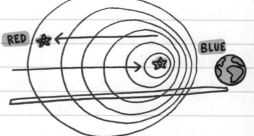

of listening, they look. If the star is moving toward us, its light wavelengths are compressed, and we perceive it as slightly bluer. And if it's moving away—as most objects in the universe are—it appears redder.

Light from galaxies outside of our local group appears to be toward the red end of the spectrum (the "**REDSHIFT**"), which means that it supports the theory that the entire universe is e x p a n d i n g.

When we see starlight in the night sky, we are observing light that probably left stars millions of years ago. Galaxies and stars are so far away from each other that even though light travels quickly, it can take millions of years for the light waves to reach Earth. We can look "back in time" to the early days of the universe by looking at stars and galaxies that are really far away!

The FORMATION of the SOLAR SYSTEM

Our solar system began 4.6 billion years ago as a nebula—a floating cloud of gas, ice, and dust.

A shockwave, probably from a nearby exploding star, caused the nebula to start rotating and condensing. As it rotated, it flattened into a disc shape, like a ball of dough spinning into a pizza crust in the air. Gravity pulled the bits of gas, dust, and ice into larger clumps of matter, which, in turn, pulled in more bits of gas, dust, and ice. The temperatures and pressure of all the matter at the center became so hot that fusion started and a star, our sun, was born.

The rest of the gas, ice, and dust of the nebula pulled together into larger and larger clumps, forming the planets, moons, and other space objects.

Because the energy from the sun was so intense, lighter elements were swept away from the inner solar system.

DUST

GAS

ICE

HEAVY

LIGHTER

As a result, the inner planets close to the sun are composed mostly of heavy elements, while the outer planets are composed mostly of lighter elements and gases.

The Importance of Gravity

Gravity is the driving force behind the origin of our solar system (and others like it). Gravity draws nebulas close together, creating heat that leads to fusion and star formation. Gravity causes space material to clump together, forming celestial bodies, like planets and moons. Gravity also causes planets to stay in orbit around the sun. THANKS, GRAVITY!

HISTORICAL THEORIES of OUR SOLAR SYSTEM

Today, we know that our solar system has eight planets and smaller objects that revolve around the sun. In the past, however, people had other ideas....

EARTH-CENTERED MODEL:

Greek scientists, such as Aristotle and Ptolemy, believed Earth was at the center of the solar system. They thought that the sun, moon, and the five planets they knew of at the time all revolved around Earth.

WE ARE THE **CENTER** OF THE UNIVERSE.

IF YOU SAY SO!

223

SUN-CENTERED MODEL: In 1543, NICOLAUS COPERNICUS published a paper saying that Earth and all other planets revolved around the sun. Only the moon, he said, revolved around Earth.

HATE TO CONTRADICT ANYONE IN A TOGA, BUT IT'S MORE LIKE THIS.

Using his observation of the planet Venus, among other observations, GALILEO GALILEI also theorized that the sun was at the center of the solar system.

These models were pretty close to our current solar system model, but both Copernicus and Galileo were ridiculed and persecuted for their work.

CHECK YOUR KNOWLEDGE

1. Out of the three main theories about the origin of the universe, which one is most credible, and why?

2. Explain how the Doppler shift works.

3. If you are standing still in a car and a train whistles past you, how does the sound change before and after it passes you?

4. How do we know the universe is expanding?

5. How did our solar system begin according to the big bang theory?

6. Why are the inner planets composed mostly of heavier elements, while the outer planets are composed mostly of lighter elements?

7. How did ancient Greek philosophers perceive our solar system?

8. How did Copernicus's and Galileo's studies change the model of the solar system?

ANSWERS

CHECK YOUR ANSWERS

1. Out of the constant state theory, the oscillating model, and the big bang theory, the big bang theory is most credible because we know the universe has changed dramatically throughout history, we don't have evidence that the universe will contract, and we know the universe is expanding.

2. The Doppler shift is the perceived change in frequency or wavelength of a sound or light wave. When the distance between the source of the wave and the person perceiving the wave is decreasing, the wavelengths appear to be shorter, and the frequency higher (and vice versa).

3. As the train moves toward you, the waves are getting compressed and the whistle sounds higher. When the train is moving away from you, the sound waves are stretched as the distance between you and the train increases, so the whistle sounds lower.

4. By studying light waves emitted from galaxies, we can recognize the redshift of light, which means that we perceive the light to have longer wavelengths than usual. This means the galaxies are moving away from us.

5. A shock wave from something such as a nearby star exploding caused a nebula to start condensing. As the nebula condensed further due to gravity, the sun was born, and the leftover matter clumped into planets.

6. The energy from the sun swept away lighter elements, so the planets close to the sun lost most of their lighter elements.

7. Greek philosophers thought that Earth was at the center of the solar system, and that everything revolved around Earth.

8. They placed the sun at the center of the solar system.

Unit

6

The Earth,
Weather, Atmosphere,
and Climate

Chapter 22

MINERALS, ROCKS, AND THE EARTH'S STRUCTURE

MINERALS and THEIR USES

A MINERAL is a solid inorganic substance that is naturally formed in nature. Minerals have CRYSTAL STRUCTURES, which means that the atoms in a mineral are arranged in an orderly pattern that repeats over and over again.

Crystal minerals are formed in a number of ways. The two most common ways are:

1. **COOLING OF MAGMA:** Molten (melted) rock, called magma, cools when it reaches the earth's surface. As it cools, its atoms form crystals, which are seen in **IGNEOUS ROCKS**.

> **IGNEOUS ROCK**
> rock formed by cooling magma

2. **FORMATION IN SOLUTION:** When you have elements in a solution and the water evaporates, the ions that are left over can form crystals. Rock candy is actually made when water evaporates and sugar crystallizes onto a stick. Also, sometimes compounds in a solution can PRECIPITATE, which means that they form a solid out of ions in a solution.

Minerals can be identified and classified according to their physical properties:

COLOR

STREAK: Scientists scrape a mineral against a white tile to produce a chalky line, called a streak. The streak shows the powdered form of a mineral and is usually a different color than the mineral itself.

LUSTER: a mineral's shininess. Metallic minerals reflect light, while nonmetallic minerals can be glassy, pearly, dull, etc.

CLEAVAGE and **FRACTURE**: The crystal structure of a mineral determines how it will break apart. Cleavage is the tendency of a mineral to break into flat sheets. Fracture is the tendency of a mineral to break into jagged, rough pieces. A mineral that fractures instead of cleaves is sturdier.

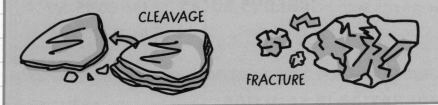

CLEAVAGE

FRACTURE

HARDNESS: The hardness of a mineral is how easily it can be scratched. Diamonds are the hardest mineral, and they are so hard that only another diamond can scratch them!

SPECIFIC GRAVITY: Does the mineral sink or float? The specific gravity of a mineral, or of any substance, is how its density compares to the density of water. If a mineral is 20 times denser than water, it will have a specific gravity of 20. A specific gravity of 1 means the mineral has the same density as water.

Uses of Minerals

The most valuable kind of mineral is a GEM, which is rare and beautiful, such as a diamond. An ORE is a mineral that contains a useful substance, such as iron, lead, aluminum, or magnesium. Ore must be processed to remove the useful material. Many minerals contain silicon and oxygen, and these minerals are called SILICATES. Most of the minerals in the earth's crust are silicates.

We also eat minerals in food to keep us strong. Many multivitamins contain a number of minerals, such as calcium.

ROCKS and the ROCK CYCLE

A ROCK is a mixture of different minerals, volcanic glass, **ORGANIC MATTER**, and/or some other materials. When you look closely at a rock, you can see different colors and sometimes sparkles, which show the different components and minerals.

ORGANIC MATTER
living or once-living things

The ROCK CYCLE shows how rocks are formed and how they change. Rocks may all seem the same at first, but they are different and complex. There are three main types of rocks, classified by how they are formed: **IGNEOUS**, **SEDIMENTARY**, and **METAMORPHIC** rock. The rock cycle shows how each type is formed in a different way:

IT'S LIKE EACH HAS ITS OWN STORY!

WEATHERING
exposing rock to air, water, and ice to break it down chemically and mechanically

Igneous rock turns into **SEDIMENT** (loose pieces of rocks, minerals, living things) with **WEATHERING** and erosion, which breaks apart rock.

Under large amounts of pressure, the sediment compacts and cements into **SEDIMENTARY ROCK**.

Heat and pressure from the earth can squeeze and deform rock into **METAMORPHIC ROCK**.

Rock can then be melted by the hot temperatures deep inside the earth to form magma.

Magma that rises close to the earth's surface is cooled and hardened back into **IGNEOUS** rock. The cycle can continue all over again in any order.

The ROCK CYCLE

EROSION AND COMPACTING

MELTING AND COOLING

IGNEOUS ROCK

SEDIMENTARY ROCK

MELTING AND COOLING

HEAT AND PRESSURE

HEAT AND PRESSURE

EROSION AND COMPACTING

METAMORPHIC ROCK

All of these processes can happen in any order. For example, an igneous rock can turn into a metamorphic rock through heat and pressure. The law of conservation of energy holds true for the rock cycle—matter changes forms, but it is not created or destroyed.

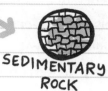

GRANITE

Igneous Rocks

Cooling magma forms igneous rocks. As the magma cools, atoms crystallize and form mineral grains. Rocks from magma that grow slowly below the surface are called INTRUSIVE igneous rocks, such as granite. Intrusive igneous rocks have larger grains. (The grains are larger because the crystal has longer to grow.)

> Think of intrusive rocks like "intruders." Intrusive rocks grow slowly and quietly under the surface, like intruders.

Rocks that result from quickly cooling lava at the earth's surface are called EXTRUSIVE igneous rocks. Magma that cools faster forms smaller mineral grains, so extrusive rocks have small mineral grains.

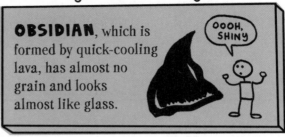

OBSIDIAN, which is formed by quick-cooling lava, has almost no grain and looks almost like glass.

OOOH, SHINY

Metamorphic Rocks

The earth squeezes and heats rocks into metamorphic rocks. The rock

BUT IT DOESN'T MELT— IF IT DID, IT WOULD BECOME IGNEOUS ROCK!

gets hot and becomes just soft enough that it deforms with intense pressure. FOLIATED metamorphic rock, like slate, has a layered structure, whereas NONFOLIATED rock, such as marble, doesn't have layers.

Sedimentary Rocks

One layer is a **STRATUM**.

Most of the rocks exposed on the earth's surface are sedimentary rocks. Sedimentary rocks are formed when sediment is compacted and cemented together. Usually sedimentary rock is formed layer by layer, with the oldest layer on the bottom. These layers are called STRATA.

The PRINCIPLE OF SUPERPOSITION says that as layers accumulate over time, the rock at the bottom is older than the rock toward the top (given that there is no overturning). Scientists use the locations of the layers relative to one another to date rocks, strata, and fossils—a process called RELATIVE DATING.

An object's relative date is basically the age of the object relative to the age of something else. It's like a clue to a mystery—if we know the age of one layer of rock, we can estimate the age of the rocks around it and get a better picture of that time period.

The EARTH'S STRUCTURE and COMPOSITION

Most rocks on the earth's surface are made of silicon and oxygen, and a small amount of aluminum, iron, and other elements. As you dig farther down into the earth, the layers are different—in fact, Earth is a lot like a peach:

CRUST: A peach's skin is like the earth's crust, which is the outermost layer of the earth. The crust is mostly soil and rock and is the thickest beneath landmasses and the thinnest under the ocean. The crust can be 70 kilometers deep at some points, but even the skin of a peach is way too thick to accurately represent the crust to scale!

MANTLE: A peach's pulp is like the earth's mantle, which is the earth's largest layer. The mantle has incredibly hot, gooey magma rock that slowly circulates in giant **CONVECTION CURRENTS**, which drag the crust around.

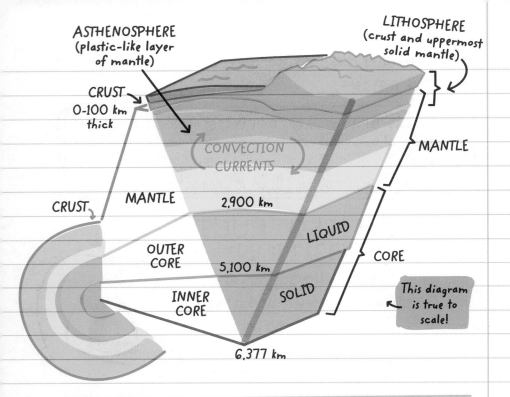

OUTER CORE: The outer shell of a peach's seed is like the earth's outer core, which is mostly molten iron and nickel. This liquid outer core gives the earth its magnetic field.

INNER CORE: The peach's seed core is like the earth's inner core, which is mostly solid iron and nickel. The inner core is warmer than the outer core, but the iron and nickel remain solid because the inner core is under an incredible amount of pressure from the layers on top of it.

Density, pressure, and temperature all increase as you get to deeper layers of the earth. Think about how much rock and other weight is sitting on top of the earth's inner core!

CHECK YOUR KNOWLEDGE

1. Minerals can be formed through the cooling of _ _ _ _ _.

2. Minerals have _ _ _ _ _ _ _ structures.

3. List the different properties used to characterize minerals.

4. What is ore?

5. Cooling magma forms _ _ _ _ _ _ _ rocks.

6. Metamorphic rock is formed by _ _ _ _ _ _ _ _ _ and _ _ _ _.

7. What are strata?

8. The layers of the earth from innermost layer to outermost layer are _ _ _ _ _ _ _ _ _ _, _ _ _ _ _ _ _ _ _ _, _ _ _ _ _ _, and _ _ _ _ _.

9. The iron and nickel that comprise the inner and outer core are _ _ _ _ _ in the inner core, but _ _ _ _ _ _ in the outer core.

10. How does sedimentary rock become metamorphic rock?

ANSWERS

CHECK YOUR ANSWERS

1. Magma

2. Crystal

3. Color, streak, luster, cleavage, fracture, hardness, specific gravity

4. Ore is a mineral that contains a useful substance, like iron.

5. Igneous

6. Squeezing, heat

7. Strata are layers of sedimentary rocks.

8. Inner core, outer core, mantle, crust

9. Solid, liquid

10. Through heat and pressure, which melts sedimentary rock until it becomes metamorphic

Chapter 23

EARTH'S CRUST IN MOTION

The earth's crust and the rigid layer of the mantle that is connected to the crust are together called the **LITHOSPHERE**. The earth's lithosphere is broken like an eggshell into large parts called PLATES (also known as TECTONIC PLATES). These plates move around on top of a plastic-like layer of the mantle called the ASTHENOSPHERE.

LITHOSPHERE
(crust and uppermost solid mantle)

> **LITHOSPHERE**
> the crust and the rigid layer of the mantle connected to the crust

The earth's surface and its geological features, such as mountains, earthquakes, and volcanoes, are all caused by lithospheric plate activity (tectonic plates that haven't had a smooth relationship).

MOUNTAIN BUILDING

Different kinds of plate activity create different kinds of mountains, like the following:

FAULT-BLOCK MOUNTAINS: When plates move away from each other, they create **FAULTS**, rock layers that are pulled apart. This sometimes causes large blocks of rock to tilt and separate, forming parallel ridges and valleys. Mountains with sharp, jagged ridges above wide, flat valleys, like the Teton Range and the Sierra Nevada, are most characteristic of fault-block mountains.

FOLDED MOUNTAINS: Plates moving together exert an enormous amount of pressure on rock from different sides, causing it to fold and squeeze together. You can usually see all of the rock layers if you look at an exposed face of a folded mountain. The Appalachian Mountains on the East Coast of the U.S. are an example of ancient folded mountains. The Himalayas are a much younger and less eroded example of folded mountains.

VOLCANIC MOUNTAINS: When the lava from a volcano cools, it creates another hard layer. After layers and layers of hardened lava pile up, the volcano can form a cone-shaped mountain, like Mount Saint Helens and dozens of other volcanoes in the Cascades.

UNDERWATER VOLCANIC MOUNTAINS: Underwater volcanic eruptions can build mounds under water. As more lava piles up, eventually the mountain reaches the water's surface, forming a volcanic island, such as Hawaii.

CONTINENTAL DRIFT

If you look at a map of the world, you'll see that some continents, like South America and Africa, seem to fit together pretty well. ALFRED WEGENER, a German meteorologist, came up with a theory of CONTINENTAL

DRIFT to explain this. It suggests that originally these continents were connected as a huge landmass, which Wegener called PANGAEA (pronounced pan-jee-uh). Scientists have since found fossils of dinosaurs and plants as well as similar rocks on the eastern coast of South America and the western coast of Africa, which brings up the question: Could the dinosaurs have walked across?

> Scientists have found fossils of the Triassic land reptile Lystrosaurus in Africa, India, and Antarctica—and thanks to Wegener's theory of continental drift, we can see why!

Plate Tectonics

The shifting and moving of plates affects the earth's surface and appearance. At the plate boundaries (where the edges of plates meet), plates can move apart, collide, overlap, or scrape past each other. Uneven heating of the mantle causes CONVECTION CURRENTS, or the cycling of heat that drags the plates around.

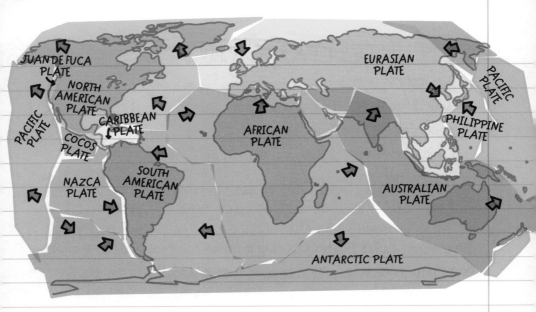

Plates Moving Apart

The boundary between plates moving apart is called a
DIVERGENT BOUNDARY. When plates move apart, magma
from the mantle gets pushed up and forms new crust to fill
the gaps between the plates. This new magma is less dense
than the surrounding area, so it usually lifts up and forms
ridges in the seafloor. Plates that move
apart can also form rift valleys,
where the earth is torn apart.

SEAFLOOR SPREADING

Using sound waves, scientists mapped the seafloor and
discovered a bunch of underwater ridges. This led to a theory
of SEAFLOOR SPREADING: As plates along the ocean bed
spread apart, hot magma is forced upward and flows through
the cracks, forming ridges of igneous rock called BASALT.

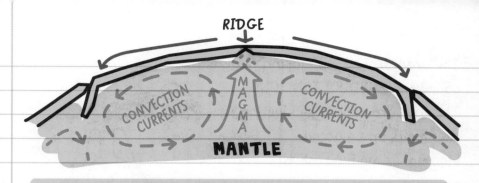

RIDGE

CONVECTION CURRENTS

MAGMA

CONVECTION CURRENTS

MANTLE

THIS IS HAPPENING **NOW** IN THE ATLANTIC OCEAN AT THE MID-ATLANTIC RIDGE—IT'S SPREADING ABOUT 2.5 CENTIMETERS EACH YEAR!

Scientists found that rocks were older as they got farther from ocean ridges, which supports the idea that new rock is formed at the ridges. The magnetic properties of rocks on the seafloor also support the theory; the earth's magnetic field switches back and forth every 200,000 to 300,000 years. As you go farther from a seafloor ridge, the rock has alternating magnetic fields, proving it was formed at different times!

Plates Colliding

The boundary between plates moving toward each other is called a CONVERGENT BOUNDARY. Massive earthquakes occur along these boundaries, often deep under the crust. There are two types of plates: OCEANIC PLATES and CONTINENTAL PLATES. Oceanic plates are denser than continental plates, so when an oceanic and a continental plate collide, the denser oceanic plate sinks into the mantle, a process called **SUBDUCTION**.

> **SUBDUCTION**
> when a plate sinks into the mantle

DENSER THINGS ALWAYS SINK BENEATH LESS DENSE THINGS.

243

The area around the sinking plate is
called the SUBDUCTION ZONE.
The rock around the subducting
slab melts into magma.
Magma, or molten rock, is
not as dense as the solid
rock of the crust and
lithosphere. So, the magma
rises to the surface,
creating a volcano.
Volcanoes spew magma—when
magma reaches the earth's surface,
however, it is called LAVA.

When two continental plates
collide, because they are of
equal density, one doesn't
get subducted. Instead, the
crusts get compressed into
each other, forming folds and
crumples, which we see as
mountains.

Oceanic plates occur at midocean ridges where molten rock
has cooled and solidified. As more molten rock erupts in the
ridge, it pushes the oceanic plate away from the ridge. As it
gets farther away, it gets colder and denser. So when two

oceanic plates collide, whichever plate is older (and therefore colder and denser) will sink underneath the younger (and therefore warmer and less dense) plate. One oceanic plate is always a bit less dense than the other.

Plates Sliding Past Each Other

When plates slide past each other in different directions, their edges can scrape, causing EARTHQUAKES. Places that experience frequent earthquakes, like California, are located on top of plate boundaries. Plates sliding past each other can also form **FAULTS**, or enormous fractures in the rock bed. The boundary between plates sliding past each other is called a TRANSFORM BOUNDARY.

FAULTS
fractures in rocks caused by plates sliding past each other

EARTHQUAKES

As rocks get strained from rubbing against other tectonic plates, they build up potential energy . . . until they break and move, releasing all this stored potential energy. This movement and breaking causes vibrations that move outward like a wave—that's an earthquake.

FROM GETTING STUCK ON EACH OTHER

Think of straining rocks like stretching a rubber band. The rubber band will keep stretching, until at some point, it breaks and releases all of the potential energy it was storing as it stretched.

SEISMIC WAVES and SEISMOGRAPHIC DATA

The energy in earthquakes is released in the form of vibrations called **SEISMIC WAVES**, which travel outward in all directions. The source of the seismic wave, which is where

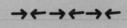

SEISMIC WAVES
the energy waves
released by earthquakes

the movement originates, is called the FOCUS. The point on the earth's surface that's closest to the focus is called the EPICENTER. The effects of the earthquake are felt closest to the epicenter because the vibrations get less intense farther from the focus.

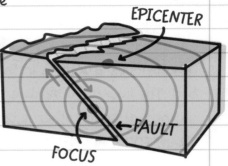

EPICENTER

FAULT

FOCUS

P-Waves and S-Waves

There are two kinds of underground seismic waves:

1. PRIMARY WAVES, called **P-WAVES**, which vibrate in the same direction as the wave is traveling

→←→←→←

2. SECONDARY WAVES, called **S-WAVES**, which vibrate perpendicularly to the direction the wave is traveling

∿∿∿

THE DIFFERENCE IN SPEED BETWEEN THESE TWO TYPES OF WAVES HELPS US PINPOINT THE FOCUS AND EPICENTER OF THE EARTHQUAKE.

Because S-waves and P-waves travel through the earth's interior, they don't affect us as much. SURFACE WAVES, which are the seismic waves that travel on the earth's surface, are slow-moving, large, and can be very destructive.

Seismograph and Richter Scale

To measure strength, or **MAGNITUDE**, of seismic waves, scientists use a **SEISMOGRAPH**, which records the seismic waves from all over the world.

> **MAGNITUDE**
> a measure of how much energy an earthquake released, as indicated by the height of the seismic wave as recorded by the seismograph
>
> **SEISMOGRAPH**
> a device that records seismic waves

Using distance information from different seismograph stations, they can figure out the epicenter of the earthquake.

The magnitude of an earthquake is measured using the RICHTER SCALE. Richter magnitudes are based on the magnitude of the seismic wave. Most major earthquakes are in the 6 to 9 range on the Richter scale. For every 1-point increase on the scale, the ground shakes 10 times as much and the earthquake carries 32 times more energy!

Tsunamis

Earthquakes that happen under water can create seismic sea waves, called TSUNAMIS.

247

As these tsunamis approach land, they can become enormous—sometimes as tall as a nine-story building—and can cause a lot of destruction. In 2004, Sumatra, Indonesia, experienced one of the worst tsunamis in history, which killed roughly 230,000 people. In 2011, a devastating tsunami swept over Japan's North Pacific Coast.

VOLCANOES

Magma, or molten rock, is less dense than the solid rock of the crust and lithosphere, so it constantly wants to rise to the surface. When rising high-pressure magma finds an opening to the surface, the magma explodes out of it. Volcanoes usually form as tectonic plates collide or drift apart to form a long crack, or RIFT. Or they can just "pop up" at a HOT SPOT, where tons of boiling magma pushes toward the surface in one spot. ← SUCH AS HAWAII

When rising high-pressure magma finds an opening, it explodes to the surface, creating a VOLCANO. Some of the magma is under so much pressure that a volcanic eruption can push lava, rock, ash, and hot gases thousands of meters into the air.

SCIENTISTS CAN PREDICT ERUPTIONS IF THEY TRACK A VOLCANO'S PAST ERUPTIONS AND USE MONITORING INSTRUMENTS ON THE VOLCANO.

CHECK YOUR KNOWLEDGE

1. What are hot spots?

2. Rocks farther from ocean ridges are _____.

3. What is the location of the source of a seismic wave (directly under the epicenter)?

4. What are folded mountains?

5. Wegener called the landmass that included all of the continents _____.

6. What are ocean waves caused by earthquakes?

7. What is the name of a theory that explains underwater ridges and the age of seafloor rocks?

8. _____ evidence from across an ocean supported Wegener's Pangaea theory.

9. The magnitude of earthquakes is measured on the _____ scale.

10. The crust and the hard part of the mantle attached to the crust is called the _____.

11. When oceanic and continental plates collide, what is the result?

ANSWERS

CHECK YOUR ANSWERS

1. Hot spots are places where large amounts of boiling magma push to the earth's surface to create a volcano.

2. Older

3. Focus

4. Folded mountains are mountains formed when plates move together and exert pressure on rocks from each side of the plate.

5. Pangaea

6. Tsunamis

7. Seafloor spreading

8. Fossil

9. Richter

10. Lithosphere

11. Oceanic plates will slide under continental plates because oceanic plates are less dense. This is called subduction. Magma is created in the subduction zone around the sinking plate. When this magma rises to the surface, it creates a volcano.

Chapter 24

WEATHERING AND EROSION

The earth's surface changes all the time. While the earth is constantly building mountains and landmasses, it is also constantly broken down by weathering and erosion.

WEATHERING

Weathering is when rocks are broken down into smaller pieces, sort of like crushing a hard candy into crumbs and pieces. The main forces that break down rocks are MECHANICAL and **CHEMICAL**.

> **MECHANICAL WEATHERING** is when physical forces break down rocks.

ICE WEDGING: Water in the cracks of rocks freezes and expands, forcing the crack to widen. This process repeats, and rocks are pushed farther apart.

PLANTS AND ANIMALS: The roots of plants can put pressure on rock, breaking it apart. Also, some animals burrow in rocks or fissures in rocks, which breaks the rocks apart.

EVEN TINY PLANTS

ABRASION: Water and wind carry particles that hit rocks, slowly scraping away their surfaces—like rubbing sandpaper on a rock.

RELEASE OF PRESSURE: As underground rocks emerge on the surface, there is less pressure on them, so they are able to expand and break apart.

THERMAL STRESS: When rocks heat up, they expand; when they cool down, they contract. This continuous process slowly stresses the rock until it cracks apart.

CHEMICAL WEATHERING is when rocks are broken down by chemical reactions—like how soda can wear away your teeth's protective layer!

NATURAL ACIDS: Carbon dioxide in the air or soil reacts with water to form carbonic acid, which can corrode (wear away) certain rocks, especially limestone. "Acid rain" speeds up this process.

PLANT ACIDS: Plant roots produce organic acids that can dissolve minerals in rocks.

OXIDATION: Oxygen can react with rocks and metals, such as iron, to break them down. Rust, formed when oxygen reacts with iron, is an example of oxidation. Most red rocks that you see are red because they have lots of iron, and therefore rust!

SOIL

Soil is the dirt you find on the ground, and it supports all plant life. SOIL is a combination of rocks weathered to small bits, organic matter from living organisms, water, and air. The layers of soil are called HORIZONS. Soils develop over the course of thousands of years, and more mature soils have more horizons, or layers.

The soil that is closest to the earth's surface contains HUMUS (not like the hummus you eat!), which is organic matter from decayed animals and plants. Humus is essential for plant growth: The nutrients from decomposing animals and plants get cycled back into the environment through humus in the soil.

Erosion

When you build a sand castle and waves wash it away, your sand castle is eroded by the waves. EROSION is the removal of weathered material. The four main forces of erosion are:

1. WATER: When it rains, the force of gravity pulls water down across the earth.

GULLIES, RIVERS, and STREAMS: The traveling water is called RUNOFF, or WATERSHED, and it forms gullies (like a gutter or drain in the earth) where it carries sediment away. Over time, these gullies can form large rivers. The faster the water moves, the heavier the particles it can transport.

SHEET FLOW: The rain falling on a sloped surface, like a hill, forms a sheet of water, which carries away loose sediment in a process called SHEET EROSION. It's like a giant waterslide.

WHEE!

2. ICE: Huge masses of ice, called **GLACIERS**, move across the earth's surface, carrying away chunks of rocks and scraping rock surfaces, wearing them down and creating grooves. Glaciers are like rivers of ice that slowly bulldoze their way down a mountain.

3. GRAVITY: Of course, gravity is the force that carries water and glaciers downhill. But gravity doesn't only cause water to move, it can also cause erosion through **MASS MOVEMENT**, or the erosion of land. Some examples are **ROCK SLIDES** and **MUDFLOW**.

ROCK SLIDE
when rocks come loose and bounce and slide down a hill or mountain

MUDFLOW
Like a rock slide, but with mud: Sediment that accumulates water forms mud and gets heavier. The added water weight pulls the mud downhill, creating a mudslide.

4. WIND: Wind blows loose rock and sand against other rock surfaces, and can transport these particles across a landscape.

DEPOSITION

DEPOSITION is the process of water or wind depositing, or dropping, sediment. Some examples are:

> **DELTAS**: triangular areas of nutrient-rich sediment deposited by rivers

> **FLOODPLAINS**: areas of sediment that are created when nearby rivers or streams flood and deposit sediment

> **MORAINES**: debris deposited by glaciers

> **TALUS DEPOSITS** or **SCREE SLOPES**: broken rocks that have fallen from nearby cliffs

> **DUNES**: hills of sand built by wind or water

TOPOGRAPHIC MAPS

TOPOGRAPHIC MAPS can contain information about where highlands, like mountains, or lowlands, like valleys, are located. The land's height above sea level is its **ELEVATION**.

The elevations are presented with CONTOUR LINES, which are lines that connect points of the same elevation.

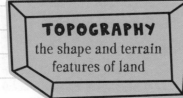

TOPOGRAPHY
the shape and terrain features of land

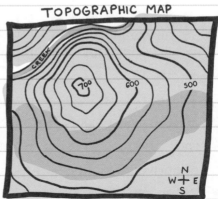

TOPOGRAPHIC MAP

CHECK YOUR KNOWLEDGE

1. Explain the difference between mechanical and chemical weathering.

2. Give two examples of mechanical weathering.

3. Give two examples of chemical weathering.

4. Define "humus."

5. What are the different ways water erodes land?

6. Explain how ice wedging works.

7. Give a real-life example of chemical weathering.

8. What do topographical maps tell us?

9. How does a floodplain form?

10. Explain the differences among weathering, erosion, and deposition.

11. How do glaciers move material?

ANSWERS   257

CHECK YOUR ANSWERS

1. Mechanical weathering is physically breaking rocks down. Chemical weathering is when rocks are broken down by chemical reactions.

2. Any two of the following: ice wedging, plant and animal action, abrasion, release of pressure, or thermal stress

3. Any two of the following: natural acids, plant acids, or oxidation

4. Humus is organic matter from decayed animals and plants.

5. Flowing water creates rivers and gullies, streams erode land, and sheet erosion pulls down dirt from land.

6. Water in cracks freezes. As water freezes, it expands, widening the crack.

7. Rust forming on iron-rich rocks

8. The shape of land and its terrain features

9. A floodplain is created when a nearby river floods and deposits sediment.

10. Weathering is when rocks are broken down into smaller pieces. Erosion is the removal of weathered rocks. Lastly, deposition is the dropping of sediment.

11. As glaciers move, they scrape the earth's surface and transport rocks, sediment, and other materials.

#7 has more than one correct answer.

Chapter 25

THE EARTH'S ATMOSPHERE AND WATER CYCLE

The EARTH'S ATMOSPHERE

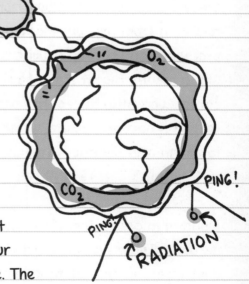

The earth's ATMOSPHERE, which is a thin layer of gas surrounding the planet, is what allows life to exist on Earth. The atmosphere is like the earth's blanket: It absorbs and traps just the right amount of heat from the sun to keep our planet at a livable temperature. The atmosphere also protects us against harmful radiation and has gases, such as oxygen and carbon dioxide, which people, animals, and plants need to survive.

Composition

WHAT WE OFTEN REFER TO SIMPLY AS "AIR"

The atmosphere is made of both gases and AEROSOLS, which are solid particles. The gases are:

78 percent nitrogen   21 percent oxygen

1 percent other gases
like argon, carbon dioxide, water vapor, carbon monoxide, **OZONE** (a colorless, toxic gas), methane, hydrogen, etc.

Each of these gases plays an important role in the atmosphere. WATER VAPOR is like a very fine mist that can create clouds and weather. Ozone absorbs ultraviolet (UV) radiation from the sun. Plants use carbon dioxide for essential processes, and carbon dioxide is also a GREENHOUSE GAS, which means that it traps heat from the sun, warming the earth. Currently, the earth's atmosphere has too much heat-trapping carbon dioxide, which is causing our overall climate to warm and change—a phenomenon called global warming, or GLOBAL CLIMATE CHANGE.

Along with gases, there are particles in the atmosphere called aerosols. These particles include salt evaporated from oceans, dust from the ground, pollen from plants, ash from volcanoes, acids, and other particles from human pollution. Aerosols can affect the weather and climate because they reflect and absorb sunlight.

Atmosphere Layers

The atmosphere has five layers (listed from closest to farthest from the ground):

THE THICKNESS OF EACH LAYER VARIES, SO THESE ARE AVERAGES.

1. TROPOSPHERE (0–16 kilometers from the ground)

- The layer closest to Earth (the tallest mountains are only about 8 kilometers high)
- Contains most of the weather
- Contains most of the air molecules
- Heated by the warmth of the earth's surface—so the higher you go in the troposphere, the colder it gets

2. STRATOSPHERE (16–50 kilometers from the ground)

- Layer above the troposphere
- Most large planes fly here.
- The ozone layer is located at the top of the stratosphere.
- Because the ozone, which is located high up in the stratosphere, absorbs UV radiation from the sun, it gets warmer as you get higher.

OZONE LAYER
a layer of gas in the atmosphere that protects humans and animals from harmful UV rays from the sun

3. MESOSPHERE (50–80 kilometers from the ground)

- Temperatures here drop drastically because it contains little ozone and matter to absorb heat.
- Meteors that enter our solar system usually burn up here. (A "shooting star" is a meteor burning in the mesosphere.)

The prefix *meso* means "middle." The *mesosphere* is the middle layer of the atmosphere.

4. THERMOSPHERE (90–500 kilometers)

- The hottest layer in the atmosphere
- Filters out gamma rays and X-rays from the sun

5. EXOSPHERE (500–10,000 kilometers)

- The outermost layer of the atmosphere
- Has almost no matter, and eventually fades into space
- **SATELLITES** orbit the earth in this layer.

> *Exo* is a Greek suffix that means "outside." The *exosphere* is the outermost layer.

BONUS CATEGORY: IONOSPHERE

> NOT TECHNICALLY A LAYER: IT RESIDES WITHIN THE OTHER LAYERS.

- An ion is a charged particle—the ionosphere is made of a layer of charged particles.
- This layer absorbs the sun's AM radio waves, while at night, in the sun's absence, the ionosphere reflects radio waves from city to city.

> RADIO RECEPTION IS BETTER AT NIGHT BECAUSE OF THE IONOSPHERE!

Ozone Layer

The oxygen we breathe is made of two oxygen atoms bonded together; ozone is made of three oxygen atoms bonded together. The ozone layer, which is in the stratosphere, protects us from the sun's UV rays—the same rays that cause sunburns and skin cancer.

> THE OZONE HOLE IS **NOT** WHAT IS CAUSING GLOBAL CLIMATE CHANGE, ALTHOUGH MANY PEOPLE GET THESE CONFUSED.

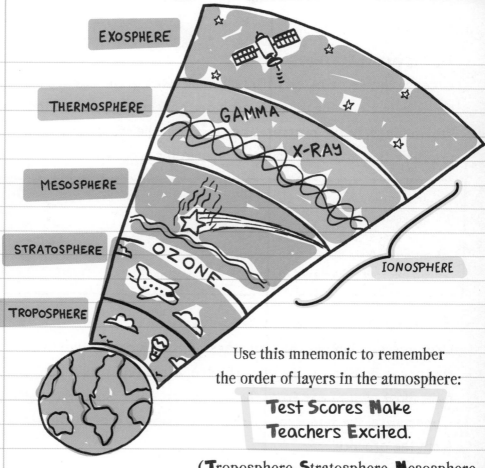

EXOSPHERE

THERMOSPHERE

GAMMA

X-RAY

MESOSPHERE

STRATOSPHERE

OZONE

IONOSPHERE

TROPOSPHERE

Use this mnemonic to remember
the order of layers in the atmosphere:

**Test Scores Make
Teachers Excited.**

(**T**roposphere, **S**tratosphere, **M**esosphere,
Thermosphere, **E**xosphere).

SAVE THE OZONE LAYER

Chlorofluorocarbons (CFCs), chemicals used in
some refrigerators and in aerosol spray bottles
(like hairspray), damage the ozone layer. Our
use of CFCs has caused a hole in the ozone layer
above Antarctica. You can see the ozone layer's
development at ozonewatch.gsfc.nasa.gov.

Pressure Changes

Because the force of gravity pulls molecules to the earth's surface, most of the air molecules are concentrated close to that surface, so air pressure is greatest in the troposphere. Air pressure decreases as you go higher in the troposphere.

> It gets harder to breathe when you are in high altitudes because air pressure decreases with altitude, so there is less oxygen in the atmosphere. Mountain climbers spend months at high-altitude camps in preparation for climbing a big peak in order to get used to the different air conditions.

WHEW!

Temperature Changes

Like pressure, temperature changes with altitude. The earth's surface is heated by the sun. The troposphere, in turn, gets most of its heat from the earth's surface. So in the troposphere, the temperature decreases as you travel farther from the ground.

The stratosphere is heated by the ozone layer, which absorbs a lot of radiation and heat from the sun. Because the ozone layer is located at the top of the stratosphere, the temperature increases as you travel higher.

The part of the mesosphere closest to the ozone layer gets the most warmth. Because the ozone layer is close to the bottom of the mesosphere, temperatures decrease as you travel higher.

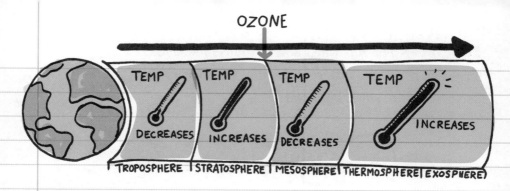

OZONE

| TEMP DECREASES | TEMP INCREASES | TEMP DECREASES | TEMP INCREASES |

TROPOSPHERE | STRATOSPHERE | MESOSPHERE | THERMOSPHERE | EXOSPHERE

Temperatures in the thermosphere and exosphere also increase as you travel farther from the earth's surface, although there are so few molecules it wouldn't feel "hot."

WATER CYCLE

Water gets cycled through the land and the atmosphere through the WATER CYCLE. The water cycle consists of evaporation, transpiration, condensation, precipitation, and runoff, repeated over and over again:

EVAPORATION is when a liquid changes to vapor through heating. The sun's rays heat water in oceans and on the ground, transforming it into water vapor that rises into the atmosphere.

Plants also release water vapors into the air through **TRANSPIRATION** or **EVAPOTRANSPIRATION**.

> **TRANSPIRATION** or **EVAPOTRANSPIRATION**
> a plant releasing water vapor into the environment

CONDENSATION is when a gas changes into a liquid through cooling. After water has been evaporated into the air, the air cools down and the water molecules clump together to form tiny droplets of liquid water, forming clouds.

PRECIPITATION is when water droplets in clouds get large and heavy and fall from the atmosphere back to Earth—as rain, snow, hail, and sleet.

When precipitation falls on the ground, it gets absorbed and funneled into streams and rivers that eventually flow back into the ocean. Water flowing above ground is called **RUNOFF**, while water flowing below the surface is called **GROUNDWATER**.

Warm air passes over the ground and the ocean, evaporating water back into the atmosphere, beginning the process all over again! So water never enters or leaves our ecosystem— it just gets cycled through different forms.

CHECK YOUR KNOWLEDGE

1. Most of the gas in the atmosphere is _____ and _____.

2. As you travel higher in the troposphere, temperatures _____.

3. The hottest layer in the atmosphere is the thermosphere, although it wouldn't feel hot because the _____ are so few and far between.

4. Describe the stratosphere.

5. Most weather is located in the _____.

6. What does the ozone layer protect us from?

7. The air pressure _____ as you get closer to the earth's surface.

8. Describe the mesosphere.

9. Describe the water cycle.

ANSWERS

CHECK YOUR ANSWERS

1. Nitrogen, oxygen

2. Decrease

3. Molecules

4. The stratosphere is above the troposphere. It is where planes fly. At the top of the stratosphere is the ozone layer.

5. Troposphere

6. Ultraviolet or UV rays

7. Increases

8. The mesosphere is above the stratosphere. Temperatures drastically drop in the mesosphere. It is the middle layer of the atmosphere.

9. If we start from the ground, first, water on the ground evaporates. This means that it turns from a liquid to a gas, and rises. Then it condenses by cooling and becoming denser liquid. This is what happens when clouds form and rains occur. Rain, snow, or any way in which water comes back down to Earth is called precipitation. Water falls on the ground and gets absorbed into oceans, plants, and streams. Then it happens all over again.

Chapter 26

WEATHER

WEATHER refers to the condition in the atmosphere at a given place and time. Weather includes information about:

AIR TEMPERATURE   **WIND**

HUMIDITY (amount of moisture in the air)   **CLOUDS**

PRECIPITATION like rain, snow, or hail

AIR TEMPERATURE

Air of different temperatures causes air pressure and density differences, creating winds and convection currents. Different air temperatures also cause water to vaporize (when it's warm) and then condense as precipitation (when it's cold).

Relative humidity levels are also affected by air temperature: Warmer air can hold more water because the molecules move around faster and don't clump into water molecules as quickly. So when cold air reaches warm air, the water in the air often condenses, causing rain.

WHEN A RAINSTORM MOVES IN, USUALLY YOU CAN FEEL THE AIR TEMPERATURE CHANGING.

Air pressure, temperature, and air density affect one another and control how air behaves. Air pressure is the push of each molecule colliding with each other and their surroundings. As the temperature rises, air molecules move more rapidly and exert increased pressure on the objects around them. Likewise, as the temperature drops, air molecules move less and exert less pressure. **AIR DENSITY** is the mass of air molecules in the given space. The denser the air, the more collisions are possible, therefore greater air pressure and higher temperatures result. This is why lower elevations usually have warmer temperatures and higher elevations are usually colder.

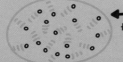

← MORE DENSE, HIGHER PRESSURE, HIGHER TEMPERATURE

LESS DENSE, → LOWER PRESSURE, LOWER TEMPERATURE

GLOBAL and LOCAL WINDS

WIND
the movement of air

Uneven heating of air in the atmosphere creates air temperature differences. Air that is warm expands and therefore is less dense and has lower pressure than colder air. **WIND** is the result of the air pressure and density differences caused by warm and cool air. Air flows from high-pressure areas to low-pressure areas, creating wind.

Global Winds

Differing air temperatures around the world cause winds that loop across the planet. The sun's rays strike the earth more directly near the equator than near the poles. So, the air heats up more near the equator than the poles. Therefore, warm air from the equator rises and moves toward the poles, while cold air from the poles moves toward the equator to replace it.

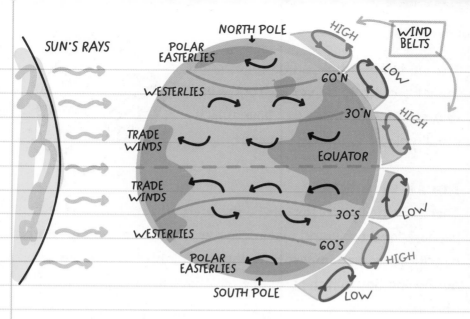

The earth's rotation, combined with these differing air temperatures, causes the movement of air from the equator and the poles to curve in different directions. This is called the CORIOLIS EFFECT. The Coriolis effect causes winds to curve to either the east or west, creating predictable wind patterns in different parts of the world.

> The winds near the equator are called the **TRADE WINDS** because early sailors used them to navigate trade routes.

Jet Stream

Although some winds blow at the earth's surface, there are also high-altitude winds, which are located in the upper troposphere. In North America, the global JET STREAM is formed at the boundary between cold and dry air from the North Pole, and warmer, moister air from farther south.

The air temperature differences cause the jet stream to be very strong—up to a steady 250 miles per hour, which usually blows from west to east.

JET STREAM

Local Winds

There are daily breezes where the ocean meets the land because land cools and warms faster than water (water stays nearly the same temperature day and night). Land is heated during the day, which heats the air above it through conduction. This warm air rises, causing convection currents with cooler air from the ocean. During the day, cooler air moves ashore and is called a SEA BREEZE. At night, air above the ocean water is warmer than the air on land, so it rises. The resulting convection current forms a wind that moves out into the ocean from the land, called a LAND BREEZE. Local winds are also caused by topography, like the different temperatures in a valley or wind funneling through a mountain pass.

HUMIDITY

Humidity is the amount of moisture, or water vapor, in the air. Usually, the humidity level is reported in RELATIVE HUMIDITY, which is the amount of humidity in the air compared to how much the air can hold. When air is at 100 percent relative humidity, the air molecules are completely SATURATED, which means they can't hold any more water vapor.

Dew Point

Water droplets, called DEW, form on grass early in the morning. Dew is formed when water condenses from the air. The DEW POINT is the air temperature at which dew forms on surfaces. The dew point depends on both the amount of water vapor in the air and the air pressure.

CLOUDS

When water vapor in the air condenses, it forms a cloud. So a cloud is an indication that the water vapor in the air has reached its dew point. Clouds form when moist air cools and water vapor condenses onto small dust or salt particles in the atmosphere, forming tiny water droplets or ice crystals.

Clouds are usually identified by their shape and altitude in the sky. The three main cloud shapes are:

1. **CIRRUS CLOUDS** form at very high altitudes where temperatures are very cold. The cold temperatures cause the water to condense into feathery-looking ice crystals.

CIRRUS

2. CUMULUS CLOUDS are puffy and located at mid-level to lower elevations. They usually show up on days with nice weather, but really tall and gray ones can cause thunderstorms.

CUMULUS

3. STRATUS CLOUDS form in large sheets, usually at low altitudes. Fog is actually a stratus cloud that is really close to the ground.

STRATUS

These cloud types can also be located at different altitudes. Different prefixes describe the height of the cloud base:

CIRRO- describes a high cloud, like most cirrus clouds

ALTO- describes a mid-level cloud, like an altocumulus cloud

STRATO- describes a low-lying cloud, like many stratus clouds

Clouds that produce precipitation, like rain or snow, often have the prefix NIMBO- or the suffix -NIMBUS attached to them. For example, a cumulonimbus cloud is a storm-producing cumulus cloud.

PRECIPITATION

When water droplets in a cloud combine and get large and heavy, they fall from the sky in the form of precipitation. Depending on air temperature and other conditions, precipitation can be: **RAIN** **SNOW**

HAIL **ICE PELLETS** **FREEZING RAIN**

AIR MASSES and WEATHER FRONTS

AIR MASSES are large bodies of air that move across land, bringing in weather. The type of weather depends on where the air mass developed. For example, if the air mass developed over warm water, it will bring in warm, humid air.

A COLD FRONT means a cold air mass is moving in to replace a warm air mass. The boundary between air masses majorly influences the weather. Cold and warm air have different densities, so the air doesn't mix—instead one air mass either rises above or sinks beneath the other air mass.

Because fronts mean a change in weather, they are an essential part of a forecast weather map. Incoming fronts have different symbols on the weather map. Some types of fronts are:

WHEN WARM AND COOL AIR MEET, THEY OFTEN CAUSE RAIN AND STORMS.

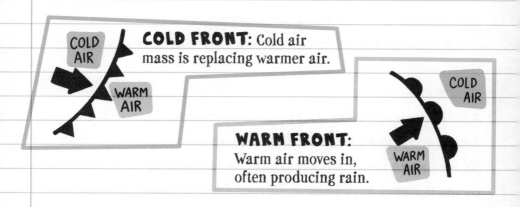

COLD FRONT: Cold air mass is replacing warmer air.

COLD AIR

WARM AIR

WARM FRONT: Warm air moves in, often producing rain.

COLD AIR

WARM AIR

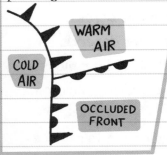

OCCLUDED FRONT: A cold and a warm air front both move in, but the cold air front moves in faster, pushing the warm air front up, often producing rain.

WARM AIR

COLD AIR

OCCLUDED FRONT

STATIONARY FRONT: Cold and warm air meet and stay put. Once either front begins to move forward, it is no longer a stationary front.

COLD AIR

WARM AIR

SEVERE WEATHER
Thunderstorms

When warm, moist air moves quickly upward and cools, electric charges form on the air molecules, creating a negative charge on the bottom of the cloud and a positive charge at the top of the cloud. The storm cloud induces a positive charge on the ground. The positive and negative charges rush toward each other, creating a bolt of electricity called LIGHTNING. Lightning is incredibly hot, expanding the nearby air. The air expands faster than the speed of sound, producing a sonic boom called THUNDER (so thunder is actually the sound of air expanding).

Tornadoes

When warm air rises quickly in cumulonimbus clouds (like when a cold front moves in), the updraft can create a funnel cloud. If it reaches the ground, it creates a temporary swirling vortex of wind called a TORNADO. Tornadoes are destructive, but they usually last only a short time and stay in a small area.

Hurricanes

HURRICANES are the most powerful type of storm, formed in low-pressure areas over tropical waters. Low-pressure areas of warm, moist air rise and cause powerful winds. The earth's rotation causes the winds and clouds to swirl in a counterclockwise direction in the northern hemisphere. The EYE OF THE STORM is the center of the storm and is, surprisingly, an area of calm.

I SHOULD BE OK...

PREDICTING WEATHER

A METEOROLOGIST is someone who studies the atmosphere and predicts weather. Meteorologists use temperature, air pressure, humidity, precipitation, and other information from satellites to predict the weather. RADAR, which stands for "RAdio Detection And Ranging," is also used to collect weather information. Radar devices send out signals that get deflected by storm clouds and rain, so they can show the level of precipitation in an area (radar maps show heavy and light rain in different colors). Using this information from many sources, meteorologists make weather maps, which are used for the forecast.

Weather Maps

Weather maps have lines called ISOBARS that connect points of equal air pressure. Because differences in air pressure cause wind, windy areas have a lot of different isobar lines. When the isobar lines are far apart, there are small differences in pressure and little wind. Lines on a weather map that connect areas of equal temperature are called ISOTHERMS. Weather maps also show air masses and fronts.

> The prefix *iso* means the "same." *Isobar* means areas of the same pressure, and *isotherm* means areas of the same temperature.

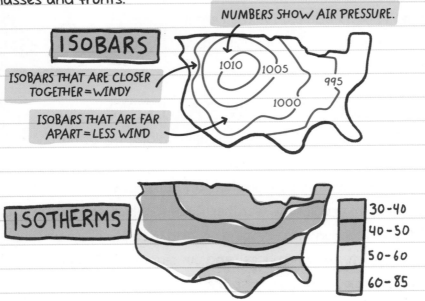

NUMBERS SHOW AIR PRESSURE.

ISOBARS

ISOBARS THAT ARE CLOSER TOGETHER = WINDY

ISOBARS THAT ARE FAR APART = LESS WIND

1010 1005
995
1000

ISOTHERMS

30-40
40-50
50-60
60-85

Some natural hazards, like severe weather, signal they are coming ahead of time. Others, like earthquakes, can be harder to predict. With all natural hazards, however, scientists can study the locations, magnitudes, and frequencies of the events to help forecast future ones. By using satellites to monitor tornadoes and severe storms, we can pinpoint areas at risk and decide where to build storm basements or levees, or use technology to protect ourselves.

CHECK YOUR KNOWLEDGE

1. Which has higher air pressure—cold or warm air? Why?

2. Why do clouds usually form over areas of low-pressure air?

3. What are cirrus clouds made of? And where are they located?

4. What are three different forms of precipitation?

5. What is the prefix for a low-lying cloud, the prefix for a storm cloud, and the suffix for a storm cloud?

6. What do we experience when a cloud touches the ground?

7. Which clouds look like cotton candy and are usually located in mid-level elevations?

8. How do you know when water vapor in the air has reached its dew point?

9. Explain how sea and land breezes work.

10. How do thunderstorms develop?

11. When isobars are spaced really close together, what do they indicate?

ANSWERS

CHECK YOUR ANSWERS

1. Warm air has higher air pressure because air molecules move around faster and collide more in warm air than cool air.

2. Lower-pressure air means warmer air. This warm air rises, and the water vapor in the air condenses, forming clouds.

3. They are made of tiny ice crystals, and are located high up in the sky.

4. Any three of the following: ice pellets, freezing rain, rain, hail, and snow

5. Strato-, nimbo-, -nimbus

6. Fog

7. Cumulus clouds

8. There is a cloud.

9. During the day, as warmed air from the land rises, sea breezes bring in cooler air. At night (when the land is colder than the water), the warmer air above the water rises, and colder land breezes move from the land out to sea.

10. When warm, moist air is forced upward quickly, it creates charges on the air molecules. This warm air condenses into a storm cloud, bringing rain. The charged cloud forms a thunder and lightning storm.

11. They indicate a lot of variation in air pressure—which translates into a lot of wind.

Chapter 27

CLIMATE

CLIMATE is the average weather conditions of an area over a long period of time, in terms of temperature and precipitation. For example, the climate in coastal Alaska is colder and wetter than the climate in central Mexico.

CLIMATE FACTORS

Latitude

MEASURED IN DEGREES (°)

LATITUDE measures the distance of a location north or south from the equator. Different latitudes get different amounts of light and heat from the sun. The sun's rays hit areas near the equator more directly, so they are generally warm. Areas near the poles, which get sunlight at low angles, receive less heat and are generally cold. Different latitude regions correspond to different climates:

TROPICS: located from 23.5° north to 23.5° south of the equator. Temperatures in this region are hot for most of the year, unless they are at high altitudes.

TEMPERATE ZONE: between 23.5° north and 66.5° north latitude lines, and 23.5° south and 66.5° south latitude lines. These areas get TEMPERATE, or moderate, weather. Most of the U.S. is located in a temperate zone.

POLAR ZONE: located at the earth's poles—to the north and south of the 66.5° latitude lines. Polar zones get little solar radiation, so they are freezing cold for most of the year.

Elevation

Elevation, or the height above sea level, also affects climate. Air in the troposphere, which is the layer of atmosphere closest to the ground, is heated by conduction with land. Because air higher up in the atmosphere has fewer molecules, there are fewer air molecules to absorb heat from the earth's surface, so temperatures are colder. Temperatures generally go down about 6.5°C for every kilometer above sea level.

THAT'S ABOUT 3.6°F PER 1,000 FEET.

Water

Locally, because water takes longer than air to heat up and cool down, coastal areas have less fluctuation in temperatures. Globally, ocean currents also affect coastal climates. Warm water from the equator forms currents that move outward, warming the air and nearby land. After traveling to the poles, the cooled water returns to the equator, cooling the air and land it passes. The GULF STREAM is a warm current that starts near the equator and moves from Florida all the way to Iceland.

ICELAND WOULD BE VERY ICY WITHOUT THE WARMING EFFECT OF THE GULF STREAM.

Mountains

Not only do mountains provide high elevations, which affect climate, they also affect rain patterns. When warm, moist air bumps into a mountain, it rises and cools. As it cools, the water condenses and precipitates to form rain. After the air has dumped all of its moisture onto the mountain, the air is left dry, forming a RAIN SHADOW (an area where very little precipitation falls).

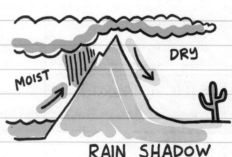

RAIN SHADOW

Cities

Cities can affect the local climate. Cities have lots of buildings and black asphalt that absorb heat from the sun, which then heats the air. Rural areas, on the other hand, have much more vegetation that can cool the area with evapotranspiration. City temperatures can be more than 5°C warmer than surrounding areas, so a city is sometimes referred to as a "heat island."

CLIMATE TYPES

CLIMATOLOGISTS (scientists who study the climate) use a classification system that uses average temperatures and precipitation levels from different regions. According to this system, there are six main climate groups:

1. **TROPICAL**: hot weather—can be either tropical wet or tropical wet and dry—along the equator. An example is the rain forest in South America.

2. **DRY**: dry, desertlike conditions. An example is the Sahara Desert in northern Africa.

3. **POLAR**: freezing cold conditions found at regions near the North and South Poles. An example is Antarctica.

4. **MILD**: moderate temperatures—usually found along coastlines. An example is the Mediterranean.

5. **CONTINENTAL**: large temperature differences between summer and winter (there is no water nearby to moderate the temperature). Examples are the midwestern United States and Canada.

6. HIGH ELEVATION: high-altitude climates. An example is the Himalayan mountain region.

GREETINGS FROM

THE Himalayas!

EL NIÑO and LA NIÑA

Once in a while, the seawater in the Pacific Ocean cools down or warms up more than usual. The unusual warming is called EL NIÑO and the cooling is called LA NIÑA. During El Niño years, the trade winds soften, so water in the Pacific doesn't move as much from east to west and, thus, very little cold water can surface from below. This causes the water along the west coasts of North and South America to be warmer than usual. The change in ocean temperature brings rainfall that causes flooding in some regions and drought in others.

WHOOSH!

During La Niña years, the opposite happens: The trade winds are very powerful, and they push the warm water from the west Pacific farther westward. As a result, a lot of cool deep-sea water surfaces. Weather in the U.S. is usually drier during La Niña years, although it varies by location.

CLIMATE CHANGE

There is a lot we don't know about our complex global climate system, but scientists agree that atmospheric particles, solar radiation changes, the earth's movements, and greenhouse gases affect climate on a global scale. The climate has changed numerous times throughout Earth's history, and it will continue to do so. How we understand, react to, and adapt to a changing climate will determine our ability to live on Earth.

Atmospheric Particles

When solid and liquid particles get into the atmosphere, they increase the amount of cloud cover and block the sun's radiation from warming the earth.

Although humans add particles to the environment through pollution, there are natural processes that also add particles to the atmosphere—like meteorite collisions, forest fires, and volcanic explosions, which spew ash and dust into the atmosphere.

Solar Radiation Changes

The sun doesn't always radiate the same amount of energy. The sun sometimes gets sunspots, which are dark spots on the sun. There is some correlation between solar energy given off and global temperatures.

The Earth's Movements

Currently, the earth is tilted 23.5 degrees on its axis. In the past, it has been tilted more or less. The earth's tilt can affect the climate because the sun's rays strike the earth at different angles depending on its tilt. Also throughout Earth's history, the movements of continents, oceans, and mountains have caused climate changes in localized areas.

Greenhouse Gases

Certain gases, like carbon dioxide, sulfur dioxide, and others, trap heat in the atmosphere. The GREENHOUSE EFFECT is the warming of the atmosphere by gases that trap heat. On one hand, greenhouse gases are essential because they trap heat and allow plants and animals to survive (such as at night when it's colder). The CARBON CYCLE, like the water cycle, has kept the amount of carbon in our global ecosystem fairly constant over a long period of time. Processes such as forest fires, volcanic eruptions, and the respiration of organisms have all added to the amount of carbon in the atmosphere. Meanwhile, absorption by plants and the oceans have taken carbon out of it.

Since the late 18th century, however, people have mined and burned enough fossil fuels (for transportation, electricity, etc.) to increase CO_2 levels way beyond their historically normal range. Because fossil fuels take hundreds of millions of years to form, this carbon isn't being absorbed fast enough to balance the amount that humans are adding. By using evidence, experiments, and historical data stretching back hundreds of thousands of years, scientists have determined that the emissions of greenhouse gases are causing global warming, which is causing an increase in the overall temperature of the earth's atmosphere.

This increase in greenhouse gases is changing our climate. The earth's average climate has been warming at a scary rate, and some effects are:

- **ICE CAPS MELTING**
- **SEA LEVELS RISING**
- **FOREST FIRES**
- **HABITAT CHANGES**
- **EXTREME WEATHER EVENTS AND PATTERNS**

CHECK YOUR KNOWLEDGE

1. How can mountains affect local climate?

2. Explain how El Niño years are different from regular years.

3. How does latitude affect the local climate?

4. Why do land areas near water experience less fluctuation in temperature?

5. How would city temperatures differ from those of nearby rural areas?

6. Define "greenhouse effect."

7. Explain the carbon cycle.

8. What has caused an imbalance of CO_2 levels in the atmosphere?

ANSWERS

CHECK YOUR ANSWERS

1. Mountains create rain patterns—a rainy side and a dry side, or a rain shadow. Also, the top of a mountain can be colder than the bottom, depending on its elevation.

2. During El Niño years, the trade winds soften, the water doesn't move as much, and cooler water can't surface, so the water warms. El Niño also causes flooding in some places and droughts in others.

3. The sun's rays hit higher latitudes at a lower angle because of the earth's tilt, so higher latitudes receive less heat and are generally colder.

4. Water cools and heats slower than land. So, in the winter, the water warms the air, and in the summer, the water cools the air.

5. City temperatures would be warmer because the asphalt absorbs heat, and there are fewer trees and plants to cool the area by evapotranspiration.

6. The greenhouse effect is the warming of the atmosphere by gases that trap heat.

7. The carbon cycle is nature's way of balancing the amount of carbon in the atmosphere. Processes like forest fires and the respiration of organisms release carbon into the atmosphere. Meanwhile, absorption by plants and the oceans take carbon out of the atmosphere.

8. Burning fossil fuels and releasing more CO_2 into the atmosphere than can be balanced by the carbon cycle

Unit 7

7

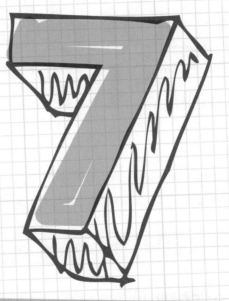

Life:
Classification and Cells

Chapter 28

ORGANISMS AND BIOLOGICAL CLASSIFICATION

What makes a living thing? An ORGANISM is anything living. But what does it mean to be living? Living things:

Are structured around the most basic living unit: a cell

Grow, change, and develop

Respond to **STIMULI** (anything that causes a reaction in organisms, such as sunlight, temperature, or other environmental factors)

Consume energy in order to live

Reproduce

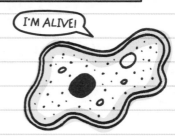

I'M ALIVE!

CLASSIFICATION

Scientists classify organisms by their structure and how closely related they are. They arrange them into groups and categories based on the features they have in common.

Classification Hierarchy

Scientists place organisms in broad to specific categories. Here is the order from the broadest grouping to the most specific grouping:

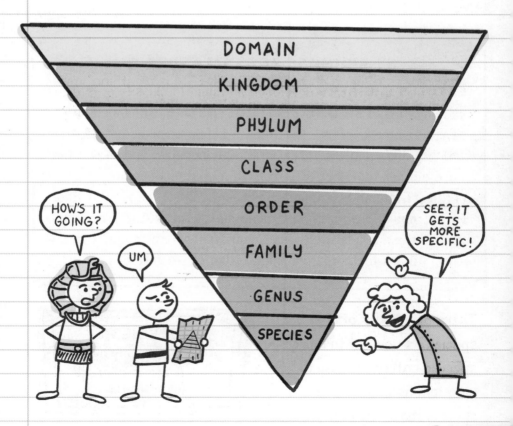

DOMAIN

KINGDOM

PHYLUM

CLASS

ORDER

FAMILY

GENUS

SPECIES

HOW'S IT GOING?

UM

SEE? IT GETS MORE SPECIFIC!

To remember the classification system, keep in mind this mnemonic:

YUM, INDEED!

Dear King Philip Came Over For Great Spaghetti!

(**D**omain, **K**ingdom, **P**hylum, **C**lass, **O**rder, **F**amily, **G**enus, **S**pecies)

BINOMIAL NOMENCLATURE

CAROLUS LINNAEUS developed a system to classify organisms using Latin and **BINOMIAL NOMENCLATURE**, which just means "a name with two terms." The first word of the term defines **GENUS**, which is the smallest group of similar species, and the second word defines the **SPECIES** itself. Binomial nomenclature is sort of like a first and last name—one is more specific than the other. For example *Tyrannosaurus rex* or *Canis lupus* (the gray wolf). Binomial nomenclature helps scientists from any country in the world know which organisms have what characteristics.

There are fewer and fewer species as you get to more specific categories—so a kingdom has many more species than a genus.

SPECIES
group of living organisms that are able to exchange genes or interbreed

Domain: Eukaryota
(organisms with complex cells)

Kingdom: Animalia

Phylum: Chordata

Class: Mammalia

Order: Carnivora

Family: Felidae

Genus: Felis

Species: *Felis catus*

KINGDOMS

Scientists categorize organisms into six general kingdoms.
Here are the main features of each kingdom:

PLANTS

- Multicellular (made of more than one cell)

- Cells are surrounded by cell walls.

- **AUTOTROPHS**, meaning "self-feeder," because they can feed themselves

- Make their food using **PHOTOSYNTHESIS**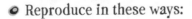

> ### PHOTOSYNTHESIS
> the production of energy using
> sunlight, carbon dioxide, and water

- Reproduce in these ways:

  - Some plants have seeds in flowers.

  - Conifers (a type of tree, like a pine tree) have seeds in cones.

  - Mosses and ferns use **SPORES**.

> ### SPORE
> a plant cell that is like a seed
> and can produce a new plant

- Many plants can also reproduce **ASEXUALLY** by cloning themselves from their roots (like aspen trees) or from runners, horizontal stems (like strawberries).

ANIMALS

- Multicellular

LIKE NUTRITION. YUM!

- **HETEROTROPHS**, meaning "other-nutritive," because they eat other (living or dead) organisms to feed themselves

- Can be separated into vertebrates or invertebrates

- **VERTEBRATES**: animals that have backbones and other bones that protect and give mobility, such as mammals, fish, amphibians, birds, reptiles

- **INVERTEBRATES**: animals that have no backbones, such as **ARTHROPODS**, which include lobsters, crabs, insects, and spiders (the largest group of invertebrates). They have body sections and an outer skeleton in the form of a hard outer body covering. Other invertebrates include mollusks, worms, and many other groups.

FUNGI

- Single or multicellular
- Include mushrooms, yeast, and mold
- Are heterotrophs
- Reproduce with spores
- Have cell walls

THEY EAT WHATEVER THEY'RE GROWING ON!

PROTISTS

- Mostly single-celled
- Some heterotrophs, some autotrophs
- Include amoeba, algae, and paramecium

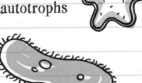

ARCHAEBACTERIA

- Single-celled
- Live in extreme environments, like hot springs and very salty water

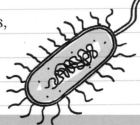

EUBACTERIA

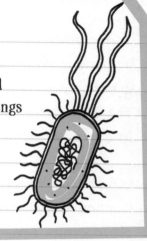

- Single-celled organism

- Include bacteria of all types, like the kind that are in soil, water, and other living things

- Some are heterotrophs and others are autotrophs.

THERE ARE MORE EUBACTERIA LIVING IN YOUR MOUTH THAN HUMANS LIVING ON EARTH! BUT MOST ARE HARMLESS.

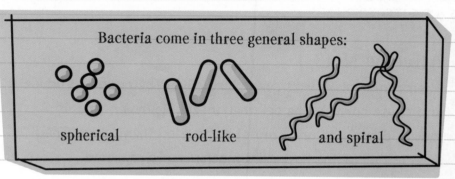

Bacteria come in three general shapes:

spherical   rod-like   and spiral

VIRUSES

A VIRUS is a strand of viral hereditary information (DNA) enclosed in a protein coat. A virus attaches itself to a healthy cell and injects its hereditary information into the cell. The virus uses the cell to assemble its identical offspring, and then it bursts the cell open, releasing all of the replicated viruses—this is called an ACTIVE CYCLE.

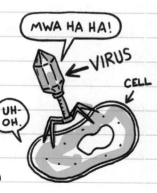

MWA HA HA!

VIRUS

CELL

UH-OH.

On the other hand, a virus can remain inactive, letting its genetic information get replicated along with the cell's genetic information—this is called an INACTIVE CYCLE. The virus can remain in the inactive cycle for a long while. At any point, however, the virus can enter the active cycle.

Viruses can infect nearly every type of organism. In humans, viruses cause the flu, chicken pox, and HIV, among other things. A virus that infects bacteria is called a BACTERIOPHAGE.

Alive or Not?

At first glance, viruses seem very alive. They can reproduce and cause harm to the cell they infect. However, viruses require a host cell and cannot survive by themselves. They must use all of the host cell's machinery to replicate.

SORTA LIKE ZOMBIES!

Immunity

It is very difficult to treat a viral infection. Usually, your body can fight it naturally, and then you get IMMUNITY, or the ability to resist infection again. When you get a virus, your cells make proteins called INTERFERONS that protect other cells from infection. When you get a VACCINE, or shot, you are actually getting a small dose of a disabled virus to help your body acquire immunity.

CHECK YOUR KNOWLEDGE

1. What characteristics do all living things have?

2. How does binomial nomenclature work?

3. List the classification hierarchy from general to most specific. (Hint: This is easiest to remember with your mnemonic device!)

4. Explain the difference between an autotroph and a heterotroph. Give examples of each.

5. Name the six kingdoms.

6. Describe a virus.

7. Why might a virus not be considered living?

8. What is immunity?

ANSWERS

CHECK YOUR ANSWERS

1. Living things consume energy, are made of cells, grow and change, respond to external stimuli, and reproduce.

2. In binomial nomenclature, the first word is the organism's genus and the second word is the species.

3. Domain, Kingdom, Phylum, Class, Order, Family, Genus, Species (**Dear King Philip Came Over For Great Spaghetti!**)

4. An autotroph is an organism that can feed itself, like plants do through photosynthesis; a heterotroph eats other organisms for food, like fungi, organisms that eat whatever they are growing on.

5. Plants, animals, fungi, protists, archaeabacteria, and eubacteria

6. A virus is a strand of genetic information surrounded by a protein coat.

7. A virus cannot survive on its own; it must use the machinery and supplies of a living cell to reproduce.

8. Immunity is the resistance to getting sick. After contracting a virus, our bodies make cells that help us prepare for and resist future infections by that virus.

Chapter 29

CELL THEORY AND CELL STRUCTURE

CELL THEORY

Cells are the basic building blocks of life. Every living thing is made of cells—the smallest living organisms are made of a SINGLE CELL. Also, different cells can perform different functions. For example, a muscle cell performs a different function than a stomach cell does.

Cells are really tiny, so they can't be seen with the naked eye. They were first discovered with the invention of microscopes, and ROBERT HOOKE observed the first cell in the 1660s.

In time, scientists put their observations together to come up with the CELL THEORY:

All organisms are made of cells (one or more).

The cell is the basic building block of life (in structure and function).

Every cell comes from another existing cell (cells divide to form new cells).

Because an organism can be made of one cell alone, think of all the functions a tiny little cell must be able to perform: It needs to be able to consume, store, and use energy, protect itself, and reproduce. Different structures within the cell help it perform all of the functions necessary to survive.

Think of a cell as a factory—each structure is like a machine that performs a different function to keep the factory running.

ORGANELLES

ORGANELLES are the parts of a cell. They do a range of things, including:

Process and release energy

Destroy and digest materials

Replicate genetic information

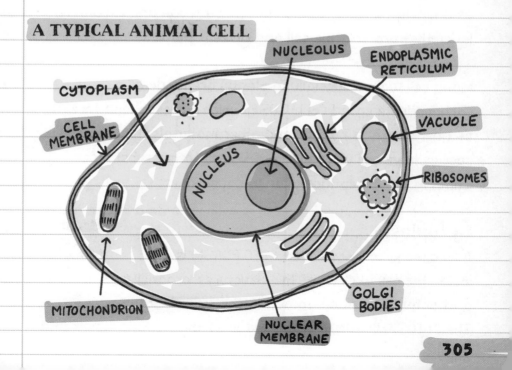

A TYPICAL PLANT CELL

CELL WALL

CELL MEMBRANE

CYTOPLASM

CHLOROPLAST

GOLGI BODIES

RIBOSOMES

NUCLEUS

ENDOPLASMIC RETICULUM

NUCLEOLUS

MITOCHONDRION

VACUOLE

A TYPICAL ANIMAL CELL

NUCLEOLUS

ENDOPLASMIC RETICULUM

CYTOPLASM

CELL MEMBRANE

VACUOLE

NUCLEUS

RIBOSOMES

MITOCHONDRION

GOLGI BODIES

NUCLEAR MEMBRANE

305

Organelles include (from the outside to the inside):

Cell Membrane

Every cell has a CELL MEMBRANE, which is a layer on the outside of the cell that holds the cell together. It also controls the flow of material in and out of the cell—like a gate to a castle. It is SEMIPERMEABLE (also known as SELECTIVELY PERMEABLE), which means it can let certain stuff through and keep other things out (or in).

Cell Wall

In addition to the cell membrane, plants, algae, fungi, and some bacteria also have a CELL WALL. Think of the cell wall as a highly fortified castle wall; it is a tough and rigid outer layer that protects the cell and gives it shape.

Many cell walls (especially in plants) are made of a carbohydrate called CELLULOSE, which comes in long threads of fiber that allow water and other materials through. Other species have cell walls made of various other substances (chitin in fungi, peptidoglycan in bacteria, etc.).

Cytoplasm

LIKE FRUIT IN A JELLO SALAD

A jellylike substance called CYTOPLASM is inside the cell wall. All of the structures, organelles, and activities are contained in the cytoplasm. The CYTOSKELETON, which is made of thin protein fibers and hollow protein tubes, maintains structure and helps things move around in the cell.

Ribosomes

RIBOSOMES are the protein-making factories in a cell. Proteins are an essential part of every cell. They are found in most structural components, and they are also a part of major reactions that take place in the cell. Ribosomes receive directions from hereditary material to make certain proteins.

Nucleus

The NUCLEUS is the control center of the cell. It houses the cell's CHROMOSOMES, which are strands made of DNA (DEOXYRIBONUCLEIC ACID), which is the code for genetic information. The nucleus also includes:

NUCLEAR MEMBRANE: a protective double membrane surrounding the nucleus that controls the flow of materials in and out of the nucleus

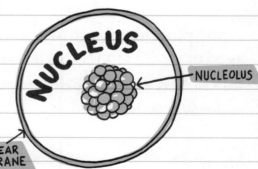

NUCLEOLUS: a small structure found inside the nucleus that makes ribosomes and transports them to the cytoplasm

Vacuoles

VACUOLES are temporary storage bubbles for the cell. They store water, food, and waste.

> IN PLANT CELLS, THESE CAN BE HUGE.

Lysosome

A LYSOSOME is like the cell's garbage and recycling facility. It has chemicals to break down food, cell waste, and foreign particles that enter the cell, such as bacteria and viruses. It digests and destroys dead cells or old cell parts, as well as recycles material to make other cells.

Mitochondria

MITOCHONDRIA are the cell's powerhouse. They release energy in food by carrying out a reaction with oxygen. Cells that need more energy, like muscle cells, have a larger number of mitochondria.

Endoplasmic Reticulum

ENDOPLASMIC RETICULUM (ER) is the transport facility for the cell. It is made of folded membranes, and it processes and moves materials.

Golgi Bodies

GOLGI BODIES are the packaging, sorting, and distributing facility. They sort proteins and other products from the ER, then package and distribute them to where they need to go.

Chloroplasts

CHLOROPLASTS (in plant cells only) are food production structures that contain **CHLOROPHYLL**, a green pigment that makes plants look green and also uses energy from the sun to change water and carbon dioxide into glucose, a simple sugar.

> There are two main types of cells:
> **PROKARYOTES** and **EUKARYOTES**.
> The main difference is that prokaryotes do NOT have a membrane-bound nucleus, mitochondria, or organelles, while eukaryotes do. Prokaryotic cells are very simple and are found in single-celled bacteria. Eukaryotic cells are much more complex and found in protists, fungi, animals, and plants.

ANIMAL CELLS vs. PLANT CELLS

Animal and plant cells are similar in many ways, but they have their differences:

Every plant cell has a cell wall, the rigid barrier made out of cellulose that surrounds the cell membrane.

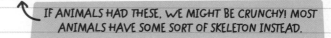
IF ANIMALS HAD THESE, WE MIGHT BE CRUNCHY! MOST ANIMALS HAVE SOME SORT OF SKELETON INSTEAD.

Plant cells have chloroplasts to produce food from sunlight.

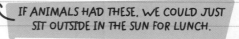
IF ANIMALS HAD THESE, WE COULD JUST SIT OUTSIDE IN THE SUN FOR LUNCH.

Plant cells usually have a large central vacuole for storage that takes up a lot of space.

IF ANIMALS HAD THESE, WE COULD GO A LOT LONGER WITHOUT WATER AND FOOD.

MULTICELLULAR ORGANISMS

Multicellular plants and animals have different cells to carry out different functions. A bunch of different cells doing a similar job are called a TISSUE. Tissues work together to form ORGANS, such as the heart, stomach, or liver. Organs working together form ORGAN SYSTEMS, such as the digestive or respiratory system.

CHECK YOUR KNOWLEDGE

1. Explain cell theory.

2. The _ _ _ _ _ _ _ is the control center of a cell.

3. What does the nuclear membrane do?

4. Plant cells have cell walls made of _ _ _ _ _ _ _ _ _ that provide structural support.

5. What do mitochondria do?

6. Plant cells have _ _ _ _ _ _ _ _ _ _ _ _, the organelle that contains a green pigment called _ _ _ _ _ _ _ _ _ _ _, which produces food from sunlight.

7. Explain what a lysosome does.

8. The cell stores food and waste in _ _ _ _ _ _ _ _.

9. Ribosomes receive directions from hereditary material to make certain _ _ _ _ _ _ _ _.

10. A bunch of different cells doing a similar job are called what?

CHECK YOUR ANSWERS

1. Cell theory states that all living things are made of cells and that they are the basic building block of life. Also, every cell comes from another existing cell.

2. Nucleus

3. The nuclear membrane is the protective wall surrounding the nucleus, and it controls the flow of materials in and out of the nucleus.

4. Cellulose

5. They provide the cell with energy.

6. Chloroplasts, chlorophyll

7. Lysosomes are like the cell's garbage and recycling facility. They can contain chemicals to break down and recycle other cell parts.

8. Vacuoles

9. Proteins

10. A tissue

Chapter 30

CELLULAR TRANSPORT AND METABOLISM

CELLULAR TRANSPORT

Cells are constantly absorbing and releasing things into their surroundings. Cells are a lot like our bodies—we are constantly drinking, eating, and expelling waste (every time we exhale, we release our bodies' carbon dioxide waste). A cell works the same way: It constantly takes in oxygen, food, and water, and expels waste.

The cell membrane is the gatekeeper of the cell's activities. The membrane is selectively permeable, which means it allows some things in and out of the cell—but not all things. (It's selective.) Things enter and exit the cell membrane through passive and active transport.

Passive Transport

Passive transport is the movement of things in and out of the cell without the use of energy. There are three kinds:

1. **DIFFUSION** is the movement of molecules from an area of high to low concentration. Molecules enter a cell if they are in a lower concentration within the cell.

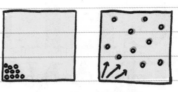

DIFFUSION

The cells are trying to find an EQUILIBRIUM (a balanced state). For example, your cells use up oxygen all the time, so the concentration of oxygen in your cells is lower than the concentration in the air. When you breathe, oxygen molecules from the air diffuse into the cells of your lungs.

Diffusion also works the other way—to expel things. For example, after using oxygen, your cells produce carbon dioxide. You exhale carbon dioxide from your cells because the concentration of carbon dioxide is greater inside the cell than it is in air.

2. **OSMOSIS** is a type of diffusion; it is simply the process of water molecules moving from a higher to a lower concentration

OSMOSIS

a membrane. When you soak dehydrated fruit, like raisins, in water, they REHYDRATE—the water passes through the cell walls to fill in the fruit. The water flows from a point of high concentration (the bowl) to one of low concentration (inside the raisin).

3. In **FACILITATED DIFFUSION**, transport proteins on the cell's membrane transport substances into and out of the cell without energy.

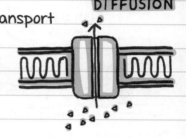

FACILITATED DIFFUSION

Active Transport

ACTIVE TRANSPORT requires energy to move a substance into or out of a cell. A transport protein called ADENOSINE TRIPHOSPHATE (ATP) binds with the molecule and transports it into the cell using the cell's energy. When a molecule is moving against its concentration gradient—in other words, when a molecule moves from an area of low concentration to an area of high concentration—energy is required.

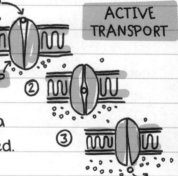

ACTIVE TRANSPORT

CELLULAR METABOLISM

The METABOLISM of a cell includes all of the chemical reactions that allow a cell to survive. Metabolism includes the chemical reactions required to release or generate energy, to produce chemicals the body needs such as proteins, and to expel waste.

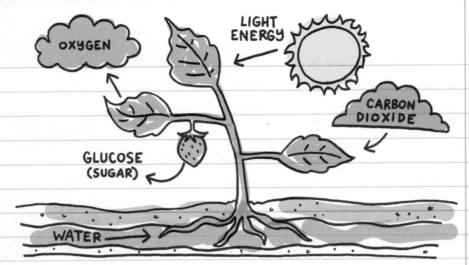

Photosynthesis

Photosynthesis is the chemical reaction a plant carries out in order to produce energy from sunlight. In photosynthesis, the green pigment in plants, called chlorophyll, uses the sun's energy to convert carbon dioxide and water into energy in the form of glucose, a sugar molecule. Photosynthesis releases oxygen as a waste product. Photosynthesis can be shown with the chemical equation:

$$6\ CO_2 + 6\ H_2O + \text{LIGHT ENERGY} \to \to \to C_6H_{12}O_6 + 6\ O_2$$

CARBON DIOXIDE   WATER   GLUCOSE   OXYGEN

Cellular Respiration

In CELLULAR RESPIRATION, glucose in food reacts with oxygen, producing carbon dioxide, water, and energy in the mitochondria, plus the waste products of the reaction: CO_2 and H_2O.

> CELLULAR RESPIRATION MIMICS OUR BODY'S OWN METABOLIC AND RESPIRATORY SYSTEMS. WE EAT FOOD AND BREATHE IN OXYGEN. THEN CHEMICAL REACTIONS BREAK DOWN THE MOLECULES AND REARRANGE THEM, RELEASING THE ENERGY WE NEED.

When you breathe in and out, you are inhaling the oxygen necessary for cellular respiration, and exhaling carbon dioxide and water, the waste products of cellular respiration. (RESPIRATION is another word for breathing, and breathing allows you to get oxygen in order to power cellular respiration.) Cellular respiration releases energy in the form of ATP.

$$C_6H_{12}O_6 + 6\ O_2 \rightarrow\rightarrow\rightarrow 6\ CO_2 + 6\ H_2O + ATP$$

GLUCOSE   OXYGEN   CARBON DIOXIDE   WATER   ENERGY

↑ PHOTOSYNTHESIS AND RESPIRATION ARE THE EXACT OPPOSITE OF EACH OTHER—COMPARE THE FORMULAS.

Fermentation

FERMENTATION is another chemical reaction that releases energy through the breakdown of food. Fermentation releases less energy than cellular respiration, and it occurs where there is no oxygen available for cellular respiration.

Fermentation is just like respiration, except it doesn't use oxygen—it also breaks down glucose molecules, releasing energy in the form of ATP.

> **FERMENTATION**
> breaking down sugars to release energy in food without using oxygen

When there isn't enough oxygen available to fuel cellular respiration, your muscles resort to fermentation for energy. One waste product of fermentation is LACTIC ACID. Muscle burn and cramps are caused by the lactic acid build-up in your muscles from the fermentation reaction. Ouch!

Production of Necessary Chemicals

The metabolism of a cell makes all of the chemicals necessary for the cell's survival. The molecules produced by the cell are:

AMINO ACIDS: the compounds that can be added together to make proteins

PROTEINS: large molecules made from stringing amino acids together

ENZYMES

ENZYMES are molecules that help a chemical reaction proceed. A certain amount of energy is required to get a reaction going, and enzymes reduce that amount of energy. Think of an enzyme as a matchmaker—when molecules react, they have to physically fit together. An enzyme physically brings the molecules together, helping the reaction proceed. Because enzymes are shaped to match specific reactants, each reaction uses a different enzyme. For example, some enzymes in your body break down food into smaller molecules while other enzymes help pass these smaller molecules into your bloodstream.

IT'S A MATCH!

ENZYME

Miss

CHECK YOUR KNOWLEDGE

1. The cell membrane is selectively permeable. What does this mean?

2. Give an example of something that the membrane is selectively permeable to.

3. Define "passive transport" and list the three forms of passive transport.

4. Compare and contrast diffusion and osmosis.

5. Explain the differences between active and passive transport.

6. What does an enzyme do?

7. How are cellular respiration and fermentation different?

8. In which organelle does cellular respiration take place?

9. What are the end products of cellular respiration?

10. Explain the process of photosynthesis.

ANSWERS

CHECK YOUR ANSWERS

1. "Selectively permeable" means some things are able to pass through the membrane, but others aren't.

2. Oxygen, carbon dioxide, etc.

3. Passive transport is the movement of material in and out of the cell, and it doesn't require energy. Passive transport can happen through diffusion, osmosis, or facilitated diffusion.

4. Diffusion is the movement of molecules from an area of high to low concentration, and osmosis is the diffusion of water molecules from a higher to a lower concentration through a membrane.

5. Active transport requires energy. In active transport, a transport protein binds to the molecule and uses cellular energy to transport the molecule. Passive transport doesn't require energy.

6. An enzyme helps a chemical reaction proceed by bringing together the reactants.

7. Cellular respiration requires oxygen, while fermentation does not. Also, cellular respiration releases more energy than fermentation.

8. Cellular respiration takes place in the mitochondria.

9. The end products of cellular respiration are energy, water, and carbon dioxide.

10. In photosynthesis, chlorophyll uses the sun's energy to convert carbon dioxide and water into glucose. Photosynthesis releases oxygen as a waste product.

#2 has more than one correct answer.

Chapter 31

CELL REPRODUCTION AND PROTEIN SYNTHESIS

CELL DIVISION and MITOSIS

When an organism grows, the total number of cells in an organism increases. Even in organisms that are no longer growing, cells are constantly dying and being replaced. Where do these new cells come from? CELL DIVISION. With cell division, one cell divides into two cells. Two cells can divide to create four cells, and then each of the four cells can divide to create eight cells, and so on. So an entire organism can grow from one cell alone.

The Cell Cycle

Each cell naturally goes through a life cycle. There are many phases of the cell cycle. One of these phases is when the cell divides, a process called MITOSIS. Mitosis is cell division that produces identical cells. In cell division, the nucleus is divided. Each DAUGHTER CELL is identical to the original parent cell. (The original PARENT CELL no longer exists at the end of mitosis.)

I'M LONELY.

MITOSIS

IT'S LIKE LOOKING INTO A MIRROR!

The other phases of a cell cycle make up the period where a typical cell spends the most time. These three phases together are called INTERPHASE. During interphase, a cell grows and duplicates its chromosomes (structures that contain all of the cell's DNA) and organelles in preparation for mitosis. The nuclei of the daughter cells will have the same number and type of chromosomes.

Scientists use the term "parent" to describe the older cell that divides or reproduces and "daughter" to describe the resulting cells.

Because mitosis is the division of the nucleus, only organisms that have nuclei can go through mitosis—so only eukaryote cells can undergo mitosis (unlike prokaryote cells, such as bacteria, which have no nucleus).

One complete cell cycle is the time from one cell division to the next. Different cells have cycles of different lengths.

ASEXUAL REPRODUCTION

ASEXUAL REPRODUCTION is when one parent organism reproduces alone, resulting in new daughter organisms that are genetically identical to the parent.

Mitosis

Cell division can be used not only for growth, but also for asexual reproduction. Organisms that use asexual reproduction are genetically identical to the parent. Many organisms, such as jellyfish, some types of worms, and many plants, use asexual reproduction at some stage of their lives. Asexual reproduction is the primary form of reproduction for unicellular organisms such as bacteria and protists.

Binary Fission

Although only eukaryotes (organisms with complex cells) can use mitosis to carry out asexual reproduction, many prokaryotes (bacteria) also reproduce using asexual reproduction. Instead of mitosis, however, prokaryotes divide using a process called BINARY FISSION. In binary fission, the cell duplicates its genetic material. The cell

BINARY FISSION

then elongates, causing the genetic material to split. The cell pinches down the middle, producing two new daughter cells identical to their parent cell.

Budding and Regeneration

THINK OF THE BUDS ON AN OLD POTATO—THAT'S ASEXUAL REPRODUCTION.

In some multicellular animals, the cell uses mitosis and cell division to produce a BUD of cells identical to the parent cell. When the bud is large enough, it can break off and live on its own. The resulting bud is identical to its parent.

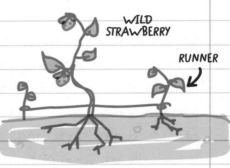

WILD STRAWBERRY

RUNNER

Plants can reproduce through VEGETATIVE PROPAGATION, which is when a plant produces RUNNERS, or horizontal stems that grow and form roots, and eventually create a new plant.

Plants can also reproduce through FRAGMENTATION, which is simply when a piece of the plant breaks off and the piece begins to grow into a new plant.

Animals that can REGENERATE, or regrow lost parts, like sea stars, can also reproduce asexually through regeneration. If a sea star is cut in half, for example, each part can regenerate into a new organism!

SEXUAL REPRODUCTION

Many organisms, including most animals and plants, reproduce sexually. In SEXUAL REPRODUCTION, a male and a female organism combine their genetic material to produce an offspring. Unlike asexual reproduction, the offspring is unique and different from each parent.

During sexual reproduction, a male SEX CELL, called a SPERM, and a female sex cell, called an EGG, join together. The joining together of a sperm and an egg is called **FERTILIZATION**, and the cell that forms from fertilization is called a **ZYGOTE**. The zygote will eventually grow and develop into an organism through mitosis and cell division.

FERTILIZATION
when a male and female sex cell unite

ZYGOTE
the cell that results from fertilization; has a complete set of chromosomes

SEXUAL vs.
ASEXUAL REPRODUCTION

Some organisms reproduce asexually, sexually, or both. What are the benefits of each?

PROS

- Sexual reproduction results in more variation. Each offspring has a unique combination of genetic material. More variation means that offspring will have different traits that can help them survive in different environments.

- Asexual reproduction requires less energy. Asexual reproduction doesn't require a mate and can be done with one parent alone. A population can expand quickly with asexual reproduction.

CONS

- In asexual reproduction, because there is no genetic variation, the population can become extinct quickly if conditions are unfavorable. If there were a parasite that targeted the organism, the population might die off quickly because every organism is identical.

- Sexual reproduction requires more effort and energy because the organism must find a mate. If an organism is unsuccessful at finding a mate, he or she will not reproduce.

DNA

Traits such as hair or eye color get passed down from parent to offspring through DNA (strands of genetic material that store hereditary information). DNA is tightly coiled around protein molecules to form chromosomes.

Think of DNA as a zipper. During cell replication, the DNA is unzipped. Each side of the zipper is later paired up with a new complementary zipper half that is identical to the other missing side of the zipper. The result is two new identical zippers. Each complete zipper contains half of an old zipper and half of a new zipper.

Complementary nitrogen bases comprise the teeth of the zipper. The complementary nitrogen bases fit together, so complementary base pairs always go together. There are four types of nitrogen bases: ADENINE, THYMINE, CYTOSINE, and GUANINE, represented by the letters A, T, C, and G. The order of these letters (nitrogen bases) is the "language" that tells a cell how to build an organism: AGGCATCGAATCG... etc., for billions of letters!

The A on one strand always pairs with the T on another, and the C always pairs with the G, which means there are always equal amounts of A and T, and equal amounts of C and G.

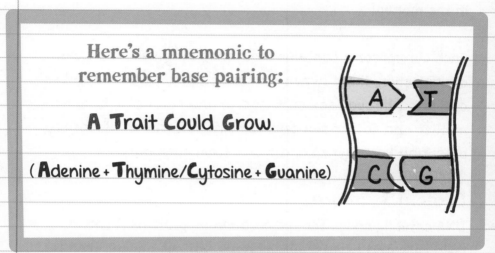

Here's a mnemonic to remember base pairing:

A Trait Could Grow.

(**A**denine + **T**hymine/**C**ytosine + **G**uanine)

Mutations

Sometimes mistakes are made when DNA is replicated. These mistakes are called MUTATIONS, and they can be caused by UV light, chemicals, and X-rays, among other things. Some mutations can cause an organism to die. Many are too small to make a difference in survival. Every once in a while, mutations can create traits that can help the organism survive. Genetic mutations are one of the ways organisms evolve.

Genes

GENES are segments of DNA strands that code for a specific trait. A gene is like an instruction manual, and DNA is the language and step-by-step directions listed in the manual.

Each chromosome contains thousands of genes. In sexual reproduction, these genes are passed down from parent to offspring through sex cells (sperm and egg cells). Because mother and father sex cells combine to form an offspring, offspring have genes and traits from each parent.

Protein Synthesis

DNA actually codes for the creation of proteins. Proteins build cells and tissues, which create various genetic traits. Proteins are complex molecules that are made by stringing together amino acids. Three base pairs (for instance, CTG or AAC) code for an amino acid. If a protein were a long beaded necklace, each bead would be an amino acid. The order, or sequence, of the amino acids determines the type of protein.

Although DNA is found in the nucleus of a cell, the proteins are made on the ribosomes in the cytoplasm. To get the information from the DNA molecule to the ribosome, the cell uses a messenger called RNA, which stands for RIBONUCLEIC ACID.

The RNA is fashioned from the DNA pattern, but unlike DNA, which contains two strands, RNA contains only one strand, like half of a DNA strand (half of a zipper). The RNA strand is like a pattern or mold from which many proteins can be made.

The other difference between RNA and DNA is the base each uses. Although RNA also uses base pairing, instead of the T (thymine) used in DNA, RNA uses a U (Uracil).

There are three different types of RNA, and each one serves a different function:

NUCLEUS
mRNA

mRNA: known as the **MESSENGER RNA**, carries the DNA code out of the nucleus to the cytoplasm

RIBOSOME

rRNA: known as the **RIBOSOMAL RNA**, it is what ribosomes are made of. Ribosomes attach to the mRNA molecule in order to begin protein production.

rRNA

AMINO ACID

tRNA: known as the **TRANSFER RNA.** Transfer RNA molecules transfer amino acids to the ribosomes.

tRNA

The Human Genome

Humans have thousands of genes. All of these genes are located on our chromosomes, and together all the genes make up what is called the human GENOME. Scientists have been working for a long time to map the location of each gene on our chromosomes. This project is called the HUMAN GENOME PROJECT. Scientists are trying to map the location of genetic diseases in order to help prevent and better understand them.

CHECK YOUR KNOWLEDGE

1. In what stage of the cell cycle do cells spend the most time? What happens in this stage?

2. What are the forms of asexual reproduction?

3. Compare and contrast asexual and sexual reproduction.

4. What is cell division used for?

5. What happens when there is a mutation in the DNA?

6. The joining together of a _____ and an egg is called _____, and the cell that forms is called a _____.

7. What are DNA's nitrogen bases, and how are they paired?

ANSWERS

CHECK YOUR ANSWERS

1. Interphase. During interphase, the cell prepares for division by growing and replicating its chromosomes and organelles.

2. Asexual reproduction can be carried out through mitosis, binary fission, budding, and regeneration.

3. In asexual reproduction, the offspring is identical to the parent. In sexual reproduction, the offspring is genetically unique. Sexual reproduction requires more energy and two parents, while asexual reproduction requires only one parent and less energy.

4. Cell division is used to replace old and worn-out cells, and also for growth. It is also used in asexual reproduction.

5. Sometimes mutations can cause an organism to die, sometimes they are helpful, but often they don't make much difference in survival.

6. Sperm, fertilization, zygote

7. A (adenine), T (thymine), C (cytosine), G (guanine). A and T go together, and so do C and G.

Unit

8

 Plants and Animals

Chapter 32

PLANT
STRUCTURE AND
REPRODUCTION

Some plants are microscopic, and some are as tall as thirty-story buildings—but all plants are made of cells that have cell walls and nearly all have a green pigment called chlorophyll, which allows them to make energy from the sun in a process called photosynthesis (energy production). Plants also have red, orange, and yellow pigments called CAROTENOIDS, which are also used for photosynthesis.

HEY, HOW'S IT GOING?

The first plants were probably green algae living under water. Then ferns, conifers, and flowering plants developed over millions of years as species adapted to living on land. Plants made the jump from living in water to land by developing structures that allowed them to grow upward and conserve water. On land, in order to conserve water, plants developed a waxy protective layer called a CUTICLE. For structural support, plants developed rigid cell walls filled with cellulose, a strong fiber.

VASCULAR and NONVASCULAR PLANTS

MOSTLY VERY SIMPLE PLANTS LIKE MOSSES

NONVASCULAR PLANTS don't have structures to help them carry and distribute water or nutrients, so each cell absorbs water and nutrients on its own.

VASCULAR PLANTS have tubelike structures that carry and distribute nutrients. Most vascular plants have seeds, but there are a few vascular plants, such as ferns, that don't.

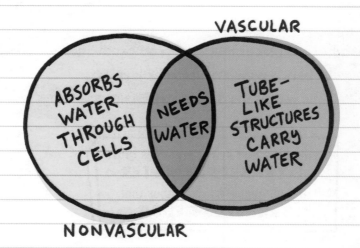

VASCULAR

ABSORBS WATER THROUGH CELLS

NEEDS WATER

TUBE-LIKE STRUCTURES CARRY WATER

NONVASCULAR

Vascular Tissue

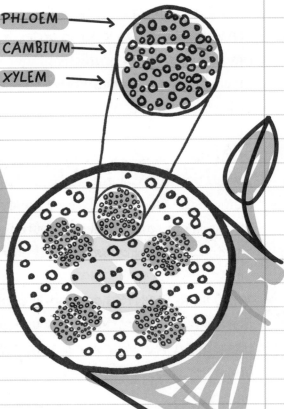

PHLOEM ⟶

CAMBIUM ⟶

XYLEM ⟶

XYLEM: tubelike cells stacked together to form vessels that distribute water from the roots to different parts of the plant. They also provide structural support.

PHLOEM: tubelike cells stacked to form tubes that distribute food for use and storage

CAMBIUM: cells that produce new xylem and phloem cells; between the xylem and phloem in some plants; increases the thickness of stems and roots

Remember that xylem produces tubes that **TRANSPORT WATER**, and phloem produces tubes that **TRANSPORT FOOD**.

SEEDLESS PLANTS

Seedless plants reproduce using SPORES, which are small reproductive units. Seedless plants can be broken down into two categories: nonvascular and vascular.

Nonvascular Seedless Plants

NONVASCULAR SEEDLESS PLANTS are only a few cells thick because each cell absorbs water and nutrients through its cell membrane directly from its surroundings.

Most nonvascular seedless plants live in damp environments where there is ample water. Nonvascular seedless plants have RHIZOIDS, which are tiny stringy structures instead of roots. Rhizoids anchor plants. Nonvascular seedless plants include mosses, liverworts, and hornworts.

Nonvascular seedless plants are often the pioneer species of a developing ecosystem, especially in wetter climates.

Vascular Seedless Plants

VASCULAR SEEDLESS PLANTS, such as ferns, ground pines, horsetails, and spike mosses, can grow larger because they have structures to distribute water and nutrients. Most of the vascular seedless plants—apart from ferns and horsetails—don't exist anymore, and we know about them only through fossils.

PLANTS THAT HAVE SEEDS

SEEDS are reproductive units adapted to land. Unlike spores, seeds have stored food resources and a seed coat for protection. It's like when parents give kids a lunchbox and coat so that they survive at school. Seeded plants can be broken down into GYMNOSPERMS, which are plants that have seeds that aren't contained in a fruit, and ANGIOSPERMS, which are plants that have seeds contained in a fruit. All of the fruits we eat are angiosperms.

> **REMEMBER:**
> Gymnosperms produce seeds that are **NOT** protected by fruits (like pine trees).
> Gymnosperms do **NOT FLOWER**.
> Angiosperms produce seeds that are protected by fruits.
> Angiosperms do flower.

All plants with seeds are vascular plants, and most have these three structures:

1. **Leaves:** the organ of the plant where photosynthesis happens. Some are flat, others are shaped like needles, and others have different shapes.

EPIDERMIS: the outer layer with a waxy cuticle that prevents water loss and protects the leaf. The leaf exchanges gases such as oxygen and carbon dioxide with the environment through openings in the epidermis, called **STOMATA**. *LIKE LIPS ON YOUR MOUTH* **GUARD CELLS** open and close the stomata. ← Leaves also can lose water through these stomata, so they usually keep them closed on hot days.

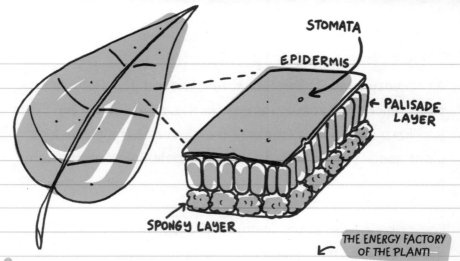

STOMATA

EPIDERMIS

← PALISADE LAYER

SPONGY LAYER

THE ENERGY FACTORY OF THE PLANT!

PALISADE LAYER: the layer beneath the epidermis that contains chloroplasts to make energy through photosynthesis

SPONGY LAYER: the layer beneath the palisade layer. It gets its name from the arrangement of cells—they are very loosely packed, leaving many air pockets to store CO_2 or oxygen, like a sponge. Most of the vascular tissue, which is the tissue that distributes water and food, is found in the spongy layer.

2. Stems: the support for leaves, branches, etc.

3. Roots: the plant structure that absorbs water, gases, and nutrients from the soil, and stores food. Structurally, roots also support the plant and prevent it from being blown or washed away.

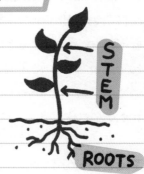

STEM

ROOTS

339

Flowering Plant Reproduction

All angiosperms flower. Seeds are formed in a flowering plant when the female part of the flower is POLLINATED, or fertilized with pollen from the male part of the plant. Most plant species have both male and female parts on the same plant.

Egg cells develop in the female reproductive part, called the OVARY. The ovary also has a long tube extending from it called the PISTIL. Surrounding the pistil are the male reproductive parts, called STAMENS. Stamens produce POLLEN, a colored "dust" that contains sperm cells. The STIGMA is the part of the plant that receives the pollen.

A seed is produced when the egg from the ovary is united with sperm from pollen, a process called POLLINATION. Pollination happens when pollen from the stamen is transferred to the pistil via the stigma. Most plants have adaptations that keep them from self-pollinating, such as different timing of maturity of sperm and egg cells, or enticing insects with nectar so the insects carry the pollen to other plants. The sperm cells in the pollen then reach the stigma and move down the pistil to reach the egg cells in the ovary.

Parent plants must scatter their seeds away from themselves so they don't compete for sun, water, or nutrients

from the soil. Plants have adapted different methods for
SEED DISPERSAL such as:

- **WIND**: Seeds are light and have feathery
  bristles so they can be carried by the wind.

LIKE WHEN
THE SEEDS ON A
DANDELION HEAD
BLOW AWAY

- **WATER**: Seeds float away down streams and rivers.

- **ANIMALS**: Seeds may hook on to an animal's fur,
  feathers, or skin. Animals may also eat a fruit and
  then disperse the seed through their droppings.

- **BURSTING**: The fruit of the seed dries out and splits
  open, thus throwing seeds in different directions.

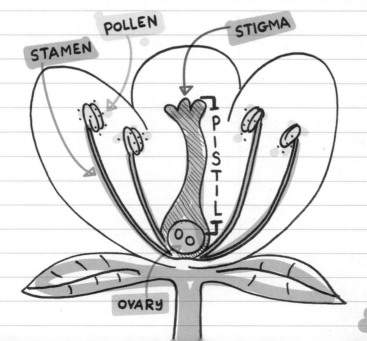

POLLEN   STIGMA   STAMEN   PISTIL   OVARY

If the seed has the proper water and temperature, it GERMINATES, or grows, using food stored in the seed. The protective coating of the seed splits open, and a primary root extends into the soil. The seed continues to develop, sprouting roots, stems, and leaves that allow the plant to make food and support itself.

CHECK YOUR KNOWLEDGE

1. What is the part of a flower that contains sperm cells?

2. Explain what roots do.

3. Give an example of a seedless vascular plant.

4. What do nonvascular plants have instead of roots?

5. Why are nonvascular seedless plants only a few cells thick?

6. What is the kind of seeded plant that flowers?

7. What is the green pigment used for photosynthesis?

8. What is the male reproductive part of a flowering plant?

9. Explain the function of a plant's stomata.

10. Plants that have seeds not surrounded by fruits are called what?

11. What does a plant's xylem do?

12. What do seedless plants use to reproduce?

ANSWERS 343

CHECK YOUR ANSWERS

1. Pollen on the stamen

2. Roots provide stability, collect water, and store nutrients.

3. Fern

4. Rhizoids

5. Because each cell must absorb nutrients and water directly from the environment

6. Angiosperm

7. Chlorophyll

8. Stamen

9. The stomata are openings in the leaf that exchange gases like oxygen and carbon dioxide with the environment.

10. Gymnosperms

11. The xylem distributes water from the roots to other parts of the plant.

12. Spores

#3 has more than one correct answer.

Chapter 33

ANIMALS: INVERTEBRATES

ANIMAL CHARACTERISTICS

Most animals have the following characteristics:

MULTICELLULAR (made of many cells)
HETEROTROPHS (they eat other organisms)
MOBILE (can move to find food, shelter, and safety)

Most animals have **SYMMETRY**, which means they look identical across a line that divides them. Humans, dogs, and many other animals have **BILATERAL SYMMETRY**, which means that if you drew a line down their bodies, both sides would look the same. Other animals have **RADIAL SYMMETRY**, which means that they have identical parts arranged in a circle, like a starfish. But there are a few **ASYMMETRICAL** animals—like a pond snail, which has a shell that curls in one direction.

INVERTEBRATES

Animals that don't have backbones are called INVERTEBRATES. Invertebrates include a wide variety of animals such as worms, sponges, clams, scallops, lobsters, and grasshoppers. The vast majority of animal species are invertebrates.

Sponges

Scientists first thought that sponges were plants because they are SESSILE, or unmoving. But unlike plants, most SPONGES are heterotrophs. Sponges filter microscopic organisms out of the water for food.

In sexual reproduction, most sponges are HERMAPHRODITES, which means each sponge has both the male and female parts. Sponges reproduce both SEXUALLY and ASEXUALLY, which means they either combine male and female DNA to produce an offspring that has new genetic information, or they reproduce asexually, so the offspring is identical to the parent.

Cnidarians (pronounced like NiDArians)

CNIDARIANS are hollow animals composed of two cell layers, and the inner cells enclose a digestive cavity. They have tentacles surrounding their mouths. ← WHICH IS ALSO WHERE THEY EXCRETE WASTE!

Cnidarians include jellyfish, sea anemones, hydras, and corals. Cnidarians shoot out stinging cells from their tentacles to capture prey, which is why a jellyfish stings.

Flatworms

FLATWORMS are long, flat worms that have bilateral symmetry. Most flatworms are parasites, which mean they live in a host, like a human or dog, for food and shelter. The TAPEWORM, one type of parasitic flatworm, lives in the host's intestines, eating its food.

Tapeworms are made of body segments with both male and female reproductive organs. As tapeworms

SOME CAN GROW MORE THAN 50 FEET!

grow, they add on new segments, growing longer and longer. The tapeworm spreads to other organisms through its eggs. A segment fills with fertilized eggs, and then breaks off. These eggs exit the host with the animal's waste, landing on grass or other plants. When other animals eat the grass or plants, the tapeworm's eggs enter the new host. **Gross!**

Roundworms

A roundworm is like a long tube layered within another. A fluid-filled cavity separates the inner and outer tubes. Roundworms have more complicated bodies than flatworms because they have both a mouth and an anus, where waste exits their bodies.

Segmented Worms

Segmented worms, also known as ANNELIDS, have bodies made of repeating rings, or segments. (Their body structure is easy to remember because of their name.) Segmented worms have closed circulatory systems, a mouth for eating, and an anus for expelling waste.

Earthworms and leeches are two examples of segmented worms. Earthworms live in soil and eat organic matter from the soil for energy. Earthworms carry out gas exchange through their skin. To help gas pass through their skin, they are covered in a thin layer of mucus. (That's why worms are so slimy.)

Mollusks

Mollusks are soft-bodied organisms that usually have a shell. A layer of tissue called a mantle surrounds their bodies. In mollusks with shells, the mantle secretes the shell. Examples of mollusks include snails, scallops, and octopuses.

Arthropods

Arthropods have jointed **APPENDAGES**, like claws, legs, and antennae. Arthropods have a hard outer body covering called an EXOSKELETON. The exoskeleton doesn't grow with the animal, so as the arthropod grows, it sheds its exoskeleton and builds

> **APPENDAGE**
> a structure that is attached to something larger. For example, an arm is an appendage because it is attached, hopefully, to a body.

a new one in a process called MOLTING. Most arthropods are insects, but there are many other kinds as well, such as spiders, scorpions, centipedes, and crustaceans. Arthropods are the largest group of animals, with more than one million species.

INSECTS

Insects are a very diverse group of organisms, but many, like ants, have bodies that can be broken down into three parts:

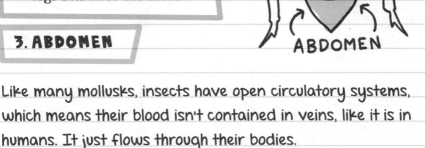

1. **HEAD**: eyes and antennae attach to the head

2. **THORAX**: wings or legs attach to the thorax

3. **ABDOMEN**

Like many mollusks, insects have open circulatory systems, which means their blood isn't contained in veins, like it is in humans. It just flows through their bodies.

Many insects, such as butterflies, ants, bees, and beetles, change drastically from the time they are young to the time they are fully grown. The physical transformation that insects undergo is called **METAMORPHOSIS**.

METAMORPHOSIS
a body transformation

Metamorphosis can either have four stages:
EGG
LARVA
PUPA
ADULT

Or three stages:
EGG
NYMPH
ADULT

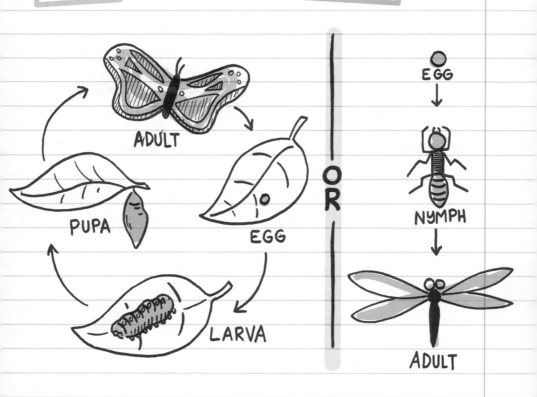

ADULT

PUPA

EGG

LARVA

OR

EGG

NYMPH

ADULT

The larva or nymph stage is all about food (a caterpillar is basically a mouth with a walking stomach behind it). The adult stage is all about reproduction. Many adult insects don't even eat at all. ← THEY'RE MISSING OUT!

ARACHNIDS

Spiders, scorpions, and ticks are all arachnids. Arachnids have only two body parts: a **CEPHALOTHORAX**, which is the head and thorax region stuck together, and an abdomen. They also have four pairs of legs.

CENTIPEDES AND MILLIPEDES

Centipedes and millipedes have long, segmented bodies. Centipedes have one pair of legs per segment, and millipedes have two pairs of legs per segment.

CRUSTACEANS

Crustaceans live in water and vary greatly in size. Most crustaceans have antennae, chewing appendages, and five pairs of legs. Crustaceans include crabs, lobsters, water fleas, shrimp, and barnacles.

Echinoderms

Echinoderms have spiny skin and radial symmetry (their body parts are arranged in a balanced way around the center). Echinoderms don't have heads or brains. They include sea urchins, starfish, sun stars, and sand dollars.

CHECK YOUR KNOWLEDGE

Match the term with the correct definition:

1. Heterotroph
2. Arachnid
3. Earthworm
4. Cephalothorax
5. Arthropods
6. Sponge
7. Roundworms
8. Cnidarians
9. Bilateral symmetry
10. Appendage

A. A segmented worm with a closed circulatory system

B. Worms that have both a mouth and an anus

C. An organism that gets its food by eating other organisms

D. Invertebrates that have exoskeletons and jointed appendages

E. Hollow animals with two cell layers, such as jellyfish, sea anemones, hydras, and corals

F. The head and thorax region of an arachnid

G. A sessile invertebrate

H. An arthropod with two body parts

I. A mirror image across one line

J. A structure that is attached to something larger

ANSWERS 353

CHECK YOUR ANSWERS

1. C
2. H
3. A
4. F
5. D
6. G
7. B
8. E
9. I
10. J

Chapter 34

ANIMALS: VERTEBRATES

CHORDATES

CHORDATES are animals that, at some
stage in their development, have a:

NOTOCHORD

a rod (such as a backbone) extending
down the length of a body for support

NOTOCHORD

NERVE CORD

a nerve that runs along the length
of the animal's body and becomes
the animal's nervous system

I WANT TUNA.

NERVE CORD

PHARYNGEAL SLIT

an opening between the body cavity
and outside of the body that is
usually present only in the early
stages of development

PHARYNGEAL SLIT

355

The largest group of chordates is vertebrates. Vertebrates are animals that have a skull and an ENDOSKELETON, which is an internal skeleton that supports the body, provides attachment points for muscles, and protects organs. An endoskeleton includes things such as your rib cage, your leg bones, and your skull.

Vertebrates can either be cold-blooded or warm-blooded animals. Cold-blooded animals are called **ECTOTHERMS**, and their body temperature changes with the temperature outside. If it is cold out, an ectotherm has a colder body temperature and is therefore less active.

ECTOTHERM
cold-blooded

ENDOTHERM
warm-blooded

An **ENDOTHERM** is a warm-blooded animal, and its internal temperature doesn't fluctuate as much. Humans, for example, are endotherms, and lizards are ectotherms.

FISH

FISH (the largest group of vertebrates) breathe underwater using GILLS, which are a structure that carries out gas exchange with water. Fish have fins on their sides to help them steer in the water, as well as on the tops and bottoms of their bodies for stability.

Fish have an endoskeleton made out of either bone or CARTILAGE, which is a hard, flexible tissue. (Your ears and nose are made out of cartilage, which is why you can smush around your nose and ears with your hands.) Most fish are bony.

Bony Fish

BONY FISH have scales and are also covered in a layer of mucus that helps them glide through water. Fish also have an internal balloonlike structure called a SWIM BLADDER. Like a balloon, the swim bladder inflates and deflates to help the fish float or sink.

Fish reproduce using EXTERNAL FERTILIZATION, which is a process of fertilizing eggs outside of the body. Female fish squirt out eggs, and then male fish pass over the eggs, releasing sperm to fertilize them.

Cartilaginous Fish

CARTILAGINOUS FISH have skeletons made mostly of cartilage. They usually have a suckerlike mouth with claws or teeth inside that help them attach to a host fish. Usually, the fish sucks the blood of other fish, sort of like a vampire fish. Sharks and rays are other types of cartilaginous fish.

AMPHIBIANS

AMPHIBIANS are animals that live part of their lives in water and part on land. Frogs, toads, and salamanders are all amphibians.

Like fish, amphibians are ectotherms. In cold weather, ectotherms become DORMANT (inactive) in order to conserve energy. In hot, dry conditions, ectotherms move underground to find cool and damp conditions where they remain dormant until the temperature outside is easier for them to handle.

Amphibians use both their lungs and their skin to carry out gas exchange. Did you ever notice how frogs are slimy? Amphibians must always be moist to carry out gas exchange through their skin.

Most amphibians use external fertilization, just like fish do. Baby amphibians look completely different from adult amphibians. Amphibians go through metamorphosis, a body transformation, as they age. Young amphibians, like tadpoles, live entirely in water. They have gills and no legs. As the young amphibian ages, it grows legs and lungs, and can often survive where there is little water. It will return to water, however, when it is time to reproduce.

REPTILES ← SHOW UP AFTER AMPHIBIANS IN THE FOSSIL RECORD

REPTILES are vertebrates that live on land. Like fish and amphibians, reptiles are ectotherms. When a lizard is cold, it will sit on a rock in the sun to warm itself. Alternatively, when a lizard is hot, it will find shelter in a cool place under a rock. In the winter, many reptiles undergo a process similar to hibernation called BRUMATION. Turtles, lizards, alligators, and snakes are all examples of reptiles.

Reptiles use internal fertilization, which means the egg is fertilized by the sperm inside the female's body. Reptiles lay soft-shelled eggs, which is an adaptation that allows them to lay eggs on land without the eggs dying. Their eggs are also AMNIOTIC. In an amniotic egg, the yolk provides the growing embryo with food. Chickens also lay amniotic eggs—the yellow part of the egg is the yolk.

359

BIRDS

BIRDS are vertebrates that have wings, legs, bills or beaks, and feathers. (In fact, birds are the only animals that have feathers.) Birds are ENDOTHERMIC, which means they must use energy to generate their own heat internally, as opposed to getting it from the environment. They also lay hard eggs, which they sit on to keep warm until the babies hatch from the eggs. Most birds, although not all, can fly. Penguins and ostriches can't fly, though penguins can swim and ostriches can run really fast.

GO GO GO!

MAMMALS ← SHOW UP EVEN MORE RECENTLY THAN OTHER GROUPS IN THE FOSSIL RECORD

Dogs, whales, humans, bears, and kangaroos are all examples of MAMMALS. Mammals get their name from the fact that they have MAMMARY GLANDS, glands that produce milk for feeding their young. Mammals, like birds, are endothermic. To help them stay warm, mammals usually have hair or fur, which insulates them so they don't have to burn as much energy to maintain their body temperature.

Mammals usually take much more time caring for their offspring than most other animals. For one thing,

360

mammals nurse their young for weeks or even months on milk they produce in their mammary glands. All mammals use internal fertilization.

There are three main types of mammals:

1. MONOTREMES: mammals that lay eggs in leathery shells. There are only five living species of monotremes: the duck-billed platypus and four species of echidnas (which look like a spiny anteater). All monotremes live in Australia, Tasmania, or New Guinea.

2. MARSUPIALS: Marsupials give birth, then allow their young to mature in a pouch, like kangaroos, opossums, and wombats.

3. PLACENTALS: mammals that fully develop with a saclike organ called the PLACENTA that feeds them within the uterus. The placenta has an UMBILICAL CORD, which is a cord that carries food, water, and oxygen to the embryo and returns waste to the mother. Your belly button is where your umbilical cord connected you to your mother!

WHERE IS THAT DARN BELLY BUTTON?

NINETY-FIVE PERCENT OF ALL MAMMAL SPECIES ARE PLACENTALS.

Mammals can be **HERBIVORES**, **OMNIVORES**, or **CARNIVORES**. Herbivores, such as cows, are plant eaters; omnivores, such as humans, eat plants and meat; and carnivores, such as mountain lions, are meat eaters.

HERBIVORE
plant eater

OMNIVORE
plant and animal eater

CARNIVORE
animal eater

Mammals are generally more capable of learning and remembering things than most other types of animals. They have complex nervous systems and large brains.

Mammals existed during the time of the dinosaurs, but they mostly lived underground as small rodents. Once the dinosaurs went extinct (about 65 million years ago), there was less competition and mammals were able to adapt and evolve into all the ecological niches left vacant by the dinosaurs. Now there is a wide variety of mammal species living in diverse habitats around the globe.

CHECK YOUR KNOWLEDGE

1. Vertebrates are animals that have an _____.

2. Vertebrates are all _____, which are animals that at some point in their lives have a notochord, a nerve cord, and pharyngeal slits.

3. Which mammals lay eggs?

4. The invertebrates that are ectotherms are _____, _____, and _____.

5. Fish can either have _____ or _____ skeletons. A shark has a _____ skeleton.

6. How do female mammals feed their young?

7. Amphibians carry out gas exchange using both their _____ and _____.

8. How do fish control whether they sink or float?

9. How do reptiles survive cold weather?

10. Name and explain the three types of feeding habits of mammals.

11. Describe some ways that ectotherms maintain proper body temperatures.

ANSWERS ▶ 363

CHECK YOUR ANSWERS

1. Endoskeleton

2. Chordates

3. Monotremes

4. Fish, amphibians, reptiles

5. Bony, cartilaginous, cartilaginous

6. Their mammary glands make milk.

7. Lungs, skin

8. Fish have a swim bladder that they can inflate or deflate to help them sink or float.

9. In cold weather, reptiles survive by entering an inactive state called brumation.

10. Mammals that eat meat are called carnivores. Mammals that eat only plants are called herbivores. Mammals that eat both plants and other animals are called omnivores.

11. Because ectotherms rely on the environment to control their body temperatures, if it is hot outside, ectotherms could go underground, dunk themselves in water, or find a shady spot to help them cool down. If it is cold outside, ectotherms could find a sunny spot or a rock in the sun to warm them.

#11 has more than one correct answer.

Chapter 35

ANIMAL AND PLANT HOMEOSTASIS AND BEHAVIOR

HOMEOSTASIS

HOMEOSTASIS refers to any behavior that allows an organism to maintain its internal balance despite what is going on outside. For example, when it is

> **HOMEOSTASIS**
> behaviors that allow a proper internal balance despite changing conditions in the environment

really hot outside, humans sweat. Sweating is a homeostatic response to heat and allows us to keep body temperatures constant. In animals, homeostasis includes all sorts of responses that maintain body temperature, blood sugar levels, and blood oxygen levels. Plants maintain homeostasis, too, which allows them to keep the right balance of water and nutrients. Homeostasis is how animals and plants respond to a change in the environment, called a **STIMULUS**.

> **STIMULUS**
> a change in the environment that triggers a response

PLANT HOMEOSTASIS and BEHAVIOR

Tropism

TROPISM is plant growth in response to a stimulus. PHOTOTROPISM is growth in response to light, so plants grow toward

windows as a result. There are many different kinds of tropism—plants can respond to gravity (roots growing downward and stems growing upward) and touch (vines latching on to walls).

Transpiration

TRANSPIRATION is when a plant releases water vapor into the environment. Transpiration is one way plants control their water balance and temperature.
It is also a form of evaporation. Leaves have tiny openings called stomata used for gas exchange.

When the stomata are opened, some water escapes and evaporates into the environment. The more frequently the stomata open, the more a plant transpires. Desert plants and conifers have shrunken stomata so less water can escape and they can conserve water.

Transpiration also serves as a cooling mechanism (sort of like perspiration) and helps pull nutrient-rich water from the roots upward to the leaves.

Dormancy

Many trees are leafless in the winter because the tree is responding to the cold by entering a state of **DORMANCY**, which is a period when the plant's growth and activity are stopped. Plants become dormant in order to conserve energy. When conditions, such as cold or dryness, are unfavorable for survival, plants

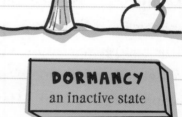

DORMANCY
an inactive state

stop growing, allowing them to live through harsh conditions. In the spring, they send stored energy in their roots back up to the branches so they can grow leaves to start producing sugar again.

ANIMAL HOMEOSTASIS and BEHAVIOR

Animal Behavior

Animal behavior is adapted to the environment, and behaviors are usually in response to a stimulus, or change, in the environment.

Behaviors can either be INNATE or LEARNED. Innate behaviors are behaviors that are genetically programmed into the animal. They don't need to be learned. For example, swimming is an innate behavior of whales—no one needs to teach a whale how to swim; it's been programmed into their DNA over millions of years of evolution. We often refer to these behaviors as INSTINCTS. Other behaviors are learned. For example, lions learn how to hunt for prey by watching their mothers in action.

Temperature Control

Animals have all sorts of mechanisms to help them control their body temperatures. When animals get hot, their blood vessels dilate, sending blood to the surface of the skin to evaporate some heat. After you exercise, your face gets all red because blood rushes to your skin.

Animals use all sorts of behaviors and responses to ensure their bodies remain at the right temperature. When you run around for a while, you probably start sweating. Sweating is one mechanism that helps control our body temperature. Dogs, on the other hand, cool themselves down by panting.

Endotherms don't rely on the environment to maintain their body temperatures. Some mammals also grow thicker coats of hair for the winter to hold in the heat their bodies are working so hard to produce, but shed their coats of fur in the springtime so they don't overheat.

Adaptations to Climate

Animals and plants adapt to their local climates. An ADAPTATION is any behavior or structure that allows an organism to survive. Cacti, for example, are adapted to life in the desert by having fleshy stems to hold water and a thick, waxy skin to prevent water loss.

IS IT SPRING ALREADY?

When it gets cold outside, some animals, such as bears, enter an inactive state called **HIBERNATION**. When an animal

HIBERNATION
a period of inactivity and slowed metabolism in cold weather

hibernates, its heart rate and breathing rate slow down, and its internal temperature drops. During hibernation, an animal finds a den or an underground burrow and enters a deep sleep. When temperatures warm up outside, the animal wakes up and comes back out.

ESTIVATION is like hibernation for hot weather. Many amphibians go underground and use estivation to survive hot summer months.

ESTIVATION
a period of inactivity and slowed metabolism in hot or dry weather

Migration

When it gets cold outside, some animals move to a warmer place. Seasonal movement is called MIGRATION. When it gets cold and food runs low, birds migrate to warmer locations, sometimes traveling up to 44,000 miles on a zigzagging roundtrip.

OH MAN, YOU GUYS ARE GONNA MISS HALLOWEEN!

Cooperative Behavior

Animals sometimes work together in order to accomplish something. For example, bees and ants cooperate to build complex colonies. Some animals, such as gorillas, live in groups with specific social ranks.

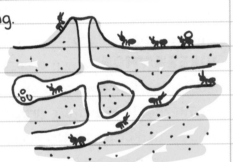

Mating Behavior

Many animal behaviors are meant to attract a mate. Many birds, for example, have elaborate mating calls and dances. The male birds try really hard to impress the females with colorful feathers and just the right dance moves.

HUMANS AREN'T THE ONLY SPECIES THAT TRY HARD TO GET DATES!

CHECK YOUR KNOWLEDGE

1. Describe some ways that animals maintain proper body temperatures.

2. What is tropism?

3. When do plants and animals become inactive?

4. What are some kinds of inactivity for plants and animals?

5. Explain cooperative behavior and give an example.

6. Explain how transpiration works.

7. Animal behaviors can either be innate or learned. Explain the difference.

ANSWERS

CHECK YOUR ANSWERS

1. Some animals grow fur when they are cold and shed when they get hot.

2. Tropism is plant growth in response to a stimulus.

3. Plants and animals enter an inactive phase when the conditions outside aren't great for growth and survival.

4. To survive temperatures, plants enter a phase of dormancy, which means they stop growing to conserve energy. In the cold, some animals hibernate, which means they find a den or underground burrow and enter a deep sleep for the winter. In really hot environments, some animals estivate, which is like hot-weather hibernation. Other animals, like birds, migrate, or travel, to find temperate weather.

5. Cooperative behavior is when animals work together in order to accomplish something, like when a group of lionesses hunt together so they have a greater chance of capturing prey.

6. Transpiration is how a plant releases water to the environment. When the plant's stomata open and close, some water evaporates.

7. A learned behavior is a behavior that an animal learns from experience or from watching other animals. An innate behavior (or instinct) is a behavior that is genetically programmed and doesn't need to be learned.

#1, #4, and #5 have more than one correct answer.

Unit 9

The Human Body and Body Systems

Chapter 36

SKELETAL AND MUSCULAR SYSTEMS

The BODY'S STRUCTURAL HIERARCHY

The body is sort of like a factory: It has an organizational hierarchy and different systems that accomplish different tasks:

The most basic unit of the body is a single cell.

← SORT OF LIKE A SINGLE WORKER IN A FACTORY

When groups of cells work together on a similar job, they are called tissues. There are all sorts of tissues in your body, such as skin, muscles, and nerves.

← LIKE A TEAM OF FACTORY WORKERS

When tissues work together to accomplish a bigger job, they are called organs. Your kidneys, heart, liver, and intestines are all organs.

← LIKE A DEPARTMENT FILLED WITH TEAMS

Even organs can work together—to form organ systems. Organ systems are made of a number of different organs working together to accomplish a task. For example, the circulatory system is an organ system that circulates blood, oxygen, and nutrients throughout your body.

↖ ALL THE DEPARTMENTS WORKING TOGETHER

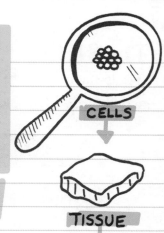

CELLS

TISSUE

TISSUE TYPES

Our bodies are made of four main tissue types:

ORGAN

1. **EPITHELIAL TISSUE**: the outer layer of tissue on your body (in other words, YOUR SKIN) and also the tissue that lines some of your body's inner surfaces

2. **CONNECTIVE TISSUE**: connects tissues. Ligaments are a connective tissue that connects bones. (Bones are another type of connective tissue.) Connective tissue also fills in spaces. The cartilage in your ears and nose is connective tissue.

ORGAN SYSTEM

3. **MUSCULAR TISSUE**: tissue that can contract and expand, creating movement

4. **NERVOUS TISSUE**: tissue that relays messages throughout your body

THE HUMAN BODY

The SKIN

Skin is the outermost layer on your body and is also the largest organ. The skin serves multiple purposes:

Protects your body from injury

Forms a barrier to prevent bacteria and organisms from entering your body

Prevents water loss

Regulates body temperature

Has nerve endings that relay information about temperature, sensation, and pain to the brain

Produces vitamin D in the presence of ultraviolet light from the sun. (Vitamin D helps the body absorb calcium.)

Releases waste. (Sweat glands also give off waste products.)

When the body is hot, blood vessels dilate and increase blood flow to the surface of the skin, releasing thermal energy. (This is why your face gets red when you exercise.) Your skin also has millions of sweat glands. When you get hot, you sweat. The sweat evaporates, cooling your body.

When the body is cold, blood vessels contract, limiting the flow of blood to your skin, preventing heat loss.

Your skin is made of three layers:
The EPIDERMIS is the
outermost layer;
the DERMIS is the layer
under the epidermis, which
has blood vessels, nerve
endings, hair follicles, and
sweat and oil glands;
the FATTY LAYER is the

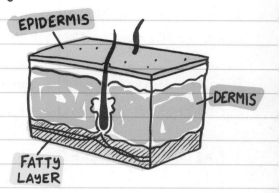

bottom layer, where your body stores the fat that insulates
and cushions your body.

MUSCULAR SYSTEM

The MUSCULAR SYSTEM controls movement—both
the kind of movement that allows you to walk and run,
and the kind of movement that you have no control over,
such as your heart beating and your stomach churning.

The muscles you can control are called VOLUNTARY
MUSCLES, and the muscles you cannot control are called
INVOLUNTARY MUSCLES. Your arm and leg muscles are
voluntary muscles, and your stomach and heart muscles are
involuntary.

Muscles create movement by contracting and relaxing. Your
muscles use energy to contract, and they produce mechanical
energy (or movement) and thermal energy (or heat).

Muscles change in size depending on how much you use them.
If you do push-ups every day, your arm and chest muscles
will grow stronger and bigger.

Kinds of Muscular Tissue

Our bodies have three kinds of muscular tissue:

1. **SKELETAL MUSCLES**: voluntary
   muscles that move bones, such as
   the muscles in your arms or legs.
   The connective tissues that attach
   skeletal muscle to bones are called
   TENDONS. Skeletal muscles usually
   work in pairs around a bone—when one
   muscle contracts, the other relaxes.

2. **SMOOTH MUSCLES**: involuntary
   muscles that work in internal organs,
   like your **DIGESTIVE TRACT**.

3. **CARDIAC MUSCLES**: involuntary
   muscles that make your heart pump.
   Cardiac muscles are found only in your heart.

SKELETAL SYSTEM

The skeletal system has many functions:

> It supports your body and gives it shape.

> It protects your internal organs,
> such as your lungs and brain!

> It stores calcium and other minerals.

The skeletal and muscular systems work together to create movement.

Cartilage

The skeleton is made of hard bones and a flexible hard tissue called cartilage.

Cartilage is a smooth, firm, and flexible tissue that is found on the ends of bones. Cartilage cushions and reduces friction between bones in your joints.

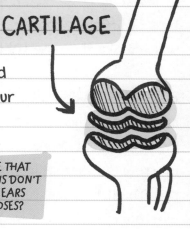

CARTILAGE

Cartilage is also found in your ears and nose.

NOTICE THAT SKELETONS DON'T HAVE EARS OR NOSES?

Bones

Though BONES seem just like hard sticks in your body, they are actually complex organs made of different kinds of tissue. A hard outer membrane called the PERIOSTEUM covers the outside of the bone. The periosteum has blood vessels and nerve endings that can signal pain.

COMPACT BONE is beneath the periosteum. Calcium and phosphorous minerals, which are deposited and stored in the compact bone, harden the bones.

SPONGY BONE is found beneath the compact bone in long bones, such as your thighbone or arm bone. Spongy bone is sort of like a hard sponge; it has tons of little air pockets, which make the bone lighter.

BONE MARROW fills bone cavities and the spaces in spongy bone. Bone marrow is either yellow or red. The yellow marrow is made of fat, while the red marrow is made of a material that produces blood cells.

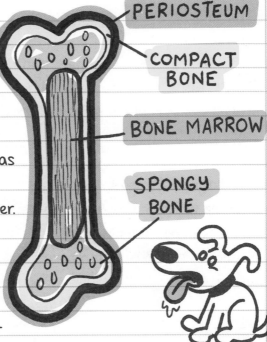

PERIOSTEUM

COMPACT BONE

BONE MARROW

SPONGY BONE

Joints

A JOINT is where bones meet, such as your knees or elbows.
LIGAMENTS, a type of connective tissue, hold the bones
together at the joints. Usually, joints allow movement,
although some joints, such as the ones in your skull, are fixed
and don't move.

Your body moves around joints. There are four main types of
joints, and each has a different kind of movement.

1. PIVOT JOINT: Bones pivot,
or rotate around a central point.
↖ IN YOUR WRISTS, NECK, AND ELBOWS

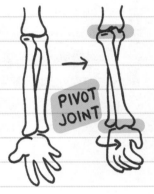

PIVOT JOINT

2. GLIDING JOINT: Bones
glide over each other.
↖ IN YOUR WRISTS, ANKLES, AND VERTEBRAE

GLIDING JOINT

3. HINGE JOINT: Bones hinge at a central point, sort of like the hinge on a door.

IN YOUR KNEES, ELBOWS, FINGERS, AND TOES

HINGE JOINT

4. BALL-AND-SOCKET JOINT: The bone is in a socket so it can rotate in a circle.

IN YOUR SHOULDERS AND HIPS

BALL-AND-SOCKET JOINT

CHECK YOUR KNOWLEDGE

1. List three functions your skin serves.

2. What types of joints are in your arm, from shoulder to fingers?

3. Where is cardiac muscle found?

4. What kind of muscles do you have control over?

5. What minerals make bones hard?

6. What's the difference between ligaments and tendons?

7. How does your skin respond when you are cold?

8. What functions does the skeletal system have?

ANSWERS

CHECK YOUR ANSWERS

1. Any three of the following: serves as a physical barrier, regulates body temperature, produces vitamin D, removes body waste, has nerve endings

2. Your shoulder is a ball-and-socket joint, your elbow is both a hinge and a pivot joint, your wrist is both a pivot and a gliding joint, and your fingers are hinge joints.

3. Only in your heart

4. Your voluntary muscles

5. Calcium and phosphorous

6. Ligaments connect bones to other bones, and tendons connect muscles to bones.

7. When you are cold, the blood vessels in your skin contract, limiting the amount of blood flow to your skin, preventing heat loss.

8. The skeletal system supports your body, gives your body your shape, protects internal organs, and stores calcium and other minerals.

Chapter 37

NERVOUS AND ENDOCRINE SYSTEMS

NERVOUS SYSTEM

Your NERVOUS SYSTEM is like your body's cell phone and email service. It gathers and relays information about your surroundings to your brain. The nervous system responds to external stimuli (changes in the environment that trigger a response).

The BRAIN, SPINAL CORD, NERVES, and SENSORY ORGANS such as your eyes, ears, nose, tongue, and skin are all a part of the nervous system.

Divisions

The nervous system is divided into two main systems:

1. The **CENTRAL NERVOUS SYSTEM (CNS)** includes your brain and spinal cord. They are called the central system because the brain is the control center for your body, and the spinal cord relays messages between your brain and your body.

2. The **PERIPHERAL NERVOUS SYSTEM (PNS)** includes all of the nerves outside the central nervous system. The word "peripheral" means away from the center, and the peripheral nervous system is outside the brain and spinal cord. The peripheral nervous system has two types of neurons: **SENSORY NEURONS** and **MOTOR NEURONS**. Sensory neurons relay information from your senses (like the temperature outside or the feeling of pain) to the brain. Motor neurons relay information from the brain to your muscles, telling your body to move—in other words, to motor. Your peripheral nervous system in turn is divided into:

- The **SOMATIC NERVOUS SYSTEM**, which controls voluntary (controllable) movements such as running, walking, and chewing.

- The **AUTONOMIC NERVOUS SYSTEM**, which controls involuntary movement, or movements your body does automatically, such as breathing and digesting food. Your autonomic nervous system also controls reflexes.

The Nervous System

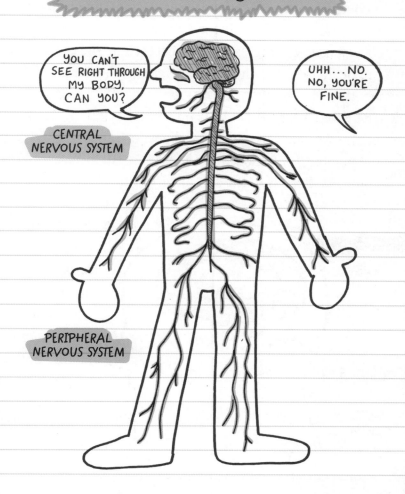

YOU CAN'T SEE RIGHT THROUGH MY BODY, CAN YOU?

UHH...NO. NO, YOU'RE FINE.

CENTRAL NERVOUS SYSTEM

PERIPHERAL NERVOUS SYSTEM

The Brain

The brain is the control center of your nervous system. The three major parts of the brain are the CEREBRUM, the BRAIN STEM, and the CEREBELLUM.

1. The **CEREBRUM** controls your thoughts and actions. It controls your perceptions of taste, sight, touch, sound, and smell. Basically, any time you use your brain consciously, you are using your cerebrum. The cerebrum can be divided into the left and right hemisphere.

2. The **BRAIN STEM** controls involuntary vital processes, such as breathing, digestion, and the pumping of your heart. The brain stem connects directly to the spinal cord.

3. The **CEREBELLUM** is at the bottom back of your brain, and it helps with coordination, balance, and motor control.

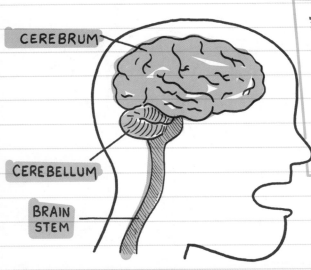

CEREBRUM

CEREBELLUM

BRAIN STEM

WITHOUT IT, YOU'D BE A KLUTZ!

Right-brained people use the right hemisphere of the cerebrum more, so they are often said to be more artistic, creative, and imaginative. Left-brained people use their left hemisphere more, so they are often said to be more logical, mathematical, and language-oriented. The left and right hemispheres are joined through a thick band of fibers called the **CORPUS CALLOSUM**.

Nerves

Nerves are the basic functioning unit of the nervous system. A nerve cell is called a NEURON, and it transmits messages called impulses. There are two main types of neurons: SENSORY NEURONS receive information such as the sensation of touch or a smell, and they transmit the information to the brain or spinal cord; INTERNEURONS relay the brain's response to motor neurons, which relay orders to your glands and muscles to take action.

A neuron is made of a cell body, an axon, and dendrites:

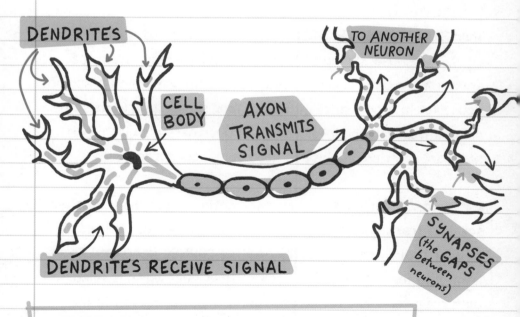

DENDRITES

TO ANOTHER NEURON

CELL BODY

AXON TRANSMITS SIGNAL

SYNAPSES (the GAPS between neurons)

DENDRITES RECEIVE SIGNAL

DENDRITES, which look sort of like tiny branches, receive an impulse, or a signal, from another neuron, and they transmit the impulse to the cell body.

The **AXON**, which looks like a much longer branch, transmits the signal from the cell body down toward the next neuron, passing the message along. The space between neurons is called a **SYNAPSE**.

When the message from the axon reaches the synapse, the axon releases a **NEUROTRANSMITTER**, or a chemical that transmits the signal to the next neuron. Dendrites receive the signal and send an impulse to the cell body, and the process begins over again.

ALL OF THIS HAPPENS IN AN INSTANT OF TIME.

Sensory Organs

Your SENSORY RECEPTORS and ORGANS, such as your eyes, ears, nose, skin, and tongue, perceive stimuli from the environment. Stimuli can be anything from something pinching your skin to a bad smell in the air. Your sensory receptors and organs transmit the information to your nerves, which then send an electrical impulse to your spinal cord and brain.

For instance, our eyes gather information about the things you see and transmit it to a nerve that sends the signal onward to your brain. The eye's LENS and the CORNEA bend and focus light onto the retina at the back of your eye, which is filled with receptors. The retina transmits the information to the OPTIC NERVE, and the optic nerve carries it to the brain, which interprets the information as images.

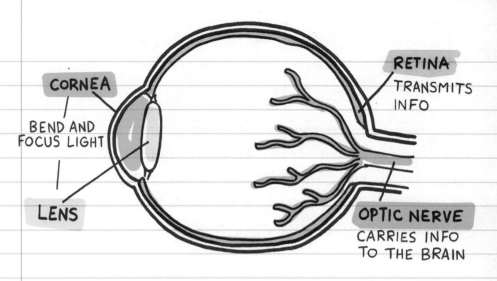

CORNEA

BEND AND FOCUS LIGHT

LENS

RETINA TRANSMITS INFO

OPTIC NERVE CARRIES INFO TO THE BRAIN

Your ear is built to perceive sound waves. It has three main parts: the OUTER EAR, MIDDLE EAR, and INNER EAR. The outer ear includes both the part of the ear you can see and the ear canal. It is built like a funnel to capture sound.

Sound waves go down your ear canal to the middle ear and reach the eardrum. The "drumbeats" caused by the vibrations shake fluid and tiny hairs in the inner ear. They sense the movement and transmit an impulse, which is taken by nerves to your brain.

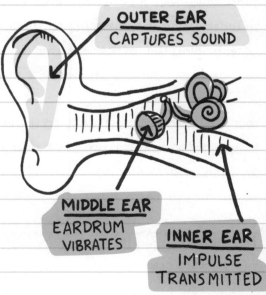

OUTER EAR CAPTURES SOUND

MIDDLE EAR EARDRUM VIBRATES

INNER EAR IMPULSE TRANSMITTED

> The fluid and hairs in your inner ear also help with your sense of balance. When you move around, the fluid moves as well, and the hairs transmit the information about the position of your head to the brain.

Your nose is lined with sensory cells called OLFACTORY CELLS that perceive smells. The inside of your nose is moistened by mucus. Smell molecules carried in the air dissolve onto the mucus, stimulating the olfactory cells.

Your tongue has tiny little sensors on it called TASTE BUDS. Taste buds perceive flavors and transmit the information to your brain. Different areas of your tongue have taste buds that are more sensitive to different taste sensations, like sweet, salty, sour, or bitter. Taste and smell are very connected. Your mouth and nasal cavity connect to each other, so when you eat something, smell molecules move up into your nose, helping you perceive taste. That's why when you have a cold and your nose is stuffed, it's much harder to taste things.

Your SKIN has sensory cells on it that can perceive temperature, texture, pressure, and pain. Again, these cells give this information to nerve cells, which send an electrical signal to your central nervous system.

ENDOCRINE SYSTEM

The ENDOCRINE SYSTEM is the body's other messaging system, but instead of sending electrical signals through a highway system of nerves, it sends chemical messages to your body through your bloodstream. The chemical messengers your endocrine system uses are called HORMONES, which are produced in ENDOCRINE GLANDS. Endocrine glands release hormones directly into the bloodstream, which carries hormones to different parts of the body. Those hormones help your body perform all sorts of jobs, from knowing when to sleep, to controlling the amount of sugar in your blood, to reproducing.

Some examples of endocrine glands are:

PITUITARY GLAND

PITUITARY GLAND

- Attached to the brain, about the size of a pea
- Controls a range of functions such as blood pressure, metabolism, and pain relief
- Produces growth hormone
- Controls other glands such as ovaries or testes

THYROID GLAND

- Below the larynx, part of your throat where your vocal cords are located
- Regulates metabolism and the amount of calcium absorbed by bones, among other things

THYROID GLAND

PANCREAS
- Produces **INSULIN**, a hormone that controls blood sugar levels

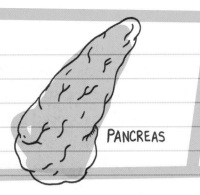

PANCREAS

OVARIES (females)
- Produce **ESTROGEN**, a female sex hormone that controls puberty and more, and **PROGESTERONE**, a female sex hormone that plays a large role in controlling a woman's ability to bear children and more

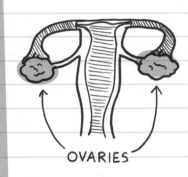

OVARIES

TESTES (males)
- Produce **TESTOSTERONE**, a male sex hormone that controls puberty, a man's ability to produce sperm, and more

TESTES

CHECK YOUR KNOWLEDGE

1. The nerves in your arm are part of the _____ nervous system.

2. What does the brain stem do?

3. List your five sensory receptors and organs.

4. Your eye uses the ____ and the _____ to bend and focus light.

5. The message a neuron sends is called an _____, and the space between two neurons is called a _____.

6. Which gland controls the other glands?

7. What do hormones do?

ANSWERS

CHECK YOUR ANSWERS

1. Peripheral

2. It is the part of your brain that controls involuntary functions.

3. Eyes, ears, nose, tongue, and skin

4. Lens, cornea

5. Impulse, synapse

6. The pituitary gland

7. Hormones are the chemical messengers of your endocrine system, which help your body perform lots of jobs, like sleeping, reproducing, and controlling the amount of sugar in your blood.

Chapter 38

DIGESTIVE AND EXCRETORY SYSTEMS

DIGESTIVE SYSTEM

The digestive system takes in food, breaks it down, and absorbs nutrients into your body. Nutrients are substances that your body uses for energy, growth, reproduction, and repair. Nutrients include vitamins, minerals, proteins, fats, and carbohydrates.

There are two types of digestion:

1. **MECHANICAL DIGESTION**: when your body physically breaks down food, such as when you chew food in your mouth. Your stomach also breaks down food mechanically when it squeezes and churns.

2. CHEMICAL DIGESTION: when your body breaks down foods using chemical reactions. Your body produces enzymes throughout your digestive tract to speed up these chemical reactions. Enzymes are special proteins that provoke chemical reactions.

Digestive Tract

The digestive tract includes:

MOUTH: Digestion begins in your mouth, where chewing (mechanical digestion) stimulates **SALIVARY GLANDS** to release saliva (chemical digestion), which breaks down food into a soft ball. The ball gets pushed down to your . . .

SALIVA ALONE CAN BREAK DOWN CARBOHYDRATES INTO SIMPLE SUGARS.

ESOPHAGUS: That's where it gets pushed down by a squeezing action, or muscle contraction, called **PERISTALSIS** into the . . .

PERISTALSIS ALSO OCCURS IN THE REST OF THE DIGESTIVE TRACT TO MOVE FOOD ALONG.

STOMACH: The stomach is a giant muscle, and it squeezes and churns the food, helping to break it down (mechanical digestion). The stomach also releases enzymes and chemicals that break the food down (chemical digestion). The food mixes with the digestive juices to produce **CHYME** (a pulpy mix of food and acid), which moves to the . . .

The Digestive Tract

SALIVARY GLANDS — release saliva, breaking down carbohydrates

MOUTH

ESOPHAGUS

STOMACH — releases digestive enzymes and chemicals to break down proteins

DUODENUM — where most digestion happens

CHYME

SMALL INTESTINE — where most nutrients are absorbed into the bloodstream

LARGE INTESTINE — where most water is absorbed into the body

RECTUM & ANUS — expel waste

SMALL INTESTINE: The first part of the small intestine is called the **DUODENUM**, and it contains digestive juices released from the pancreas and liver, called **BILE**. While bile breaks up fats, the pancreas releases digestive juices that chemically break down carbohydrates, fats, and proteins. The duodenum is where most of the digestion in your body takes place. Nutrients are also absorbed into the bloodstream in the small intestine. Next stop for chyme is the . . .

LARGE INTESTINE: This is where most of the water is absorbed into your body. As the water in the chyme gets absorbed, undigested parts harden into waste. The end of the large intestine has a part called the **RECTUM**, which leads to the **ANUS**—the last part of the digestive tract. Together, they control when we go to the bathroom to expel fecal material (waste).

Nutrition

Our body needs the right balance of foods in order to stay healthy.

PROTEINS: Our bodies use proteins to rebuild and grow cells. They are made of amino acids that your body can rebuild into new proteins. Proteins are found in meat, eggs, beans, peas, nuts, and dairy products.

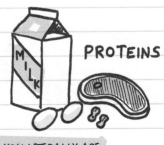

PROTEINS

YOU LITERALLY ARE WHAT YOU EAT!

CARBOHYDRATES: Our bodies burn carbohydrates for quick energy. They can be sugars, starches, or fibers. Simple sugars can provide fast

CARBOHYDRATES

energy but run out quickly, while more complex carbohydrates (starches and fibers) provide longer-lasting energy because your body has to break them apart before it can use them. Carbohydrates are found in bread, pasta, potatoes, sugar, fruit, and vegetables.

FATS: Fats provide the body with energy, insulation, and cushioning.

FATS

They also help your body absorb certain vitamins. Fats are found in fish, meat, nuts, oil, and eggs.

VITAMINS: Vitamins are nutrients your body needs for growth and cell function. Your body needs only small

VITAMINS

quantities of these nutrients. Different vitamins are found in every type of food, but some foods have more than others.

MINERALS: Minerals are needed to maintain proper body function as well. Calcium, phosphorous, potassium, sodium, iron, and iodine are all examples of minerals your body needs. Minerals are found in spinach, dairy, bananas, nuts, eggs, meat, and seafood.

MINERALS

401

EXCRETORY SYSTEM

Your EXCRETORY SYSTEM removes waste from your body in order to help it maintain homeostasis. Your body has a number of different waste systems. In your digestive system, food that is left undigested is excreted from the end of your large intestine. When you exhale, you also excrete carbon dioxide, a waste product of respiration. Your skin excretes extra salt, water, and other substances through your sweat.

Urinary System

The URINARY SYSTEM filters your blood and gets rid of waste and excess water, salt, and minerals. The kidneys are the main organs of the urinary system. Your blood constantly gets filtered by millions of tiny filtration units in the kidney called NEPHRONS.

Any liquid filtered out by the kidneys is collected and funneled into the URETER, which is a tube that leads from the kidney to the BLADDER, where URINE is stored. The bladder stretches to hold urine until it leaves the body through a tube called the URETHRA.

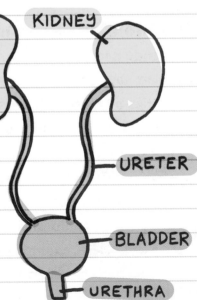

KIDNEY

URETER

BLADDER

URETHRA

CHECK YOUR KNOWLEDGE

1. What is chyme?

2. What does your body burn for quick energy?

3. Most nutrients are absorbed in the _ _ _ _ _ intestine.

4. What connects the kidney and the bladder?

5. What does our body use to rebuild and grow cells?

6. What is peristalsis?

7. What are nephrons?

8. Water is absorbed in your _ _ _ _ _ intestine.

9. Give an example of mechanical digestion and an example of chemical digestion.

10. Where is urine stored?

ANSWERS ➤ 403

1. Chyme is food combined with digestive juices.

2. Carbohydrates

3. Small

4. Ureter

5. Proteins

6. Peristalsis is a muscle contraction that sends food down your esophagus.

7. Nephrons are filtration units in your kidneys.

8. Large

9. When you chew food with your teeth, you mechanically digest it. Saliva is the first step in chemical digestion of your food.

10. In the bladder

#9 has more than one correct answer.

Chapter 39

RESPIRATORY AND CIRCULATORY SYSTEMS

RESPIRATORY SYSTEM

Cellular respiration is a series of reactions that breaks down glucose, a simple sugar, releasing chemical energy for your body to use. In order to use this sugar or "burn these calories," your body needs oxygen (like a fire needs oxygen for combustion). Cellular respiration uses oxygen and releases carbon dioxide and water as waste products. Blood is the delivery system that carries oxygen to all your cells from the lungs and returns to the lungs with carbon dioxide waste.

Respiratory Tract

You breathe air in through your mouth and nose.

From there, the air moves into your **PHARYNX**, which is a passageway in your throat that leads to both your stomach and lungs. The **EPIGLOTTIS** is a flap (the little punching bag in the back of your throat) that prevents food from going into your airway, but when you breathe, the epiglottis remains open.

From there, air moves into the **LARYNX**, a part of the air passage where your vocal cords are located.

The air then moves into the **TRACHEA**, which is lined with cartilage to keep it firm and ensure it doesn't collapse. The trachea also has tiny hairlike structures and mucus to trap bacteria, dust, or any particles that shouldn't be going into your lungs.

THESE LITTLE HAIRS (CALLED **CILIA**) PASS ALL THAT GUNK UPWARD FOR YOU TO SPIT OUT, BLOW OUT YOUR NOSE, OR SWALLOW. (BETTER TO DIGEST IT THAN HAVE IT CLOGGING UP YOUR LUNGS! STILL...GROSS!)

Next, the air moves into tubes leading to your lungs called **BRONCHI**. The word "bronchi" looks kind of like "branch," and that is exactly what happens to the bronchi: They branch into smaller tubes called **BRONCHIOLES**.

Bronchioles connect directly to **ALVEOLI**, millions of tiny air sacs. Oxygen from the air in the alveoli moves into the blood in the capillaries to be distributed throughout your body so respiration can happen in all of your cells. At the same time, carbon dioxide waste in the blood moves into air in the alveoli to be exhaled.

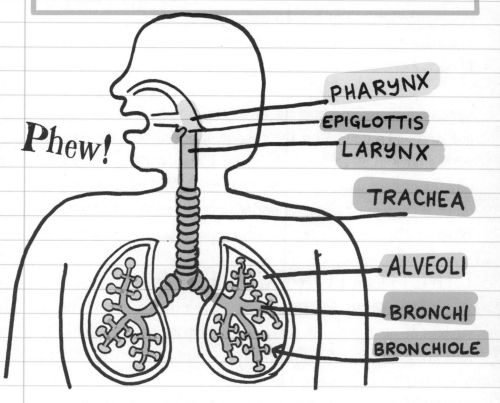

Phew!

PHARYNX
EPIGLOTTIS
LARYNX
TRACHEA
ALVEOLI
BRONCHI
BRONCHIOLE

SMOKING kills the cilia in your trachea, which is why smokers have a gross-sounding cough. They have to physically hack all that gunk out of their pipes. Super gross!

Breathing

BREATHING is the mechanical process of taking in air. You breathe automatically—you don't have to think about breathing. If you need more oxygen, you breathe faster (which is why you get out of breath when you exercise—your body needs more oxygen to burn more calories for energy).

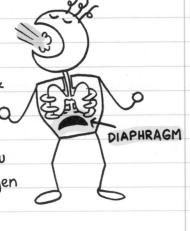

DIAPHRAGM

When you squeeze a sponge, all of the air and water rushes out, and when you let go, the sponge expands and the air rushes back in. Breathing works the same way. Air gets pulled into your chest when your chest expands, and pushed out when it contracts. A muscle under your rib cage called the DIAPHRAGM controls this expanding and contracting motion.

CIRCULATORY SYSTEM

Your CIRCULATORY SYSTEM is sort of like the transportation system of your body. It carries and distributes things like nutrients, sugars, and oxygen to different parts of your body and collects waste for removal.

Blood

If your circulatory system is the transportation system of the body, blood is the vehicle. Blood is the liquid that actually transports oxygen, nutrients, waste, and other substances.

Waste from your body is picked up and transported by blood to your kidneys. Carbon dioxide waste is carried in your blood to your lungs, where it is exhaled. Your blood also has cells from your immune system that fight diseases and heal injuries.

BLOOD CONTAINS:

PLASMA: the liquid in your blood that carries most of the substances that need to be transported, like sugar (glucose), nutrients, minerals, vitamins, carbon dioxide, and waste

RED BLOOD CELLS: cells that carry oxygen to your body's cells

WHITE BLOOD CELLS: cells from your immune system that fight disease

PLATELETS: cell fragments that clot blood (stop the bleeding when you get a cut)

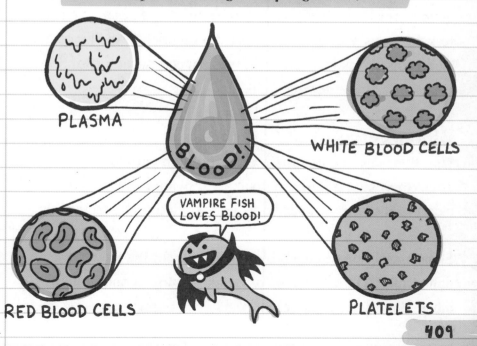

PLASMA

WHITE BLOOD CELLS

BLOOD!

VAMPIRE FISH LOVES BLOOD!

RED BLOOD CELLS

PLATELETS

Heart

Your heart is the engine of the circulatory system. It pumps blood to different parts of your body. Your heart is made of four chambers: a LEFT and RIGHT ATRIUM, and a LEFT and RIGHT VENTRICLE.

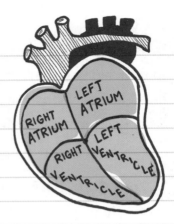

Oxygen-rich blood flows from your lungs to the left side of your heart, first through the left atrium and then to the left ventricle. From there it is pumped to the rest of your body through the aorta, a large powerful artery. The OXYGENATED blood moves through your body, releasing oxygen and collecting carbon dioxide. The DEOXYGENATED blood returns to your heart through the right atrium and gets pumped back to your lungs from your right ventricle. Once in the lungs, the blood collects oxygen and releases carbon dioxide, starting the process over again.

Blood Vessels

Blood vessels are like the roads and highways of the circulation system. When your body pumps oxygenated blood to the rest of your body, it is carried by blood vessels.

Blood vessels that carry blood away from the heart are called ARTERIES. Because arteries need to regulate how much blood flows to each part of your body, they have thick

Blood's Journey Through the Body

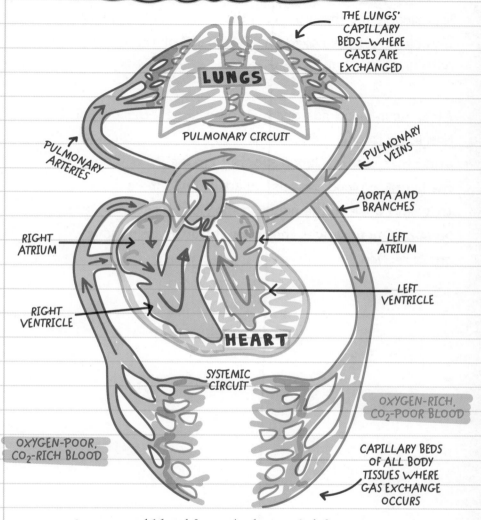

THE LUNGS' CAPILLARY BEDS—WHERE GASES ARE EXCHANGED

LUNGS

PULMONARY CIRCUIT

PULMONARY ARTERIES

PULMONARY VEINS

AORTA AND BRANCHES

RIGHT ATRIUM

LEFT ATRIUM

LEFT VENTRICLE

RIGHT VENTRICLE

HEART

SYSTEMIC CIRCUIT

OXYGEN-RICH, CO_2-POOR BLOOD

OXYGEN-POOR, CO_2-RICH BLOOD

CAPILLARY BEDS OF ALL BODY TISSUES WHERE GAS EXCHANGE OCCURS

Oxygenated blood from the lungs → left atrium
→ left ventricle → aorta to other arteries → capillaries
(exchange of oxygenated blood for deoxygenated blood)
→ right atrium → right ventricle → lungs for oxygenation
and then the cycle begins again

muscular walls that can expand and contract to let more or less blood flow through. From the arteries, blood moves into tiny blood vessels called CAPILLARIES that deliver blood directly to the cells in your body.

After your blood has dropped off oxygen, glucose, and nutrients to your cells and picked up carbon dioxide and other wastes, blood starts to make its trip back to the heart in blood vessels called VEINS. To keep blood traveling back to the heart in the right direction, veins have one-way valves that allow blood to only move in one direction.

CHECK YOUR KNOWLEDGE

1. What are alveoli?

2. What is the path air takes through the respiratory tract?

3. What is the epiglottis?

4. What kind of gas exchange takes place in the lungs?

5. What is the muscle that controls inhalation and exhalation?

6. Describe the vessels that blood travels through from the time it leaves your heart to the time it returns.

7. Which cells carry oxygen?

8. After blood gets oxygenated in the lungs, what part of the heart does it go to first?

ANSWERS ▶ 413

CHECK YOUR ANSWERS

1. Alveoli are tiny air sacs. Your lungs are made of millions of alveoli, where gas exchange takes place.

2. When you breathe in, air moves through your mouth and nasal cavity down your throat to your pharynx, then your larynx. From the larynx, it travels to your bronchi, which branch into your bronchioles. Bronchioles lead directly to the alveoli of your lungs. Air then goes back out the same pathway.

3. The epiglottis is a flap that closes to prevent food from going into your airway. When you breathe, the epiglottis remains open.

4. Your blood picks up oxygen and expels carbon dioxide.

5. The diaphragm

6. Blood leaving your heart travels through arteries to capillaries. Nutrient and gas exchange with surrounding cells takes place in capillaries. After traveling through capillaries, blood returns to the heart through veins.

7. Red blood cells

8. Left atrium

Chapter

IMMUNE AND LYMPHATIC SYSTEMS

The IMMUNE SYSTEM protects and fights against infection and disease. Your immune system is like your own personal army, battling against harmful invaders.

> **PATHOGEN**
> a bacterium, virus, or other particle/organism (such as fungi or protists) that can cause disease

NONSPECIFIC IMMUNITY

Just like an army, your immune system has different tactics for protecting your body. Physical barriers are the first line of defense: ← *SORT OF LIKE THE WALLS OF A CASTLE*

> Your skin provides a physical barrier that prevents **PATHOGENS** from entering your body.

The mucus and cilia in your respiratory system trap and remove pathogens as they enter your airways.

Saliva and the acid in your stomach kill many types of bacteria.

THIS IS LIKE MEDIEVAL DEFENDERS DUMPING BOILING OIL ON THE INVADERS FROM ABOVE!

Despite these defenses, pathogens can sometimes find a way into the castle of your body through cuts or other means. No sweat—your body has a backup system lined up to fight them.

White Blood Cells

Pathogens that make it into your body are confronted by white blood cells, which are fierce warriors against invaders. White blood cells digest and destroy bacteria and other pathogens that make it into your body. There are a number of different types of white blood cells, and each has a different task. MACROPHAGES, for instance, are white blood cells that use brute force to engulf and destroy any pathogens they encounter.

PASSIVE and ACTIVE IMMUNITY

Your body can get immunity either passively or actively. When your body fights off an infection or disease, it produces ANTIBODIES in response to the pathogen. Your body keeps these antibodies in store to fight the pathogen if it returns, providing immunity. ACTIVE IMMUNITY is when your body produces the antibodies that give you immunity.

You can also get immunity from antibodies produced by another body. Immunity gained by receiving antibodies is called PASSIVE IMMUNITY because the immunity was passively received—your body didn't work for it. A baby, for example, receives passive immunity from his or her mother during pregnancy, and later from the mother's breast milk.

Vaccinations

During a vaccination, a small amount of an inactivated pathogen is injected into your arm. Your body mounts an immune response to the pathogen, producing antibodies. These antibodies remain in your blood, prepared to fight off the real pathogen if they encounter it again.

Inflammation

After you scrape your knee or get a cut, sometimes the area can get red, puffy, warm, and tender. This redness and swelling is called INFLAMMATION. When cells get damaged, either from infection or through injury, they release a chemical that increases blood flow to the area, causing inflammation. With increased blood flow, more white blood cells can get to the area to start fighting off pathogens.

LYMPHATIC SYSTEM

The LYMPHATIC SYSTEM is sort of like a drainpipe—it collects fluid (called LYMPH) from your body and filters the fluid in small lumps of tissue scattered throughout your body called LYMPH NODES.

Lymph nodes also produce a type of white blood cell called a LYMPHOCYTE. As blood passes through the lymph nodes, lymphocytes attack and remove pathogens from your body. Your neck has many lymph nodes, so when you are sick, they often swell up with all of these little lymphocyte warriors.

ATTACK!

DISEASES

Human disease can be caused by a number of things. Some examples of pathogens and the diseases they cause are:

> Certain species of bacteria cause strep throat,
> ear infections, tuberculosis, or pneumonia.

> Viruses cause the flu, colds, polio,
> measles, warts, or AIDS.

> Certain species of protists cause malaria,
> dysentery, or giardiasis.

> Certain species of fungus cause athlete's foot,
> yeast infections, or other diseases.

Although bacteria can be killed and removed from your body with antibiotic drugs, once you have been infected with a virus it often remains with you for life!

Infectious Disease

When you get a cold from a friend, a virus traveled from your friend to you. An infectious disease is a disease that can travel from one infected organism to another. Some diseases can be spread through air, water, food, or physical contact between two organisms. Other diseases, like HIV, are spread through body fluids, like blood. Bacteria and viruses can also survive on surfaces, like doorknobs and handrails. Washing your hands is the easiest and most effective way to keep yourself free from disease.

Noninfectious Diseases

Noninfectious diseases are diseases that aren't caused by pathogens and can't be spread from person to person. Diabetes, genetic diseases, and cancer are all examples of noninfectious diseases. CANCER is a noninfectious disease where cells have a mutation in their DNA that causes the cell to reproduce uncontrollably, making copies of itself that are also cancerous. These cells grow and eventually form tumors and growths that can interfere with normal body processes. To fight cancer, doctors try to remove or kill the cancerous cells (usually with surgery, chemicals, or radiation).

CHECK YOUR KNOWLEDGE

1. Explain why inflammation occurs.

2. When you get sick, your _____ _____ swell up with lymphocytes.

3. What is an infectious disease?

4. When you get a _____, a small amount of a pathogen is injected into your arm to give you immunity.

5. Explain the difference between passive and active immunity.

6. What does your immune system do?

7. List four pathogens.

8. Give an example of a noninfectious disease.

ANSWERS

CHECK YOUR ANSWERS

1. When your cells get injured, they increase the blood flow to the area, so more blood cells can fight off the pathogens.

2. Lymph nodes

3. An infectious disease is a disease that can be passed from one organism to another.

4. Vaccination

5. When you get antibodies from another organism, it is called passive immunity. When your body makes the antibodies itself, it is called active immunity.

6. It protects and fights against infection and disease.

7. Viruses, bacteria, protists, and fungi

8. Diabetes

#8 has more than one correct answer.

Chapter 41

HUMAN REPRODUCTION AND DEVELOPMENT

REPRODUCTIVE SYSTEM

When humans reproduce, the male and female sex cells unite to form a zygote (a cell that results from fertilization and has a complete set of chromosomes) that eventually develops into a baby.

Male and female bodies have different reproductive systems, each with specific adaptations to facilitate the combining of genetic material. ← ROMANTIC, EH?

Male Reproductive System

The MALE REPRODUCTIVE SYSTEM is composed of a number of organs, some internal, and some external. The male reproductive system includes:

PENIS: an external organ that contains a tube called the URETHRA. **SEMEN** and urine exit the body through the urethra.

SEMEN
male reproductive fluid

SCROTUM: an external saclike organ that contains the testes

TESTES: produce sperm and testosterone, a male sex hormone

SPERM is the male sex cell, and is made of a head and a tail—the head has genetic information (DNA), and the tail gives the sperm mobility. When sperm are ready to leave the body, they travel from the testes through ducts up behind the bladder, where they are mixed with SEMINAL FLUID, a fluid that helps sperm move and provides them with energy. The combination of seminal fluid and sperm is called semen. Semen exits the body through the urethra, a tube in the penis.

HEY! NO SNICKERING!

THIS IS SCIENCE!

PENIS

URETHRA

TESTES

SCROTUM

MALE

Female Reproductive System

The FEMALE REPRODUCTIVE SYSTEM includes the ovaries, uterus, and vagina, among other things.

OVARIES: tiny organs that look like almonds connected to the uterus. They produce and release eggs, and they also produce sex hormones, such as estrogen and progesterone.

FALLOPIAN TUBES: tubes that connect the ovaries to the uterus. Eggs leaving the ovaries travel to the uterus through the fallopian tubes.

EGGS and **OVULATION:** The female sex cells (eggs) contain genetic information (DNA). Females are born with all of their eggs—about 1 to 2 million eggs.

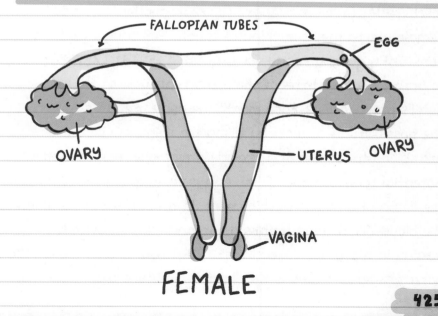

FALLOPIAN TUBES

EGG

OVARY

UTERUS

OVARY

VAGINA

FEMALE

About once a month, a female **OVULATES**, which is when a mature egg is released from either the right or left ovary. The egg travels down the fallopian tubes, with the help of short hairlike cilia, where it has the chance to be fertilized by a sperm.

UTERUS: a hollow organ where a fertilized egg can develop. The uterus is connected to the fallopian tubes and also to the vagina.

VAGINA: a canal that connects the uterus to the outside of the body, sort of like the doorway to the female reproductive system. Sperm enter through the vagina, and a baby exits the uterus through the vagina as well.

THE MENSTRUAL CYCLE: About once a
month, the female body undergoes changes called the MENSTRUAL CYCLE to prepare for reproduction. The adult female uterus thinks it's kind of a hotel for babies, and it's constantly getting ready for a guest, a FERTILIZED EGG, to arrive. You can think of the menstrual cycle as the hotel's preparations. Each month the body prepares for the possibility of a guest by filling the lining of the uterus with blood to cushion and provide a nice environment for a potential fertilized egg. If an egg is fertilized, it attaches to the lining and begins development. If an egg is not fertilized, the blood-filled lining breaks down and exits through the vagina in a process called MENSTRUATION. It's as though the hotel, or uterus, changes the sheets for future zygote guests.

HUMAN DEVELOPMENT and LIFE

Fertilization

Human development begins at FERTILIZATION. Fertilization is when the male and female sex cells come together, forming a cell that has a complete set of chromosomes, called a zygote. Male and female sex cells (sperm and egg) have only 23 chromosomes each, so when they combine the zygote has a full set of 46 chromosomes; half from mom, half from dad.

The process of fertilization starts when sperm are deposited in the vagina. The sperm swim up the vagina until they reach the egg, usually in the fallopian tubes. Although there can be up to 300 million sperm deposited in the vagina racing toward the egg, only one sperm can fertilize an egg.

TWINS

FRATERNAL TWINS are formed when two eggs are released at the same time by the ovaries, and both are fertilized. Because fraternal twins

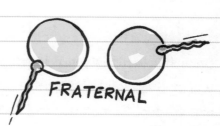

FRATERNAL

develop from different eggs and sperms, they are genetically no more similar than siblings.

IDENTICAL TWINS develop from a single egg and sperm. During development, the zygote splits in two, then each of these cells develops into separate embryos. The result is two identical babies who share all the same genetic material.

IDENTICAL

Development

The period of time between the formation of the zygote and birth is called PREGNANCY. It takes nine months for the zygote to fully develop, so pregnancy usually lasts about nine months. During that time, the zygote develops inside the mother to become first an **EMBRYO**, and then a **FETUS** (after two months). The fetus continues to grow and develop until it is a fully formed baby.

> **EMBRYO**
> a zygote attached to the uterus

> **FETUS**
> an embryo more than eight weeks old

Birth

Once the fetus is fully developed, it is ready to enter the world. Generally, the mother gives birth to the child through her vagina. Sometimes the child must be removed through a surgery called a CESAREAN SECTION. When the baby is born, the umbilical cord is cut, and the baby begins to breathe on his or her own.

Human Development

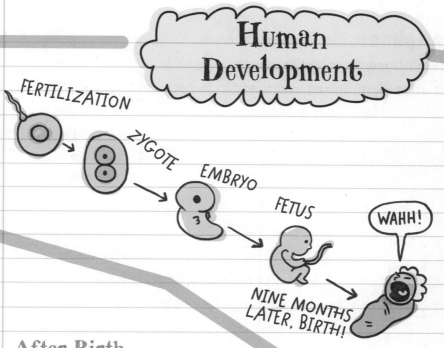

FERTILIZATION

ZYGOTE

EMBRYO

FETUS

WAHH!

NINE MONTHS LATER, BIRTH!

After Birth

As the baby develops, he or she goes through the following stages:

NEONATAL PERIOD: The first four weeks after being born, a baby's body adapts to life outside the uterus.

NEONATAL

INFANCY

INFANCY: A baby learns how to crawl, stand, and finally walk. Brain development during this time is incredibly rapid as the infant explores his or her new world.

CHILDHOOD: Children learn how to coordinate their bodies, speak, get dressed, draw, run, write, and read. Childhood ends at puberty, which usually starts happening when a child is around twelve.

CHILDHOOD

ADOLESCENCE

ADOLESCENCE is when the body goes through puberty. During puberty, boys get taller and stronger, their voices drop, and they grow facial and pubic hair. Girls also grow taller and stronger, and grow breasts, pubic hair, and develop hips. Brain development can be rapid during these adolescent years, too.

ADULTHOOD starts after adolescence and is the last stage of development. As an adult, your bones stop growing. As adults get older, their bones and muscles become weaker, and their skin begins to wrinkle. Keeping the body and brain active throughout helps slow the aging process and is important for health.

ADULTHOOD

CHECK YOUR KNOWLEDGE

1. What are ovaries?

2. What is ovulation?

3. After two months, an embryo is called a _____.

4. Sperm mixed with seminal fluid is called _____.

5. Where is the hereditary information stored in the male sex cell?

6. How do urine and semen exit the body?

7. How does the egg travel from the ovaries to the uterus?

8. A zygote develops into an _____ when it implants in the uterine wall.

9. Pregnant women give birth after about ____ months.

10. The scrotum contains the _____.

11. List some changes that boys and girls go through in puberty.

ANSWERS 431

CHECK YOUR ANSWERS

1. Ovaries are the female reproductive organ that releases sex hormones.

2. Ovulation is when the egg is released from the ovary.

3. Fetus

4. Semen

5. In the head of the sperm

6. Through the urethra

7. Through the fallopian tube

8. Embryo

9. Nine

10. Testes

11. Boys grow taller and stronger, their voices drop, and they grow facial and pubic hair. Girls also grow taller and stronger, and grow breasts, hips, and pubic hair. Brain development happens in boys and girls during this time as well.

#11 has more than one correct answer.

Unit 10

History of Life:
Heredity, Evolution,
and Fossils

Chapter 42

HEREDITY AND GENETICS

Genetics is the study of how genes interact and how traits are passed down from parent to offspring. A large part of the way you look and act is determined by genetics. The passing of traits from one generation to the next is called HEREDITY.

TRAITS and ALLELES

Genetic traits include essentially every characteristic about an organism. Some of the most observable traits in humans include hair, eye, and skin color, as well as height, but other traits are more behaviorial, such as sleep cycles, aggression, and other instincts.

ALLELE
one form
(or variation)
of a gene

A gene is a segment of a chromosome, encoded by DNA. Genes come in pairs called **ALLELES**, and each allele is a variation of that gene. If one of the genes, or alleles, is more powerful than the other, it can cover up the traits of the weaker allele. The stronger allele is known as the **DOMINANT ALLELE**. The allele that gets masked is called the **RECESSIVE ALLELE**. The recessive allele is expressed only when both alleles are the recessive form. Scientists use a letter to represent each gene of an allele. The capital letter represents the dominant allele, while the lowercase letter represents the recessive allele.

DOMINANT ALLELE
the allele that is always expressed

RECESSIVE ALLELE
the allele that can be masked by the dominant allele. Only expressed when both alleles are the recessive form.

For example, the letter "R" can represent a pea allele for being round or wrinkled.

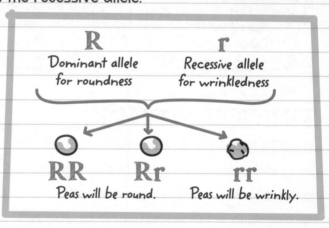

R
Dominant allele for roundness

r
Recessive allele for wrinkledness

RR   Rr
Peas will be round.

rr
Peas will be wrinkly.

When one allele is dominant and the other is recessive, the dominant allele gets expressed in the trait, while the recessive allele doesn't. So the actual alleles of an organism can't be predicted from looking at its traits alone. The genes an organism has are called its **GENOTYPE**, and the traits it expresses are called its **PHENOTYPE**. You can't observe an organism's genotype, but you can observe its phenotype.

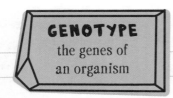

GENOTYPE
the genes of
an organism

PHENOTYPE
the visible traits or genes that
are expressed in an organism

When an organism has two of the same allele, like two dominant alleles or two recessive alleles, it is called **HOMOZYGOUS** for that trait. When the organism has two different alleles (one recessive and one dominant allele), it is called **HETEROZYGOUS**.

like the RR or rr peas

like the Rr peas

HOMOZYGOUS
an organism that
has two of the
same allele

HETEROZYGOUS
an organism that has different
alleles—one dominant and
one recessive

GREGOR MENDEL

GREGOR MENDEL, an Austrian scientist and monk, was one of the first people to extensively study genetics. Mendel gardened in a monastery, and he started noticing patterns in the way pea plants inherited certain traits, such as the color of seeds, flower color, and the shape and color of pods. He traced a trait through different generations to determine which traits were dominant and which traits were recessive. Listed on the next page are Mendel's main ideas.

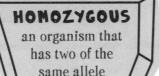

Each trait is controlled by two genes, called alleles.

An allele can be either dominant or recessive.

When chromosomes separate during reproduction, each sex cell gets one allele for a trait. So when the sex cells of parents combine, the offspring randomly gets one allele from each parent.

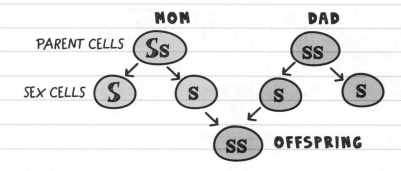

MOM   DAD

PARENT CELLS   Ss   SS

SEX CELLS   S   S   S   S

SS   OFFSPRING

PUNNETT SQUARES

By crossbreeding thousands of plants, Mendel was soon able to predict the probability, or the likelihood, that a particular plant would inherit certain qualities.

A PUNNETT SQUARE is a tool to figure out the probability that an offspring will express a certain trait. For instance, a tall plant that is heterozygous for tallness could be represented as Tt, a tall plant that is homozygous could be represented as TT, and a short plant that is homozygous could be represented as tt.

In a Punnett square, the alleles of each parent are written across the top and next to one side of a ← square. Each of the boxes represents the possible alleles of an offspring. Because one of each parent's alleles is given to the offspring, each interior box gets one allele from each parent, like so:

In this case, the parents happen to be both heterozygous for tallness. So there are three possible ways to produce a tall offspring (TT, Tt, and Tt), and one combination could express the recessive phenotype for the short trait (tt).

Because each box represents an offspring, the probability of parents Tt and Tt having an offspring with the genotype TT is $\frac{1}{4}$ or 25 percent, Tt is $\frac{1}{2}$ or 50 percent, and tt is $\frac{1}{4}$ or 25 percent. In terms of phenotype, or expressed trait, $\frac{3}{4}$ or 75 percent would be tall, and $\frac{1}{4}$ or 25 percent would be short.

These only represent the probability, or likelihood, of each outcome. These parent plants that produced four offspring might not have exactly three tall and one short offspring. They might have two and two. Or four and zero. But plants that had four hundred offspring would likely have around three hundred tall and one hundred short.

SEX DETERMINATION

Punnett squares can also be used to show the chances of having a male or female offspring. Of our 23 pairs of chromosomes, one pair is different from all of the rest, and it determines our sex, or whether we are male or female. The chromosomes that determine sex are called the X chromosome and the Y chromosome. A female has two Xs (XX) and a male has one X and one Y (XY).

Punnett Square Showing Sex Determination

MALE

	X	Y
X	XX	XY
X	XX	XY

FEMALE

Because half of the offspring are XX and half are XY, the chances of having a male offspring or a female offspring are each 50 percent. Because the female will always contribute an X, the male's contribution determines the sex of the child.

Complex Inheritance

Although Mendel made many advances in genetics, often inheritance is more complex than the Mendelian model. Sometimes, for example, a number of genes work together to produce a single result such as skin color. There are multiple genes that contribute to skin, eye, and hair color. Our traits are complicated!

Also, for some traits, one allele is not completely dominant and does not mask the recessive allele. Instead of complete dominance, parts of both traits are expressed in an offspring, a form of inheritance that is called INCOMPLETE DOMINANCE. Sometimes, neither allele is dominant over the other, which we call a CO-DOMINANT TRAIT. In both of these cases, being heterozygous results in some sort of blending.

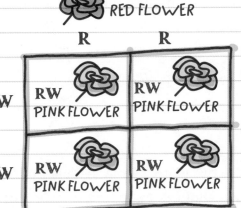

RR
RED FLOWER

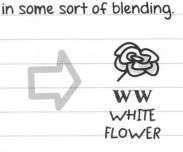

WW
WHITE FLOWER

Environmental Effects

Indeed, not all traits are always expressed. Some traits can be brought out by the combination of the environment and genetics. Genetics can put someone more at risk for developing a trait, but environmental factors may be necessary for that trait to be expressed. For example, some humans are genetically more predisposed to being overweight. Whether the person is actually overweight depends on outside factors such as eating and exercise habits. Also, most environmentally acquired traits cannot be passed on through heredity. If you get a tan or learn the drums, your child won't be born tan or with better rhythm.

GENETIC DISORDERS and DISEASES
Chromosomal Abnormalities

Sometimes an offspring inherits an incorrect number of chromosomes. One common chromosomal disorder is called DOWN SYNDROME, in which the offspring inherits three copies of human chromosome 21 instead of two. People with Down syndrome can usually lead normal lives, but they may have learning disabilities, physical abnormalities, and/or heart problems.

Recessive Genetic Diseases

While genes pass down traits such as hair and eye color, they can also pass down genetic diseases, such as cystic fibrosis, a lung disease. Most of the genetic diseases are recessive, which means they are masked by other alleles and they don't show any symptoms unless you happen to inherit both recessive alleles.

Sex-Linked Diseases

If a genetic disease is carried on the X or Y chromosome, the disease is called a SEX-LINKED DISORDER. Sex-linked disorders affect one sex more than the other. For example, color-blindness is a sex-linked recessive disorder carried on the X chromosome. Because males have only one X chromosome, if it carries the allele for color-blindness, the male will be color-blind. Because females have a second X chromosome, they are color-blind only if they receive the allele on both X chromosomes, which is highly unlikely.

GENETIC ENGINEERING

Scientists can use biological or chemical processes to alter the genes of a cell, a process called GENETIC ENGINEERING. Using genetic engineering, scientists can make crops that can grow in more conditions and are resistant to certain chemicals or pests. With genetic engineering, scientists have

HERBICIDE IS A CHEMICAL THAT KILLS WEEDS.

developed frost-resistant tomatoes and herbicide-resistant corn plants. Crops that have had their genes altered are called GENETICALLY MODIFIED ORGANISMS (GMOs).

CHECK YOUR KNOWLEDGE

1. Define "phenotype."

2. Define "genotype."

3. _____ _____ are used to show offspring's possible genotypes and the probability of each happening.

4. The main principles of Mendelian genetics are:
   A. Each trait is controlled by two genes called _____.
   B. Alleles can either be dominant or _____.
   _____ alleles mask _____ alleles.
   C. Each offspring gets one allele from each _____.

5. Explain incomplete dominance.

6. If a mother and a father are both carriers of cystic fibrosis, each having genotype Cc, the chances of them having an affected child with genotype cc is ____. ← (HINT: DRAW A PUNNETT SQUARE.)

7. When a gene is carried on the X or Y chromosome, it is called a ___-_____ trait.

8. Define "genetic engineering."

9. A male offspring receives one __ chromosome from the mother and one __ chromosome from the father.

10. An organism with alleles Aa is called _____, while one with aa or AA is called _____.

ANSWERS ▸ 443

CHECK YOUR ANSWERS

1. A phenotype is how alleles are expressed (what a trait "looks like").

2. A genotype is the actual alleles present (what genes are).

3. Punnett squares

4. **A.** Alleles
   B. Recessive, dominant, recessive
   C. Parent

5. Incomplete dominance is a type of inheritance where the offspring's trait is somewhere between the mother's and the father's traits, such as a pink flower forming from white or red parent flowers

6. $\frac{1}{4}$ or 25 percent

   PARENT 2

	C	c
C	CC	Cc
c	Cc	cc

   PARENT 1 { C, c

7. Sex-linked

8. Genetic engineering is the modification of genes through biological or chemical processes.

9. X, Y

10. Heterozygous, homozygous

Chapter 43

EVOLUTION

THEORY of EVOLUTION

Many of the species we know on Earth today existed in a very different form millions of years ago. The change and development of a species over the course of many generations is called EVOLUTION.

LAMARCK'S THEORY of ACQUIRED CHARACTERISTICS

JEAN-BAPTISTE LAMARCK formed one of the first theories of evolution. Lamarck proposed that traits developed over the course of an organism's lifetime were passed down to the next generation. It's true that traits are passed down from generation to generation—but ALL of them? Not according to Mendel's experiments.

CHARLES DARWIN and NATURAL SELECTION

A scientist named CHARLES DARWIN developed the most important theory of evolution, a theory based on NATURAL SELECTION. Much of today's understanding of evolution is based on Darwin's initial findings and ideas.

GRRR!

The theory of natural selection describes how species change over time to adapt to their environment. All organisms compete for survival. Space and food are limited, so organisms with traits most suited to an environment will beat out other organisms for survival, a concept called SURVIVAL OF THE FITTEST. The trait that gives an organism a survival advantage is passed on to its offspring when it reproduces. So it should really be thought of as survival and reproduction of the fittest.

EXTINCT? YOU STINK!

When a species isn't fit for its environment, either because the environment has changed or because outside competition for survival has increased, the species might become **EXTINCT**. Extinction is when all members of a species die.

EXTINCTION
when all the members of a species die

The Main Points of Natural Selection

Individuals of the same species have different traits.

Organisms compete with one another for survival.

Individuals with traits that help them survive reproduce more successfully. These successful individuals pass their helpful traits down to their offspring.

In time, individuals with the helpful variation may become a separate species as their numbers grow, or if they become isolated from the original population.

HOW ARE NEW SPECIES FORMED?
Variation and Adaptation

Evolution is the process of organisms becoming genetically different. Evolution has led to a wide diversity of organisms on Earth today. Individuals within a population have **VARIATIONS**, or genetic differences, in their traits.

VARIATION
genetic differences between individuals within a species

ADAPTATION
inherited variations that make an organism better suited to its environment

When the variation is helpful to the species, it is called an **ADAPTATION**. Scientists call helpful variations adaptations because the organism with the trait is better adapted to its environment. For example, birds have hollow bones that

447

that make them lighter and help them fly. Sometimes the genetic differences are small, but if the changes are large, organisms can become distinct from a **COMMON ANCESTOR** over many generations.

COMMON
ANCESTRY
a shared biological
ancestor

Genetic Mutations

Genetic mutations happen all the time, altering the DNA of an organism and producing new traits. Often the DNA mutation is harmful to the organism, and it hurts its chances of survival. But every so often, a mutation can increase the organism's chances of survival and reproduction. In time, individuals with the adaptation may become another species.

Geographic Isolation and Migration

Sometimes a population of organisms becomes isolated from the rest of the population by geographic features, like mountains, rivers, or oceans. The isolated population might develop different genetic mutations and variations in a new environment. After many generations, the isolated

population can start to look totally different from the rest of the species (its ancestors) and may eventually become a new species, unable to breed with the original population.

Selective Breeding

New species or breeds can be created by mating only certain individuals in a population. For example, if you wanted to create a breed of black dogs from a population of dogs with different-colored coats, only the black dogs would be bred with one another, until alleles for all other fur colors were eliminated from the breed. Humans have used selective breeding to create hundreds of dog breeds, along with many other animals. We've used selective breeding extensively with plants, especially for crops. Selective breeding is like natural selection, except humans are doing the selecting, not nature.

HOW QUICKLY DO THINGS EVOLVE?

Although all scientists agree that species change and organisms adapt, there are different views on how fast it happens. Some scientists think evolution tends to be a really slow process that takes millions of years—this is an evolutionary model called GRADUALISM. Other scientists think that evolution happens in spurts, explained in a theory called PUNCTUATED EQUILIBRIUM. There is evidence to support both of these theories, and it is likely that a combination of these two models has produced the diversity of life on Earth.

EVIDENCE of EVOLUTION
Fossils

Most evidence of evolution was originally
found in fossils. Fossils can preserve the structure
of an organism in many ways, and they give us
a really good idea of what certain organisms
looked like throughout Earth's long history. However, the fossil
record isn't complete. The conditions needed
to preserve an organism as a fossil are rare,

AND FOSSILS ARE HARD TO LOCATE!

so there will always be gaps in the fossil record. But it is
becoming more complete with each new discovery.

One area of evidence for evolution is EMBRYOLOGY, the study
of embryos. Comparing the embryological development of
multiple species helps us understand that many species
share characteristics in their early development. All of these
vertebrates, for instance, have muscles arranged in groups
or bundles, and a tail. Also, they each have hard, protective
coverings over the brain. So, we're not so different after all!

EMBRYONIC SIMILARITIES

FISH	SALAMANDER	TORTOISE	CHICKEN	PIG	COW	RABBIT	HUMAN

Structural Clues

Living species also give us clues about evolution. For example, many species today have **HOMOLOGOUS STRUCTURES**,

HOMOLOGOUS STRUCTURES
similar body structures

or similar body structures. Some examples of homologous structures are human arms, bird wings, whale flippers, dog forearms, and frog forelimbs. The similarity between body structures gives us information about the origin of each species and about shared common ancestors.

VESTIGIAL STRUCTURES, which are body structures that no longer have a function, provide more clues about evolution. A vestigial structure is a remnant (leftover) from an ancestor species. The vestigial structure was once a

VESTIGIAL STRUCTURES
body structures that no longer have a function but provide clues about the ancestors of a species

functioning and important part of the ancestor species, but it's no longer important. For example, humans don't have tails, but we still have a tailbone, called the coccyx. Our appendix and tonsils are also vestigial—they are two organs that we no longer use but still have.

DNA Clues

Our DNA also holds many evolutionary clues. Scientists compare the DNA of different species in order to find similarities.

DNA similarities can tell us information about common ancestry. Mutation rates can also be used to track the changes in species over time. DNA analysis has deepened our understanding of evolution and even forced us to reclassify species as more or less related than we originally thought!

PRIMATE EVOLUTION

PRIMATES form a group of mammals that includes humans, monkeys, apes, and lemurs. Primates have shared characteristics that differentiate them from other mammals, which suggests that they have a common ancestor. Some of these characteristics include:

Opposable thumbs, which allow you to grab a glass or the monkey bar

Binocular vision, which allows you to see distances and depth

Rotating shoulders, which allow you to swing your arms above your head

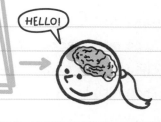

Relatively large brains, which allow you to process visual information and manage social interactions.

HELLO!

Humanlike primates that walked on two legs, called HOMINIDS, first appeared 4 to 6 million years ago. One of the oldest hominid fossils, nicknamed LUCY, was found in Africa. There are now thousands of hominid fossils that have been found and analyzed. Hominid fossils from 1.5 to 2 million years ago show more humanlike characteristics. A fossilized hominid was found next to some tools, so the hominid was named HOMO HABILIS, which means "handy man."

Today, modern humans are part of the species HOMO SAPIENS SAPIENS. *Homo sapiens sapiens* evolved from the species HOMO SAPIENS, which means "wise human."

⤹ (DOES THE EXTRA "SAPIENS" MEAN SUPER-WISE HUMAN?)

Homo sapiens sapiens is the only Hominid species that hasn't yet gone extinct. The first *Homo sapiens* appeared 400,000 years ago, and they branched off into two human groups: NEANDERTHALS and CRO-MAGNONS. Neanderthals were short and heavy with big brow bones and small chins. They lived in caves, made tools, and hunted animals. While Neanderthals are similar to us, they were probably a branch of human evolution and not our direct ancestors. Cro-Magnons, on the

other hand, are thought
to be our direct ancestors.
They looked almost like us.
They also lived
in caves, had tools, and even
made cave paintings!

CHECK YOUR KNOWLEDGE

1. Who developed the evolutionary theory of natural selection?

2. _ _ _ _ _ _ _ _ _ _ is a trait variation that helps an individual survive and reproduce.

3. Explain punctuated equilibrium.

4. Define "vestigial structures" and give an example.

5. Body parts that are similar in structure are called _ _ _ _ _ _ _ _ _ _ structures.

6. Genetic _ _ _ _ _ _ _ _ _ are one way variations occur.

7. _ _ _ _ _ _ _ created the now-disproved theory of acquired characteristics.

8. Define "extinction."

9. _ _ _ – _ _ _ _ _ _ _ _ are early *Homo sapiens* and believed to be our direct ancestors.

10. Explain selective breeding.

ANSWERS

1. Charles Darwin

2. Adaptation

3. Punctuated equilibrium is the theory that evolution happens in rapid spurts between long periods of little evolutionary change.

4. Vestigial structures are structural leftovers that no longer serve a function. Human tonsils are vestigial structures.

5. Homologous

6. Mutations

7. Lamarck

8. Extinction is when all of the individuals of a species die.

9. Cro-Magnons

10. Selective breeding is when certain individuals of a species are mated for certain qualities.

Chapter 44

FOSSILS AND ROCK AGES

FOSSILS

FOSSILS are preserved imprints or remains of prehistoric organisms. Much of what we know about the history of life on Earth comes from fossil remains.

Fossils can tell us both about the physical structure of an organism and about how and where it lived. Only a tiny percentage of organisms become fossilized. Usually, other organisms consume and decompose the body, returning its nutrients to the soil. However, when the organism is buried quickly or it has hard parts such as bones, shells, or teeth, it is more likely to be preserved.

457

THE DIFFERENT WAYS ORGANISMS BECOME FOSSILIZED

MINERAL REPLACEMENT:

The bones, teeth, and shells of many organisms have spaces occupied by air or soft material, such as blood vessels. After the organism dies, the spaces get filled in with minerals from groundwater that then harden.

MINERAL REPLACEMENT

CARBON FILMS:
An organism buried in sediment gets squeezed and heated by the earth, which pushes out all of the gas and liquid from the body. This squeezing leaves a thin film of carbon on the surrounding rocks, forming a silhouette, or outline, of the organism.

CARBON FILMS

COAL:
The coal we burn for heat is actually made of fossilized plant remains. However, because the remains have become completely compressed and carbonized, it doesn't contain much useful information.

THAT'S WHY WE CALL THEM "FOSSIL FUELS."

COAL

MOLDS AND CASTS: Once an organism that has been buried underground decomposes and dissolves, there is a space left in the surrounding rock called a **MOLD**. Sediment and minerals make their way into the mold. As the sediment and minerals harden, they create a **CAST**, or copy of the original organism.

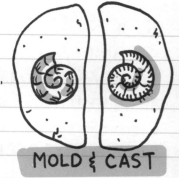

MOLD & CAST

ORIGINAL REMAINS: Sometimes the original remains of organisms are preserved. Insects have been found preserved in hardened tree resin, called **AMBER**, millions of years later. Parts of extinct species, such as the woolly mammoth, have been found frozen underground. Remains of organisms have also been found in the tar pits of California.

ORIGINAL REMAINS

TRACE FOSSILS: Sometimes footprints, trails, and burrows of animals can become fossilized. These fossils are especially interesting because they can provide information about the behavior and movement of an organism.

TRACE FOSSILS

ROCK AGES
Absolute Dating

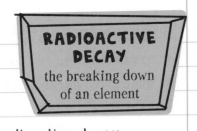

RADIOACTIVE DECAY
the breaking down
of an element

When scientists need to know the
ABSOLUTE DATE, or exact age of
a rock, they can date the rock using radioactive decay.
RADIOACTIVE DECAY is when an element breaks down. All
rocks contain unstable elements, such as isotopes of carbon,
potassium, uranium, and others. One of those isotopes—
carbon-14, or C-14—is present in living organisms. It decays
slowly, but predictably, so scientists can measure the amount
present in a fossil and work back to learn how old it is.
This absolute dating detective work is sometimes called
CARBON DATING or RADIOACTIVE DATING.

Relative Dating

Absolute dating is an accurate way to find the age of a rock
layer, but the technique doesn't work on sedimentary rocks,
which is where nearly all fossils are buried. (Sedimentary
rocks are made up of bits of other rocks, so absolute
dating would give the ages of all the different bits of
sediment—not when it was formed into a sedimentary rock.)
RELATIVE DATING of rocks compares the age of one rock
to another. Scientists determine the sequence of rocks and
estimate the age based on their order and the fossils present.

Usually, things buried deeper underground are older. The
PRINCIPLE OF SUPERPOSITION states that when

undisturbed, the oldest rocks are at the bottom, and the youngest rocks are at the top. New rock is formed when sediment gets compressed into

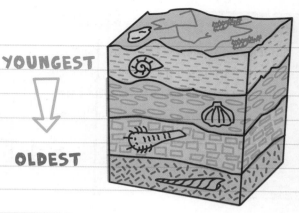

YOUNGEST

OLDEST

horizontal sheets. New sediment accumulates on the older rock layers, which is why younger rocks are on top of older ones. Using this principle, scientists can determine the relative ages of rocks. The principle of superposition only works when rock layers haven't been disturbed. Sometimes, a fault can break apart rock layers, or shift, fold, or invert (flip) layers. Other times, magma may slowly push up from within the earth and push into cracks or push rock out of the way—a process called INTRUSION. The igneous rock that comes from below may in fact be younger than the layers on top.

Unconformities

Rocks form in layers that are part of complete sequences, which is how superposition is able to give the relative age of a rock. Sometimes, however, rock layers can erode or be washed away, forming a gap in the layer sequence. These gaps are called UNCONFORMITIES. Unconformity can happen in three major ways:

ANGULAR UNCONFORMITY:
Sometimes rock layers get pushed upward, forming a tilt or roll. As the rock erodes, it takes away some of the raised rock layers, so the layers are no longer parallel. New sediment gets deposited on top forming new rock layers. The result is a gap in the rock sequence.

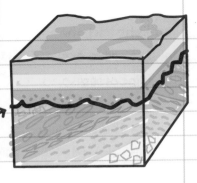

DISCONFORMITY: when new rock layers form over older rock layers that have been eroded, leaving a gap in the sequence. Unlike angular unconformity, the rock layers are all still parallel, but they are missing a layer.

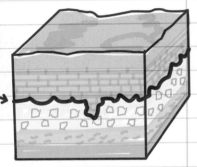

NONCONFORMITY: when sedimentary rocks form over a different kind of rock, like metamorphic or igneous rock, that has been eroded.

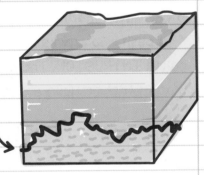

Index Fossils

Some organisms lived on Earth only during a short and specific time period. When these organisms are found as fossil remains, they are called INDEX FOSSILS because they provide a reference used to date rocks and other, nearby fossils.

CHECK YOUR KNOWLEDGE

1. Define "fossils."

2. List the different ways organisms become fossilized.

3. What are the parts of animals most likely to be preserved?

4. Preserved footprints are called _ _ _ _ _ fossils.

5. A term for using radioactive decay to determine the age of once-living fossils is _ _ _ _ _ _ _ _ _ _ _ _ _.

6. When a fossil dissolves and leaves an empty space, it creates a _ _ _ _, which can be filled in with sediment to create a replica of the fossil, called a _ _ _ _.

7. A fossil that forms a silhouette of the organism is a _ _ _ _ _ _ _ _ _ _.

8. Explain intrusion.

9. What is the isotope scientists use to find out how old a fossil is?

10. Explain the principle of superposition.

11. Define "index fossils."

ANSWERS 463

CHECK YOUR ANSWERS

1. Fossils are preserved imprints or remains of prehistoric organisms.

2. Mineral replacement, carbon films, coal, molds and casts, original remains, and trace fossils

3. Hard parts, such as bones, shells, or teeth

4. Trace

5. Carbon dating

6. Mold, cast

7. Carbon film

8. Intrusion happens when igneous rock or magma pushes up from within the earth and disturbs the existing layers of rock.

9. Carbon-14, or C-14

10. The principle of superposition says that the oldest rocks are at the bottom, and the youngest rocks are near the surface.

11. Index fossils are fossils that provide a reference used to date rocks and nearby fossils.

Chapter 45

HISTORY OF LIFE ON EARTH

TIME SCALES

The GEOLOGIC TIME SCALE is a time scale organized according to when certain organisms lived on Earth. The geologic time scale includes four major time divisions:

EONS: the longest subdivision, which can last up to hundreds of millions of years. Determined by the prevalence of certain fossils.

ERAS: the next-longest subdivision. An era marks a major shift in the types of fossils present.

PERIODS: Periods are divisions within an era. Periods mark stages within an era when different kinds of life existed.

EPOCHS: the shortest subdivision, lasting several million years. An epoch divides periods into smaller units and is also determined by life-form changes.

GEOLOGIC TIME SCALE

EON	ERA	PERIOD
Phanerozoic	Cenozoic	Quaternary
		Tertiary
	Mesozoic	Cretaceous
		Jurassic
		Triassic
	Paleozoic	Permian
		Carboniferous — Pennsylvanian
		Carboniferous — Mississippian
		Devonian
		Silurian
		Ordovician
		Cambrian
Precambrian		Proterozoic
		Archaean

RECENT

OLDEST

The geologic time scale is based on the appearance and disappearance of life-forms. Life-forms appear and disappear as they evolve and/or become extinct due to factors like environmental changes. Organisms compete with one another for resources, and individuals most suited to the environment survive, as explained by Darwin's theory of natural selection. Species that are no longer fit for their environment must either move or adapt, or go extinct.

OVER 99% OF ALL SPECIES THAT HAVE LIVED ON EARTH ARE NOW EXTINCT!

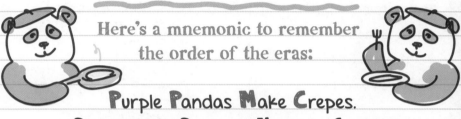

Here's a mnemonic to remember the order of the eras:

Purple Pandas Make Crepes.
(**P**recambrian, **P**aleozoic, **M**esozoic, **C**enozoic)

EVOLUTION of the EARTH

Earth has not always looked the way it does today. Plate tectonics and water levels have continually changed the earth's appearance. Before the Mesozoic era, much of Earth was covered in water. By the end of the Paleozoic era, sea levels dropped and the continents were squeezed together into a huge landmass named Pangaea. Pangaea began spreading and separating into the continents we know today by the middle of the Mesozoic era. The continents are still moving today.

THE PRECAMBRIAN ERA COVERS MORE THAN 80 PERCENT OF EARTH'S HISTORY. (NOT MUCH HAPPENED WITH LIVING THINGS IN THE FIRST 4 BILLION YEARS!)

EARTH'S

Scientists divide the earth's history into four eras. Starting with the earliest, about 4.6 billion years ago, they are:

1. PRECAMBRIAN

Spans from 4.6 billion years ago to 541.1 million years ago, which is the vast majority of the earth's existence (more than 80 percent of it!).

WE'RE #1!

The first organisms appeared! Cyanobacteria, which are single-celled bacteria, made energy through photosynthesis, releasing oxygen into the atmosphere.

The ozone layer began to appear as well. The combination of oxygen and ozone in the atmosphere slowly created an environment that allowed more life-forms to develop.

By the end of the Precambrian era, some simple multicelled organisms had begun to evolve.

HISTORY

2. PALEOZOIC

Spans 544.1 million to 252 million years ago.

Many organisms with shells or **EXOSKELETONS** started appearing.

EXOSKELETON
The prefix *exo* means "outside," and a skeleton is a firm structure. So an exoskeleton is a hard outer body structure.

Vertebrates, plants, amphibians, and reptiles evolved. (Much of Earth was covered in shallow water during the Paleozoic era, so most animals were aquatic.) Simple land animals evolved about halfway through this era.

Pangaea formed at the end of the era, creating mountains as continental plates collided.

The end of the Paleozoic era was marked by mass extinctions: Ninety percent of all marine animals and 70 percent of all land organisms became extinct.

Because organisms during the Precambrian time didn't have bones or other hard parts, there aren't many fossil records. There are many more records of the Paleozoic era.

Reptiles were one of the few types of organisms to survive from the Paleozoic into the Mesozoic era because they were well adapted to land. Scientists aren't sure of what caused the mass extinctions, though they could be the result of Pangaea's formation, the lowering of ocean levels, and the formation of deserts.

3. MESOZOIC

← "THE AGE OF REPTILES"

Spanning about 252 million to 66 million years ago (about 4 percent of Earth's history).

Pangaea split first into two landmasses and eventually into what we now know as our continents.

EURASIA

NORTH AMERICA

AFRICA

SOUTH AMERICA

INDIA

AUSTRALIA

ANTARCTICA

PANGAEA

Dinosaurs evolved during this era.

The first birds and mammals also appeared during the Mesozoic era, although mammals were mostly small and underground.

Angiosperms (flowering plants) and gymnosperms (seeded plants) first appeared.

The end of the Mesozoic era was marked by another round of mass extinctions, probably caused by a meteor colliding with Earth, which sent an enormous amount of dust and smoke into the atmosphere!

THAT AIN'T GOOD.

The dust and smoke blocked out sunlight and altered Earth's climate, which caused plants to die and subsequently caused animals that depended on the plants for food to die as well.

4. CENOZOIC

← "THE AGE OF MAMMALS"

The era we currently live in! It began about 65 million years ago (less than 2 percent of Earth's history).

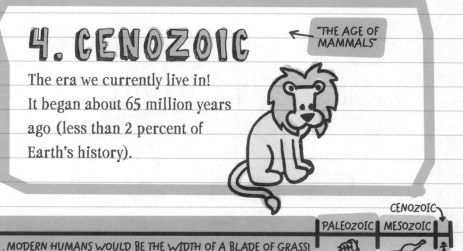

... MODERN HUMANS WOULD BE THE WIDTH OF A BLADE OF GRASS!

PALEOZOIC | MESOZOIC | CENOZOIC

Modern mountain ranges, like the Himalayas, formed.

Mammals became much larger and more dominant than their predecessors, perhaps because of lack of competition from the dinosaurs.

Early modern humans first evolved ← around 200,000 years ago.

ONLY ABOUT 0.000044% OF EARTH'S HISTORY. WE HAVEN'T BEEN AROUND VERY LONG!

MMM, DO I SMELL CREPES?

CHECK YOUR KNOWLEDGE

1. List geological time divisions from longest to shortest.

2. When did the continents as we know them appear?

3. Why were there mass extinctions at the end of the Paleozoic era?

4. What is the geologic time scale based on?

5. Which era saw a mass extinction, probably caused in part by a meteor or comet impact?

6. What era are we currently living in?

7. Describe the earth's surface before the Mesozoic era.

8. What was the first organism to appear on Earth? How did it create energy?

ANSWERS

1. Eon, era, period, and epoch

2. During the Mesozoic era, after Pangaea split and continued to spread

3. The continental plates came together to form the large landmass Pangaea. Parts that were under water previously became land. Many marine organisms couldn't survive on land, so they became extinct. Reptiles, which were more capable of living on land, survived.

4. The geological time scale is based on the disappearance and appearance of life-forms.

5. The Mesozoic era

6. The Cenozoic era

7. It was covered in water.

8. Cyanobacteria. It made energy through photosynthesis.

Unit 11

Ecology:
Habitats, Interdependence, and Resources

Chapter 46

ECOLOGY
AND ECOSYSTEMS

ECOLOGY is the study of the relationships between organisms (living things) and their environments.

> **ECOLOGY**
> the study of the interactions between organisms and their environments

ECOSYSTEMS

Ecologists study **ECOSYSTEMS**. An ecosystem includes all of the organisms and environmental factors in a certain area. It is simply a unit and can be of any size. As small as your backyard right up to . . . the largest ecosystem in the world, the **BIOSPHERE**, which includes every part of Earth where organisms can survive, such as the earth's crust, its waterways, landforms, forests, and the atmosphere. The biosphere is all of the ecosystems on Earth combined.

> **ECOSYSTEM**
> the living and nonliving factors that work together and interact in an area

476

An ecosystem can be broken down into **BIOTIC** factors, which are the living and once-living parts, and **ABIOTIC** factors, which are the nonliving parts. Some abiotic factors are air, water, soil, sunlight, temperature, and climate.

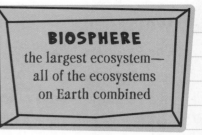
BIOSPHERE
the largest ecosystem—
all of the ecosystems
on Earth combined

BIO = LIFE!

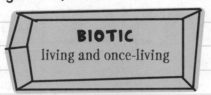
BIOTIC
living and once-living

ABIOTIC
nonliving

ABIOTIC FACTORS
Air

The atmosphere, the air that surrounds Earth, is an important abiotic factor. Animals breathe in oxygen and exhale carbon dioxide. Plants use carbon dioxide for essential processes, like photosynthesis, which uses sunlight, CO_2, and water to produce sugar molecules for energy. After using carbon dioxide, plants release oxygen back into the environment. Animals then breathe in oxygen for respiration, which converts sugar molecules into energy.

Water

Almost all life processes, such as photosynthesis, respiration, and digestion, involve water. Many plants and animals rely heavily on water not only for sustenance but also for shelter. Water is a habitat for fish and frogs and many other organisms.

Soil

Soil consists of a mixture of rock and mineral particles, water, and dead organisms. Different soils have different nutrient qualities, so different soils support different types of plant life.

Sunlight

The root of almost all our food can be traced back to sunlight. Plants and algae capture the sun's energy and use it to produce chemical energy in the form of sugars. Animals then eat plants to get energy.

Temperature and Climate

Most animals and plants can survive only in a certain temperature range. Temperature is affected by the amount of sunlight a region receives, the angle of that sunlight, elevation, if large bodies of water are nearby, ocean circulation, and

other factors. Climate is also affected by the timing and amount of wind and precipitation an ecosystem receives.

BIOTIC FACTORS

The biotic factors of an ecosystem include all of its living and once-living parts. Each organism has its own role in the ecosystem, called a NICHE, and its own living environment, called a HABITAT. All the organisms of a species that live in an area are called a POPULATION. The different populations of species living in an area are called a COMMUNITY. The community in your local park includes all of the plants, bugs, mice, raccoons, and birds living there.

LEVELS of ORGANIZATION in an ECOSYSTEM

Ecosystems can be broken down into levels (from smallest to largest):

ORGANISM: one member of a population
(a single lake trout in Lake Michigan)

POPULATION: the total number of one type of organism (a species) in a certain area (all the lake trout in Lake Michigan)

COMMUNITY: all of the populations that interact in an area (the different types of fish, bacteria, leeches, water bugs, algae, and plants that live in Lake Michigan)

> **ECOSYSTEM**: all of the communities and nonliving factors in an area (Lake Michigan as a whole)

> **BIOME**: a region that can include a number of ecosystems (the temperate deciduous forests)

> **BIOSPHERE**: all of the ecosystems on Earth combined

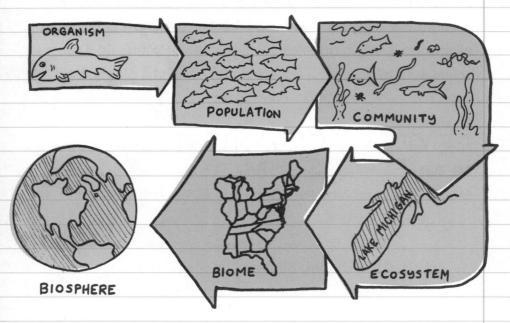

POPULATIONS

POPULATION DENSITY is how close together members of a population live. Populations are denser when more organisms occupy a smaller area. Given the same population density, populations can still space out differently. Some populations clump together, and others are spaced out across an area.

Limiting Factors

The number of organisms in a population depends on the amount of resources available. Because resources limit the population, they are called LIMITING FACTORS. They include:

WATER   SUNLIGHT   FOOD   LIVING SPACE

Organisms compete for these resources and depend on them for survival.

Niche

In order to survive, every organism finds its own niche, or role in the community. An organism's niche includes:

WHAT AND WHEN IT EATS
WHEN IT'S ACTIVE
WHAT IT USES FOR SHELTER
HOW IT REPRODUCES

> IF TWO ORGANISMS HAVE THE SAME NICHE, THEY WILL BE IN DIRECT COMPETITION WITH EACH OTHER.

Carrying Capacity

CARRYING CAPACITY is the largest number of organisms an ecosystem can support. The carrying capacity of an ecosystem is determined by limiting factors and by factors such as the number of other organisms living in the ecosystem. For example, if a drought killed off a large portion of the grass in the area, the number of sheep that can rely on that grass for food will also decrease. The total number of sheep that the remaining grass can support is the new carrying capacity.

UH-OH.

Biotic Potential

Without limiting factors, how quickly would a population grow? The BIOTIC POTENTIAL is the highest rate of reproduction possible by a species in ideal living conditions. Dogs have higher biotic potential than humans because dogs give birth to several puppies at once and humans usually only give birth to one child at a time. Dogs are also able to reproduce within a year of being born. Humans obviously take a bit longer.

BACTERIA SPECIES MAY REPRODUCE EVERY 20 MINUTES!

Population Growth and Migration

The population growth rate depends on the number of births and deaths in the population. Zimbabwe has an annual human population growth rate of 2.3 percent, but Greece has a population growth rate of −0.06 percent (which means the population is shrinking).

Population numbers can also be affected by MIGRATION, which is when a population moves from one habitat to another, like birds flying south or north. Some migrations are caused by a more permanent change in habitat or climate that forces a population to move elsewhere.

CHECK YOUR KNOWLEDGE

1. List the levels of the ecosystem from smallest to largest.

2. What's the difference between a biotic and an abiotic factor? Give some examples of each.

3. What is a limiting factor? List four limiting factors.

4. How do organisms avoid competing for the same limiting factors?

5. What is the carrying capacity of an ecosystem?

6. If penguins lay one egg a year, and robins lay five to ten eggs a year, which animal has a higher biotic potential?

7. Describe how population density affects organisms.

8. Describe how the abiotic and biotic factors of a desert and a forest differ.

ANSWERS

1. Organisms, population, community, ecosystem, biome, and biosphere

2. Biotic factors are the living and once-living parts of an ecosystem, such as plants and animals. Abiotic factors are the nonliving factors of an ecosystem, such as sunlight, water, air, temperature, climate, and space for growth.

3. A limiting factor is a limited resource that restricts the number of organisms that can survive in a population. Some limiting factors are space, food, sunlight, and water.

4. Organisms find their own niche, or role in the community. Each organism adapts itself to different feeding and living behaviors.

5. The carrying capacity is the largest population that an ecosystem can support.

6. The robin has a higher biotic potential.

7. When population density is really high, resources are more strained.

8. A desert gets more sunlight, is drier, and has cacti and grasses to support insects and animals. A forest gets more water and, therefore, has more tree habitats to support insects and animals.

#8 has more than one correct answer.

Chapter 47

INTERDEPENDENCE AND THE CYCLING OF ENERGY AND MATTER

RELATIONSHIPS AMONG POPULATIONS

The reliance on other populations for survival within a community is called INTERDEPENDENCE. Populations exist in constantly shifting balances. Some relationships help keep communities in balance; other relationships can change those communities.

Competition

Different organisms compete for the same resources, such as water, space, and sunlight. Well-adapted members of a community are more likely to survive and reproduce under heavy competition for resources.

Predation

Populations change because of PREDATOR AND PREY RELATIONSHIPS. PREDATORS are animals that eat other animals, and PREY are the animals being eaten. For predators, the amount of prey is a limiting factor.

Cooperation

Members of a population often cooperate in order to help one another survive. Some monkeys hunt in teams to increase the chances of success. In some herds, animals warn one another about the presence of a predator.

Symbiosis

Sometimes, organisms from different species interact with each other in a way that benefits one or both of them. This is called SYMBIOSIS. Symbiosis happens in three different ways:

1. **MUTUALISM**: Both species benefit from associating with each other. For example: an oxpecker eats the ticks that attach to zebras. The oxpeckers get food, and the zebras get cleaned.

2. COMMENSALISM: One organism
benefits from the relationship while the
other remains unaffected. Clown fish, which
are resistant to stings from sea anemones, use sea anemones
for protection, and the sea anemones are unaffected.

3. PARASITISM: One organism benefits while the other is
harmed. Usually, one organism, the PARASITE, feeds off
another organism, called the HOST. Hookworms enter their
hosts, such as a dog or human, and feed off nutrients in the
host's small intestine. The hookworm feeds itself by stealing
nutrients from the host.

Feeding Relationships

Every organism needs a source of energy to survive.
There are two main types of organisms:

> **1. Those that produce their own energy**

> **2. Those that eat other organisms for energy**

Producers

Producers make their own food.
Plants, algae, and some bacteria
are all producers. Most producers

> Producers are also known
> as **AUTOTROPHS**
> (auto = self; troph = feed).

produce energy through photosynthesis, which is the creation
of sugar molecules through a chemical process that requires
carbon dioxide, water, and sunlight.

Consumers

Consumers are also known as **HETEROTROPHS** (hetero = others; troph = feed).

Consumers consume other organisms for energy. The main types of consumers are:

HERBIVORES: plant eaters. Herbivores eat producers, like plants. Cows are herbivores. They eat only plants.

YUM! GRASS AGAIN.

RUDE!

CARNIVORES: meat eaters. Carnivores eat other consumers. Sharks are carnivores, meaning they get their food from eating other fish and mammals.

OMNIVORES: plant and animal eaters. Omnivores eat both other animals and plants. Most humans are omnivores—they eat producers, like fruits and vegetables, and consumers, like cows and chickens.

KISS THE OMNIVORE

DECOMPOSERS: omnivores that eat dead organisms and other waste. Decomposers like fungus and bacteria break down waste, dead plants, and animals for food. Decomposers are really important because they recycle nutrients back into the ecosystem.

CHEMOTROPHS: organisms that get energy directly from chemicals without using the sun. Chemotrophs are typically bacteria or single-celled protists. For example, methanogens are a type of bacteria that live at the bottom of the ocean near deep-sea volcanic vents. They create energy through a chemical process with the molecules in their environment, rather than through photosynthesis.

Here are a few ways to remember which consumer eats what: Herbivore has the word **"herb"** in it, which is a plant. Carnivore has the prefix **"carni,"** which comes from the Latin word for meat. Omnivore has the prefix **"omni,"** which means "everything." Omnivores eat **EVERYTHING**.

WOLVES

FOXES

BIRDS

FOOD CHAINS

A **FOOD CHAIN** shows where different organisms get their food. Food chains trace energy sources across different organisms.

SPIDERS

GRASSHOPPERS

In this food chain, the grass is the producer, the grasshopper is the **PRIMARY CONSUMER**, or the consumer at the bottom of the food chain; the spider is the **SECONDARY CONSUMER** because it eats the primary consumer for energy; the

GRASS

TERTIARY CONSUMER, the third level up on the food chain, is the bird and any carnivores beyond, like the fox and wolf.

FOOD WEBS

In the real world, energy exchanges are much more complicated than a single food chain. The same organism can be a part of multiple food chains. Scientists use FOOD WEBS to show all of the feeding relationships and overlapping food chains.

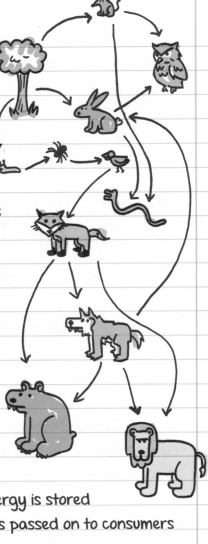

ENERGY and MATTER CYCLES

Energy and matter are constantly being transformed and recycled through the environment.

Energy Cycle

Energy enters food webs through producers, which produce energy from either sunlight or chemicals. Energy is stored in tissues and cells, and this energy is passed on to consumers when they eat other organisms.

Energy is passed through ecosystems through food chains and food webs. At each level of the food chain, most of the energy is transformed into movement and heat. Only about 10 percent of the energy from one level gets passed on to the next.

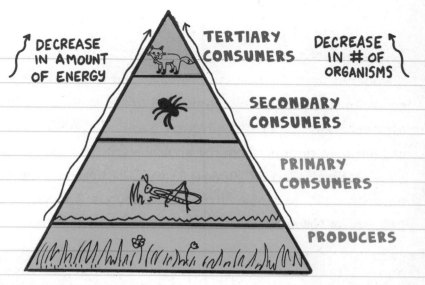

An ENERGY PYRAMID shows the energy at each feeding level of an ecosystem.

Water Cycle

Water constantly gets cycled through the environment—from rain to rivers, oceans, and plants to the sky again through evaporation . . . and back again. Even animals consume and release water as part of the water cycle.

Nitrogen Cycle

Nitrogen is used for building proteins, so it is one of the most essential elements for all plants and animals. Although the atmosphere is 78 percent nitrogen, plants and animals can't use nitrogen directly from the environment. Instead, they rely on a process called NITROGEN FIXATION, which converts nitrogen gas into usable nitrogen compounds. The NITROGEN CYCLE is as follows:

Nitrogen from the atmosphere or soil enters the nitrogen cycle through **NITROGEN FIXERS** such as bacteria.

Plants absorb the nitrogen compounds and use them to build cells.

Animals get nitrogen by eating plants.

Animal waste returns some nitrogen compounds back to the environment.

When an animal or plant dies, decomposers release their nitrogen back to the soil.

Plants absorb nitrogen compounds from the soil, starting the process anew.

Other bacteria change nitrogen compounds back into gas, restoring nitrogen gas to the environment.

CARBON CYCLE

Carbon dioxide (CO_2) and oxygen (O_2) are continually absorbed and emitted back into the environment through the CARBON CYCLE. In the atmosphere, carbon attaches to two oxygen molecules to create carbon dioxide, or CO_2.

Plants, algae, and bacteria use CO_2 from the environment to make carbon-rich sugar for energy through photosynthesis. A waste product of photosynthesis is oxygen.

Organisms such as humans break down sugar molecules for energy through a process called respiration. In respiration, organisms breathe in oxygen and release CO_2.

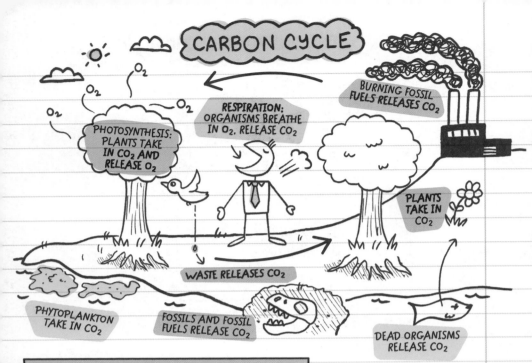

Burning fossil fuels and trees also releases CO_2 back into the environment.

Fungi and bacteria decompose animal waste and animal and plant bodies, which releases CO_2 back into the environment.

Plants take in CO_2, starting the process over again.

The ocean cycles a lot of carbon dioxide through a variety of physical and biological processes. One way is that CO_2 diffuses into the water surface from the atmosphere. CO_2 also enters into the **OCEAN CARBON CYCLE** when tiny organisms like **PHYTOPLANKTON** use it for photosynthesis and become part of the ocean's food chain. Furthermore, ocean life also produces waste, dies, and decomposes—all of which release CO_2.

GREEK FOR "DRIFTING PLANTS"

JUST LIKE ON LAND!

CHECK YOUR KNOWLEDGE

1. A producer and primary consumer are at the bottom of the food _ _ _ _ _ _.

2. Organisms use oxygen to burn sugar and release carbon dioxide through the process of _ _ _ _ _ _ _ _ _ _ _ _.

3. A food _ _ _ shows all of the complex feeding relationships in an ecosystem.

4. Explain commensalism.

5. Most energy enters the ecosystem through the process of _ _ _ _ _ _ _ _ _ _ _ _ _ _ _ _.

6. Give an example of cooperation.

7. An energy _ _ _ _ _ _ _ shows the energy at each feeding level of an ecosystem.

8. Grass is a _ _ _ _ _ _ _ _ because it makes its own energy source.

9. A lion is a _ _ _ _ _ _ _ _ because it hunts and eats prey.

10. Define "interdependence."

11. The type of consumer that eats both plants and animals is an _ _ _ _ _ _ _ _.

ANSWERS

CHECK YOUR ANSWERS

1. Chain

2. Respiration

3. Web

4. Commensalism is a symbiotic relationship where one organism benefits and the other is unaffected.

5. Photosynthesis

6. An example of cooperation is when members of a herd alert each other to the presence of a predator.

7. Pyramid

8. Producer

9. Predator

10. Interdependence is the reliance on other populations for survival within a community.

11. Omnivore

#6 has more than one correct answer.

Chapter 48

ECOLOGICAL SUCCESSION AND BIOMES

ECOLOGICAL SUCCESSION

Land is always developing and changing. A once-empty field can one day become a forest. The organisms that live in an area change with time as well. The development and change of an area over time is called ECOLOGICAL SUCCESSION.

Primary Succession to Climax Community

The process of succession that begins in an area where there were previously no plants is called PRIMARY SUCCESSION. Primary succession usually begins with bare rocks such as lava. The first organisms to move in are called **PIONEER SPECIES**. (Sort of like the American pioneers, who were the first immigrant settlers to move out west.)

Some pioneer species are:

MOSSES　　**LICHEN**　　**FUNGI**

As pioneer species grow, they release acids that break down rocks, forming soil. (Soil is made of rock particles, water, and organic matter, which is dead organisms.) As the pioneer species die, they contribute organic matter to the soil. In time, the soil becomes rich enough to support other plant life, such as grasses and herbs.

> **PIONEER SPECIES**
> the first species to move into an area, such as moss, lichen, or fungi

The presence of grass and other plant life draws small animals that eat plants to the area. As small animals move in, so do the larger animals that prey on the smaller animals. All of these animals add nutrients to the soil through their waste and remains, which are decomposed by bacteria in the soil. The richer, older soil can support larger plants, such as bushes and shrubs. These larger plants often outcompete the smaller plants, such as grasses. In time, the soil gets even richer until it can finally support trees. The trees grow and multiply until they outcompete many of the shrubs and bushes. The trees mature, and the land reaches a point where few new species can COLONIZE, or move into the area. When an area has reached this mature phase, it is called a **CLIMAX COMMUNITY**. But even in a climax community, changes and disturbances are happening all the time. A single tree may die or blow over, creating

new opportunities for other
organisms. A creek may flood,
or a brushfire may start—all
creating opportunities for new
species to colonize the area.

Secondary Succession

Unlike primary succession, where organisms need to start from
scratch, SECONDARY SUCCESSION is the development of an
area where soil already exists. Secondary succession usually
happens in an area that recently experienced a wildfire,
windstorm, insect attack, or other disturbance.

BIOMES

BIOMES are regions that have similar living and nonliving
features. In other words, biomes have similar ecosystems,
climates, vegetation, and wildlife.

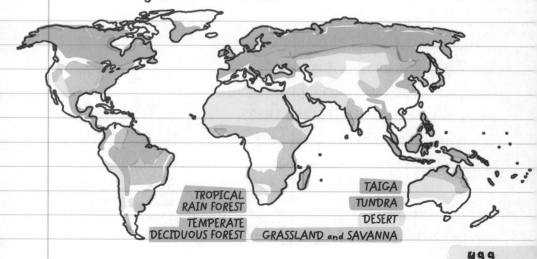

TROPICAL
RAIN FOREST

TEMPERATE
DECIDUOUS FOREST

GRASSLAND and SAVANNA

TAIGA

TUNDRA

DESERT

Tundra

The **TUNDRA** is a cold desert, like the
Arctic. Tundra biomes are generally treeless

TUNDRA
cold desert

because the soil is not rich enough to support trees; subfreezing
temperatures slow down decomposition, so it takes longer for
nutrients to enter the soil. Lichens, moss, grass, and
small shrubs generally live in the tundra.

Beneath the soil there is
a layer of ground that
is always frozen, called

PERMAFROST

PERMAFROST (like the words "permanent" and "frost" combined).
During the short summer, when some plants grow and flower,
the tundra fills with bugs, hawks, owls, grouse, mice, lemmings,
caribou, reindeer, and musk oxen. The ALPINE TUNDRA is like the
ARCTIC TUNDRA except that it is found in high-altitude places,
like above the tree line on mountains.

Taiga and Coniferous Forests

The **TAIGA** is south of the tundra and
is a cold, forested region. The trees in the
taiga are mostly CONIFEROUS TREES,
which are trees that are cone-bearing.
Many remain green year-round.

TAIGA
cold coniferous
forest

In the southern part of the taiga, the trees
can be so dense that very little sunlight gets to the ground,

500

meaning few small
plants live in this
part of the taiga. The
animals that live in

A Christmas tree is a coniferous tree. Conifers have waxy needles for leaves and grow seeds in cones.

the taiga include bobcats, wolves,
foxes, lynxes, rabbits, moose, elk,
and porcupines.

Deciduous Forest

A **DECIDUOUS FOREST** contains a variety of mostly
deciduous trees and plants. Deciduous trees are trees that
lose their leaves each year. Deciduous forests are located in
temperate regions, such as the eastern coast
of the United States, Central
Europe, and areas of Asia.

The deciduous forest
biome has a long
growing season
because it gets plenty of rain
and has pretty moderate
temperatures. Raccoons, black
bears, birds, mice, rabbits,
woodpeckers, and foxes are
some of the animals that live in
deciduous forests.

DECIDUOUS FOREST
forest mostly made of
trees that lose their leaves
(in temperate regions)

Temperate Rain Forest

TEMPERATE RAIN FORESTS are forests in temperate regions (temperatures around 50°F) that receive a lot of rain—such as forests in New Zealand and some parts of the United States, like Washington State. Black bears, cougars, and amphibians are a few of the species that live in temperate rain forests.

TEMPERATE RAIN FOREST
forest that receives a lot of rain (in temperate regions)

Tropical Rain Forest

TROPICAL RAIN FORESTS are located near the equator. They have warm temperatures and get lots of rain. Tropical rain forests house more species than any other biome. Some examples of the species that live in tropical rain forests include monkeys, jaguars, leopards, snakes, beetles, ants, crickets, parrots, and toucans.

TROPICAL RAIN FOREST
hot rainy forest located close to the equator

The rain forest is separated into levels. Each level provides a different habitat for animals.

EMERGENTS: at the treetops of the tallest trees that stick out (emerge) above the layers; home to birds and insects

CANOPY: the upper part of trees; home to birds, reptiles, and mammals such as monkeys

UNDERSTORY: under canopy leaves but not touching the ground; home to insects, reptiles, and amphibians

FOREST FLOOR: the lowest zone; home to bugs and large mammals

← EMERGENTS →

← CANOPY →

← UNDERSTORY →

← FOREST FLOOR →

THAT'S THE SIZE OF A FOOTBALL FIELD EVERY SECOND! →

The rain forest is rapidly shrinking. Every second, 1.5 acres of rain forest are cut down for wood and to clear space for farming.

503

Grasslands and Savannas

GRASSLANDS and **SAVANNAS** are in

temperate and tropical regions, but they get less rain than tropical and temperate rain forests. Grasslands are too dry for trees, but they can still support a variety of grasses and smaller plants. Many animals of the grasslands and savannas are grazers, such as bison and prairie dogs.

> A **SAVANNA** is like grassland, but it has a few trees. Africa has a large savanna called the Serengeti. Giraffes, zebras, and elephants live in the savanna.

> **GRASSLANDS**
> areas in temperate and tropical regions that don't receive much rain

Desert

DESERTS are areas with very little rain and usually extreme temperatures, like hot days and cold nights. Cacti, bushes, kangaroo rats, lizards, snakes, vultures, and armadillos are some of the organisms that have adapted to the dry conditions. With so little moisture in the ground, plants have to space out to reduce competition. Many of the animals survive by hiding under rocks during the hot day and being active during the cooler nights.

> **DESERT**
> very dry land that gets both hot and cold temperatures

FRESHWATER ECOSYSTEMS
Streams, Rivers, Estuaries

Faster-moving streams usually have more oxygen, so they can support fish species and insect larvae. Slower-moving streams allow more sediment to settle at the bottom, providing nutrients for plant growth.

Places where freshwater rivers flow into oceans are called ESTUARIES. Nutrients deposited by rivers make them very fertile. Snails, shrimp, crabs, and clams are some of the species that live in estuaries. If sediments pile up enough here, a river DELTA can form.

Lakes and Ponds

Many fish and plants live in ponds and lakes. Reeds and cattails are plants that live along the edges of ponds. Algae and PLANKTON, single-celled algae, live near the water's surface. Plants generally survive better in shallower water, so ponds and shallow lakes have the most plant life.

Wetlands ← SOUND EXACTLY LIKE WHAT THEY ARE: WET LAND.

WETLANDS, also known as swamps, are rich in animal and plant life such as beavers, alligators, turtles, cranberries, and more. They are important "filters" in the ecosystem, too.

SALTWATER ECOSYSTEMS

Most of the water on Earth is saltwater. SALTWATER ECOSYSTEMS are mostly in oceans, but they are also in saltwater lakes. The ocean is divided into three zones:

OPEN OCEAN ZONE

INTERTIDAL ZONE

CORAL REEF

1. **OPEN OCEAN ZONE:** The largest ocean zone is divided into layers depending on depth; different organisms live at different depths. Animal larvae and plankton live near the surface, the highest level in the open ocean zone.

2. **INTERTIDAL ZONE:** Seashore that is covered in water at high tide but not at low tide. Snails, barnacles, crabs, and other shelled animals live in intertidal zones.

3. **CORAL REEFS:** Coral is a small animal that grows intertwined with other coral and the calcified shells and skeletons of dead coral. Coral reefs are huge entwined structures. Coral reefs provide a habitat for a wide diversity of organisms, such as starfish, fish, shrimp, and sponges.

LIKE A GIANT APARTMENT COMPLEX FOR TINY ANIMALS

THAT'S WHY PEOPLE CALL THE CORAL REEF THE "TROPICAL RAIN FOREST OF THE SEA."

CHECK YOUR KNOWLEDGE

1. _____ succession often happens on a newly formed volcanic island.

2. Define "pioneer species."

3. After a forest fire, an area is redeveloped through _____ succession.

4. Define "climax community."

5. The _____ ____ _____ is the biome that houses the largest number of species.

6. Describe a coral reef.

7. A _____ ____ is the kind of tree that loses its leaves in the fall, and a _____ ____ always remains green.

8. The _____ is the biome just south of the tundra, home to coniferous forests.

9. The majority of saltwater and freshwater organisms live near the _____ of lakes or oceans.

10. Why don't grasslands have any trees?

ANSWERS

CHECK YOUR ANSWERS

1. Primary

2. The first species to enter an area

3. Secondary

4. A place that has been fully colonized where few new organisms can move into

5. Tropical rain forest

6. Coral reefs are interlaced underwater structures made of live coral built onto the calcified shells and skeletons of dead coral.

7. Deciduous tree, coniferous tree

8. Taiga

9. Surface

10. Grasslands can't support tree life because of the dry conditions.

Chapter

NATURAL RESOURCES AND CONSERVATION

NATURAL RESOURCES

A **NATURAL RESOURCE** is anything found in nature that is useful to us and to animals. Water, sunlight, food, air, crude oil, cotton, gold, and trees are all natural resources. Natural resources that can be recycled or replaced by nature quickly (within 100 years or so) are called **RENEWABLE RESOURCES**. Resources that can take up to millions of years to replace are called **NONRENEWABLE RESOURCES**.

Unfortunately, much of the energy we use to power our everyday lives comes from fossil fuels, a nonrenewable resource. Humans have a huge impact on the environment—too often in the form of pollution.

> **RENEWABLE RESOURCES**
> sunlight, trees, water, wind
>
> **NONRENEWABLE RESOURCES**
> metals, minerals (like diamonds), and fossil fuels such as coal, crude oil, and natural gas

509

SOIL POLLUTION and EROSION

The average person in the United States produces about 1,600 pounds of garbage a year. And most of it goes into LANDFILLS, areas of land where we deposit our garbage.

By cutting down trees and plowing fields, humans leave land more susceptible to erosion, or the wearing away of soil by rain, rivers, and winds. Erosion moves and washes away loose soil, which ends up in rivers or streams, where it can cloud the water. This prevents organisms such as plankton from receiving sunlight for photosynthesis, which in turn affects the whole food chain! Plus, erosion means that harmful fertilizers and chemicals from farms can get washed into rivers and oceans, affecting entire ecosystems.

WATER POLLUTION

Harmful chemicals from our homes, farms, and factories seep into our water sources. Sometimes raw sewage gets mixed into the waterways. Ocean water gets contaminated as rivers and streams flow into oceans, carrying their pollutants with them. Oil tankers carrying oil across the ocean sometimes have huge oil spills that kill thousands upon thousands of organisms such as birds and fish.

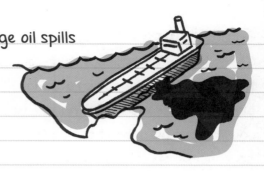

Dead Zone

Water contaminants cause major problems for aquatic life. Fertilizers and raw sewage cause algae to grow rapidly. When algae die, bacteria break them down. However, these bacteria consume so much of the water's oxygen that fish and other aquatic organisms can't survive, causing a DEAD ZONE.

> About 70 percent of Earth is covered in water, so it's hard to think of water as a limited resource. However, only a small portion of the earth's water is the kind of freshwater we can use for drinking, cooking, and bathing. And we use **A LOT** of it—the average American uses around 100 gallons a day! We also must treat and clean the water before it can be used again, which requires a lot of energy, too.

AIR POLLUTION

We pollute air when we burn wood or fossil fuels. Sunlight reacts with air pollutants to create SMOG, a combination of smoke and fog that can make it difficult to breathe and can irritate eyes. A lot of air pollution comes from automobiles that burn gas or diesel. Air pollution also comes from power plants that burn coal, natural gas, or even biofuels.

Greenhouse Effect

THESE ARE CALLED **GREENHOUSE** GASES.

Gases in the atmosphere, such as carbon dioxide, ← trap heat from the sun's radiation. They help to warm our planet. But too much greenhouse gas in the environment is causing our planet to heat up too much—this is called the greenhouse effect. Global warming is causing the ice caps to melt, water levels to rise, and weather patterns to become more extreme. Even though you can't see the extra CO_2 in the air, it is still very harmful air pollution.

Acid Rain

Pollutants in the air, such as sulfur and nitrogen oxide from automobile exhaust,

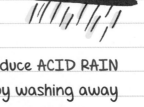

react with water in the atmosphere to produce ACID RAIN (rain that is acidic). It destroys plant life by washing away nutrients from the soil, and it can turn lakes and ponds acidic, which causes fish and other organisms to die. Acid rain can even damage buildings and statues, especially if they're made of limestone or other carbonaceous rocks.

Ozone Depletion

The ozone layer is a layer of gas in the atmosphere that protects humans and animals from the sun's harmful UV rays, which cause sunburns and skin cancer.

> Don't confuse the greenhouse effect and the hole in the ozone layer! The greenhouse effect affects global climate, while the hole in the ozone layer leaves us vulnerable to UV rays.

Chlorofluorocarbons (CFCs) are air pollutants that destroy the ozone layer. CFCs leak into the environment from freezers, air conditioners, and aerosol spray bottles.

> Scientists use the scientific method and engineering process to monitor human impact on the environment, such as air and water quality monitoring, and taking a representative sample of living things.

CONSERVATION

How can you help prevent the horrible effects of pollution? Pollute less and be conscious of your energy use. A good rule to follow for conservation is **The Three R's**:

REDUCE: Reduce the amount of trash you produce and the amount of energy that you consume. This is the best way to conserve natural resources and reduce pollution.

REUSE: Buy products that you can use more than once. Try to avoid disposable items that use up natural resources and produce extra trash.

RECYCLE: Recycling is a process that reuses and changes used materials into things that can be of use. Although it requires energy to recycle things, overall, recycling saves energy as well as landfill space and reduces our need for more natural resources. Lots of things can be recycled: plastic, metal, glass, paper, and compost.

WHAT CAN BE RECYCLED

PLASTIC bottles and containers can be recycled into all sorts of products: rope, carpet, fleece, paintbrushes, and more!

METAL in the form of aluminum soda cans, food cans, steel, iron, and copper can all be melted down and reused. A large portion of the steel used in building skyscrapers, appliances, and cars is recycled.

GLASS from bottles or jars can be melted down to form new bottles or jars.

PAPER can be recycled into other paper products, such as toilet paper, cardboard, paper towels, newsprint, and stationery. Recycling paper saves both energy and water!

ORGANIC MATTER, such as fruit and vegetable scraps, leaves, and grass, can be **COMPOSTED** (turned back into soil). Composting saves landfill space and produces good, fertile soil that can be used to grow plants!

BIODIVERSITY refers to the variety of life on Earth and the types of ecosystems that these species create. ECOSYSTEM SERVICES are the positive benefits that wildlife and ecosystems provide to people, such as soil formation and nutrient recycling. For example, wetlands are crucial for water purification—they can remove 20 to 60 percent of metals in water and eliminate lots of nitrogen entering the water. Because biodiversity and ecosystem services are in danger, scientists are engineering ways to balance our ecosystems, such as restoring wetlands and creating BIODIVERSITY PARKS—special environments designed to support diverse life forms. Scientists must present ideas that are affordable, socially acceptable, and scientifically sound in order to support the ecosystems and biodiversity necessary for our planet and humankind!

CHECK YOUR KNOWLEDGE

Match the term with its correct definition:

1. Recycle

2. Compost

3. Fossil fuels

4. Acid rain

5. Greenhouse gases

6. Renewable resources

7. Landfill

8. Dead zone

9. Nonrenewable resources

10. The three R's of conservation

11. Chlorofluoro-carbons (CFCs)

A. Coal, natural gas, and crude oil—all sources of energy

B. Collecting organic matter and allowing it to decay into soil

C. Gases such as carbon dioxide that trap heat in the atmosphere

D. An area of land where garbage is deposited

E. Fossil fuels, metals, and minerals—resources that can take up to millions of years to replace

F. Chemicals found in freezers, air conditioners, and aerosol spray bottles that degrade the ozone layer

G. An area of water depleted of oxygen where almost no aquatic life can live (caused by runoff of fertilizers and raw sewage)

H. When air pollution reacts with water in the atmosphere to produce rain that can damage plants, organisms, and even buildings

I. Reprocessing materials to be reused as something else

J. Resources that can be replaced or recycled quickly (within 100 years or so)

K. Reduce, reuse, recycle

ANSWERS 517

CHECK YOUR ANSWERS

1. I
2. B
3. A
4. H
5. C
6. J
7. D
8. G
9. E
10. K
11. F

INDEX